Strategy as Practice

Strategic management is taught in business schools as a fundamental aspect of management. It has also come to be regarded as a significant area of academic research over the past three decades. However, in that time research in strategy has largely migrated to a concern with strategy as that which organizations have, rather than strategy as that which managers do. In other words, the activity of managing and developing the strategy of organizations by the people concerned with actually doing it has become marginalized. *Strategy as Practice* reverses this trend by analysing what people do in relation to the development of strategy in organizations. In so doing it provides insights into current issues in strategy that require a more micro level of understanding. This pragmatic approach also helps to integrate different aspects of strategy research and provides insights that will help managers work more effectively.

Gerry Johnson is the Sir Roland Smith Professor of Strategic Management at the Lancaster University Management School.

Ann Langley is Professor of Strategic Management and Research Methods at HEC Montréal.

Leif Melin is Professor of Strategy and Organization at Jönköping International Business School, Jönköping University.

Richard Whittington is Professor of Strategic Management at the Saïd Business School, University of Oxford.

Strategy as Practice

Research Directions and Resources

Gerry Johnson

Ann Langley

Leif Melin

Richard Whittington

CAMBRIDGE
UNIVERSITY PRESS

CAMBRIDGE UNIVERSITY PRESS

Cambridge, New York, Melbourne, Madrid, Cape Town, Singapore, São Paulo

Cambridge University Press
The Edinburgh Building, Cambridge CB2 8RU, UK

Published in the United States of America by Cambridge University Press,
New York

www.cambridge.org
Information on this title: www.cambridge.org/9780521681568

First published 2007

Printed in the United Kingdom at the University Press, Cambridge

A catalogue record for this publication is available from the British Library

ISBN   978-0-521-86293-6   hardback
ISBN   978-0-521-68156-8   paperback

Contents

Part I

Part II   Illustrative papers

Part III

Figures

Preface

There has always been an interest by some strategy scholars in the activities of managers as they relate to the development of strategy. Henry Mintzberg's work in the 1970s and the case study work of Andrew Pettigrew and some of the authors of this book in the 1980s show this. It is an interest that has continued. For example Andrew Pettigrew and Georg von Krogh co-ordinated EGOS workshops in 1999, 2001 and 2002 on Acting and Thinking Strategically that attracted scholars with a bias towards researching such activities. It was from these EGOS workshops that several strands of research started to converge; these are discussed more fully in chapter 1.

One workshop was concerned with what strategists actually do – with strategizing. The second examined the gap highlighted by resource-based theorists: the need to understand the activities that underpin the distinctive competences bestowing competitive advantage on organizations. The third looked at the continuing interest in processes of strategy development in organizations. Given that all three of these interests placed an emphasis on the activities of people in organizations, it was decided to find out just how much interest and research was going on in the field by promoting a special issue of the *Journal of Management Studies* and inviting papers on these topics. The initiative actually started with a 'research conversation' on the themes at an EIASM conference in 2001 where over fifty academics representing these three strands met to present their research and arguments. Many of the papers developed from this event found their way into the *Journal of Management Studies* Special Issue (Johnson, Melin and Whittington 2003) and, since then, Strategy as Practice has 'taken off'.

Strategy as Practice has established itself as a significant social movement (McAdam, McCarthy and Zald 1996), able to mobilize many researchers and access important channels. Thus the www.strategy-as-practice.org list has, at the time of writing, approaching a thousand participants and the movement has streams at EGOS, the British Academy of Management and the Strategic Management Society. The first research monograph on Strategy as Practice has been published (Jarzabkowslei 2005) and there are forthcoming special issues of *Human Relations* (Jarzabkowski, Balogun and Seidl 2007) and *Long Range Planning* (Cailluet and Whittington 2007). There has also been an increasing number of publications that have taken a practice focus, as well as work that has no explicit affiliation with this emerging perspective but which is nonetheless highly relevant. Much of this is referred to throughout this book. Less tangibly, but just as important, the vibrancy of discussion and debate about strategy practice has begun to attract more and more interest. It is time now to review progress, to identify some challenges and opportunities for the next generation of research, and to offer resources and guides to help this next generation forwards. These are the aims of this book.

Apart from the authors, there have been others who have been especially helpful in bringing together the various strands in the book. In particular we would like to thank and acknowledge the many members of the Strategy as Practice network who have helped, but in particular Julia Balogun, Paula Jarzabkowski and David Seidl, Hugo Guo and Lorna Carlaw, who helped substantially with the preparation of the manuscript, and our publishers at Cambridge University Press who have been so patient with us.

Gerry Johnson, Ann Langley, Leif Melin and Richard Whittington

Authors' biographies

GERRY JOHNSON is the Sir Roland Smith Professor of Strategic Management at the University of Lancaster Management School. He received a BA in Social and Physical Anthropology from University College London and his PhD from Aston University. He has worked as a marketing executive, as a management consultant and as an academic at Aston University, Manchester Business School, Cranfield School of Management and Strathclyde University Graduate School of Business. He is also a Senior Fellow of the UK Advanced Institute of Management Research.

His research interests are in the field of strategic management practice, in particular with processes of strategy development and change in organizations. He has published in *Academy of Management Review*, *Academy of Management Journal*, *Journal of Management Studies*, *Strategic Management Journal*, *Organization Studies*, *British Journal of Management* and *Human Relations*. He serves on the editorial boards of *Strategic Management Journal* and *Journal of Management Studies*. He is also co-author of Europe's best-selling strategic management text *Exploring Corporate Strategy* (Prentice Hall, 2005).

ANN LANGLEY is Professor of Strategic Management and Research Methods at HEC Montréal. She took her undergraduate and master's degrees in the UK (Oxford and Lancaster respectively) and obtained her PhD at HEC Montréal in 1987 after working for some years as an analyst both in the private sector and in the public sector. From 2003 to 2006, she was Director of MSc and PhD programs at HEC Montréal. She was Professor of Strategy at Université du Québec à Montréal from 1985 to 2000.

Her research deals with innovation, leadership and strategic change in complex pluralistic organizations, with a more specific emphasis on the health care sector. She also has a particular interest in process research methods and has published on this theme in *Academy of Management Review*. Her empirical work has appeared in journals such as *Academy of Management Journal*, *Administrative Science Quarterly*, *Human Relations*, *Journal of Management*

Studies, Organization Studies, Organization Science and *Sloan Management Review*. She is currently senior editor for *Organization Studies*.

LEIF MELIN is Professor of Strategy and Organization at Jönköping International Business School (JIBS), Jönköping University. He received his PhD from Linköping University, where he later became a Professor of Strategic Management. He is the founding Director of CeFEO, the Center for Family Enterprise and Ownership at JIBS, and he has also served as Dean and Managing Director of JIBS.

His research interests are in the field of strategizing and organizing in organizations, especially the role of ownership and strategic leadership in strategic change activities, and strategic practices in continuously growing business firms. He has published in international book volumes and journals, including *Strategic Management Journal, Journal of Management Studies* and *Family Business Review*. He is currently serving on the editorial board for several international journals, such as *Strategic Organization, European Management Review, Journal of World Business* and *Long Range Planning*.

RICHARD WHITTINGTON is Professor of Strategic Management at the Said Business School and Millman Fellow, New College, University of Oxford. He was previously at the University of Warwick and has held visiting appointments at HEC Paris, the University of Toulouse and the Harvard Business School.

His current research is focused on Strategy as Practice, with projects on strategic issue management, learning to strategize and the historical evolution and diffusion of strategy as a practice. He has published seven other books, including the seventh edition of *Exploring Corporate Strategy, Handbook of Strategy and Management* and *The European Corporation: Strategy, Structure and Social Science*. He is a Senior Editor of *Organization Studies* and is on the editorial boards of *Academy of Management Review, Organization Science* and several other journals.

Acknowledgements

Every attempt has been made to secure permission to reproduce copyright material in this title and grateful acknowledgement is made to the authors and publishers of all reproduced material. In particular, the publishers would like to acknowledge the following for granting permission to reproduce material from the sources set out below:

'Technology as an Occasion for Structuring: Evidence from Observations of CT Scanners and the Social Order of Radiology Departments' by Stephen R. Barley, *Administrative Science Quarterly*, 1986, 31, 78-108. Extracts reproduced by permission of the Johnson Graduate School of Management, Cornell University.

'Making Fast Strategic Decisions in High-Velocity Environments' by Kathleen M. Eisenhardt, *Academy of Management Journal*, 1989, 32 (3), 543-576. Extracts reproduced by permission of the Academy of Management.

'In Search of Rationality: The purposes behind the use of formal analysis in organizations' by Ann Langley, *Administrative Science Quarterly*, 1989, 34, 598-631. Extracts reproduced by permission of the Johnson Graduate School of Management, Cornell University.

'Business Planning as Pedagogy: Language and Control in a Changing Institutional Field' by Leslie S. Oakes, Barbara Townley and David J. Cooper, *Administrative Science Quarterly*, 1998, 43, 257-292. Extracts reproduced by permission of the Johnson Graduate School of Management, Cornell University.

'Sensemaking and Sensegiving in Strategic Change Initiation' by Dennis A. Gioia and Kumar Chittipeddi, *Strategic Management Journal*, 1991, 12 (6), 433-448. Extracts reproduced by permission of John Wiley and Sons, Inc.

'Strategizing as Lived Experience and Strategists' Everyday Efforts to Shape Strategic Direction' by Dalvir Samra-Fredericks, *Journal of Management Studies*, 2003, 40 (1), 141-174. Extracts reproduced by permission of Blackwell Publishing.

'Organizational Restructuring and Middle Manager Sensemaking' by Julia

Balogun and Gerry Johnson, *Academy of Management Journal*, 2004, 47(4), 523-549. Extracts reproduced by permission of the Academy of Management.
'From Metaphor to Practice in the Crafting of Strategy' by Peter T. Bürgi, Claus D. Jacobs and Johan Roos, *Journal of Management Inquiry*, 2005, 14, 1, 78-94. Extracts reproduced by permission of SAGE Publications.

Part I

1 Introducing the Strategy as Practice perspective

Introduction

Even a quick skim through a journal that publishes research on strategy reveals a common characteristic. Conventionally, strategy researchers assume that strategy is something *organizations have*. Organizations have differentiation strategies, diversification strategies and joint-venture strategies; they have strategic planning processes, decision processes and change processes. In this view, strategy is a property of organizations. We take a different perspective: strategy is something that *people do*. Strategy is an activity. For example, differentiation strategies involve people doing things differently and in ways difficult to imitate; strategy processes involve people making strategies.

Quite probably those who research strategies and strategy processes will readily agree that 'doing' in relation to strategy is important, but often they seem not to recognize the full significance of this as a research issue. Either they tend to *assume* what people do, attributing behaviour on the basis of observed outputs and deducing from these the actual activity; or they raise 'doing' to a level of *abstract categorization*, such as planning or change. We are concerned with what people do, literally and directly. As such, Strategy as Practice is essentially concerned with strategy as activity in organizations, typically the interaction of people, rather than strategy as the property of organizations. It is interested not exclusively in the fate of organizations as wholes, but also in the practical performance of the people who engage with them. In this way our focus is on two surprisingly neglected questions: what do the people engaged in strategizing actually do and how do they influence strategic outcomes? By taking these seriously there are at least four major benefits to be gained.

The first is that researchers will address what people, usually managers, actually do to manage strategies. In this respect they will truly engage with strategic management practice and, in so doing, with the 'how' of managing strategy that we argue has rather gone missing. Since this practice is what the managers in classrooms are directly concerned with, we can also teach them better the more we recognize their everyday reality. The second, as we shall explore later in this chapter, is that this engagement with practice can offer a deeper level of explanation for some of the major strategic issues traditionally researched in strategy. Traditional abstraction often approaches these issues at only a superficial level; Strategy as Practice can get to grips with concrete details. Third, we shall argue that this concern with Strategy as Practice provides an integrating mechanism for the strategy field as a whole. What people do in relation to strategy straddles all the various themes of strategy research and helps adds insight into more macro-level concerns in the field. The fourth benefit arises from the other three. Strategy as Practice offers a rich and exciting research agenda that can take researchers in many directions, overcoming traditional boundaries within the academic discipline and reaching out directly to practitioners who have for too long stood outside the discipline.

In taking this stance, we build on a number of traditions. The pragmatist tradition of the early twentieth century (Mead 1934; Boydston 1970 on Dewey; James 1975–88) asked much the same question about human behaviour. Early research in the strategy field itself, not least that undertaken by Henry Mintzberg (1973), took seriously the question of what managers actually do. The process tradition in strategy research has acknowledged the importance of people and what they do, although as we shall argue later in this chapter it has somewhat removed itself from a primary interest in 'doing'. The 'practice turn' in the social sciences exemplified by Giddens (1984) and Bourdieu (1990) also usefully informs our interests. There is, then, no lack of theoretical and empirical tradition underpinning the Strategy as Practice domain. We do not claim to be entirely original. However, what we do lay claim to, and what people have become excited about, is that whilst the strategy field has moved far away from this interest in what people do, Strategy as Practice seeks to bring that back centre stage.

This movement in the wider field of strategy research away from the question of what people do in relation to the strategy or organizations has occurred since the 1970s. Prior to that there was no academic subject, 'Strategy', taught at business schools. What was then known as 'Business Policy' built on Barnard's (1938) interest in strategy challenges facing general managers. As such the standard classroom question for students in their case-based courses was: 'What would you do?' as a general manager faced with a problem. And the classroom debate would be about *both*: 'Why and how?', with the emphasis as much on 'how' as on 'why'. However, there was little academic research to back up either the 'why' – the rationale for strategy – or the 'how' – what managers might do to manage strategic issues. In so far as there were academic books and papers on 'how', they were largely concerned with 'business' or 'corporate' or 'long-range' planning.

It was not until the 1970s that the subject 'Strategy', became known and studied as such, but the next three decades saw its rapid growth. In 1972 what was then the BPP (Business Policy and Planning) division of the Academy of Management was half the size of the three largest divisions. By 1979 there were still only 6% of papers in *Academy of Management Journal, Academy of Management Review* and *Administrative Science Quarterly* with Strategy in their titles. By 1991 however what was renamed BPS (S being Strategy) was second only to OB (Organizational Behaviour), and it has remained so, with more submissions to the annual Academy conference than any other division (Hambrick and Chen 2005). By the same date the *Strategic Management Journal* had become one of the top five ranked management journals, all the major general management journals featured strategy papers heavily and there were professors of Strategy or Strategic Management in virtually all business schools.

During this time, however, the subject of Strategy became dominated by a concern for strategy as what organizations have and the evidence supporting the rationales of strategies. In this migration to the 'why' of strategy the subject has taken on a number of characteristics and lost others. The focus has very largely become 'the firm', not only substantively as a unit of analysis, but metaphorically; academics write in papers and talk in their lectures of 'the firm deciding' on a strategy, for example. People and what they do have gone missing. This has gone hand in hand with a tendency to assume that strategy is made or results from one-off decisions. This is so not only for those who study what strategies are (the 'content school') but also to a considerable extent amongst those who see themselves as part of the 'process school' and study strategic decision making and strategic planning. In fact we know that strategies are rarely the result of one-off decisions, but rather the outcome of quite complex processes. Nor can strategic decisions be regarded simply as being taken at the top of organizations and implemented down through a hierarchy, though in much of the strategy literature this is still often assumed. Further, despite the widespread acknowledgement of the bounded rationality of management decisions (Cyert and March 1963; Bromiley 2004), there has been a tendency to regard strategies as being decided upon through relatively formal structures and systems, with less attention given to the messiness of interpersonal relations and political processes. Those interested in Strategy as

Practice, on the other hand, recognize as an important foundation to the understanding of strategy practice the complexity of the processes that give rise to a strategy and the potential influence of many organizational members in doing so, not only through formal organizational processes but also in their more everyday activities.

Our intention is to refocus the subject on the 'how' question as it relates to strategy: to recover the old sensitivity to the real predicaments of people in their strategy making. This does not mean we wish to relegate the question of 'why'. But it does mean that we are seriously concerned about the practice of 'strategic management' or, if we need to differentiate ourselves, we are concerned with 'strategizing' (Whittington 2003) as the practice of managing strategy. In this we accept that the challenge for us is not just to aid managers in their strategic thinking, but to help improve strategic management practice.

In all of this we take a lesson from history. The Harvard Business Policy course, once a model throughout business schools, came to be accused of chronic inductivism and unwillingness to systematize. The Business Policy approach was supplanted in all the major business schools, including Harvard (Greiner, Bhambri and Cummings 2003). If Strategy as Practice is to influence either or both the academic world and the world of management, it has to be based on sound and convincing academic inquiry offering the kinds of systematic data and guidance expected now in both contemporary teaching and, especially, research. This is the motivation for this book. Our purpose is to provide scholars interested in Strategy as Practice with the conceptual base on which to develop their interest, the theoretical and methodological tools to consider how to design their research, and examples of published papers that might help them in this as well as show ways in which their work might be written up.

This chapter contributes to this purpose in several ways in the sections that follow. In the next section, we provide background on the development of Strategy as Practice and show its importance in the context of some other areas of strategy research. We then consider a particular characteristic of research in Strategy as Practice, the inevitability of plurality in terms of levels of analysis, the people involved as research subjects, the dependent variables of the research and the theories employed. The core of the chapter then provides a framework within which existing and future work can be located so as to suggest directions for future research. Building on this, there is then a brief section that provides conceptual clarity on some fundamental concepts.

The need for Strategy as Practice[1]

The concern of this book and the research with which it is concerned was initially defined in the Special Issue of *Journal of Management Studies* as 'an emphasis on the detailed processes and practices which constitute the day-to-day activities of organizational life and which relate to strategic outcomes. Our focus therefore is on micro-activities that, while often invisible to traditional strategy research, nevertheless can have significant consequences for organizations and those who work in them' (Johnson, Melin and Whittington 2003: 3). Here we amend this definition for two reasons. First because we are interested in more than the literal meaning of 'day to day'; we are also interested in what people do more occasionally in board meetings, strategy away-days, or other episodes (Hendry and Seidl 2003) that contribute to strategy development. Also, because whilst our central concern is certainly with what people do in relation to strategy and therefore with what academics regard as 'the micro', our interest is also in the context in which they do it. We therefore conceive of Strategy as Practice as a *concern with what people do in relation to strategy and how this is influenced by and influences their organizational and institutional context.*

The centrality of human action and interaction within this definition requires us to make an overarching observation about our ontological position in relation to mainstream work in strategy. An underlying problem in the study of strategy is that, in seeking to meet the challenge of rigour posed in the late 1970s (Schendel and Hofer 1979), scholars have very largely drawn on theoretical positions unsuited to the understanding of the role of human action. Human action comes to be something that is deduced or assumed from findings or insights drawn from much more macro levels of economic or sociological inquiry: strategies are theorized as somehow disembodied. At the extreme, this is exemplified in the remark of a strategy colleague: 'I am interested in strategies, not what people do.' Because a practice-based perspective invites us to see strategies and strategizing as human action, as doing, and because it places human interaction at the centre, it takes a different ontological position from mainstream strategy research. Indeed we argue that the issue is not so much whether current theories or methods that

[1] This section of the chapter draws extensively on the arguments advanced in the introductory paper to the Special Issue of *Journal of Management Studies* (Johnson, Melin and Whittington 2003) that originally set out the case for what has become known as Strategy as Practice.

dominate management research are more or less appropriate. The more fundamental issue is that the placing of practice at the centre requires a fundamentally different view of what strategy as a subject is about. We now consider this in relation to some of the imperatives for taking such an approach.

The rationale

There are *economic, theoretical* and *empirical* reasons why we need to reassert a balance in favour of what people do in relation to the strategies of organizations. In this section we consider these.

First, from an *economic* perspective, markets are becoming more open, market entry more common, resources increasingly tradable, information more readily available, labour more mobile. A resource-based view (Barney 1986, 1991) suggests that as a consequence the transparent becomes a precarious foundation for competitive advantage. If sustainable advantage can be achieved and sustained it is likely this is because such advantage is lodged in the interactive behaviours of people in organizations that resource-based view (RBV) theorists sometimes refer to as 'micro assets' that are hard to discern and awkward to trade.

Moreover, there may be a shift to a more 'hypercompetitive' environment in which speed, surprise and innovation can be winning bases of competitive advantage (D'Aveni 1995; Brown and Eisenhardt 1997). Fast and innovative responses to competition require organizational decentralization, so that strategic decisions are taken, or strategic influence is exercised, by those who are close to customers or suppliers or to organizational skills (Zenger and Hesterley 1997; Whittington et al. 1999) and who may be more at the periphery of organizations than at their apex (Johnson and Huff 1997; Regnér 2003). This increasing pace of change has also tended to shift strategy making from well-defined systems of episodic planning and decision making into a much more continuous process (Eisenhardt and Brown 1999), rooted in more everyday practices and, again, involving more people throughout organizations. To understand what managing strategy entails in such conditions means that research has to address the activities of organizational actors in such contexts and how these influence strategic outcomes.

At the *theoretical level,* there are also reasons for more attention to be given to what people do in relation to strategy within organizations. For example the *resource-based view* has been critically examined for failing to deliver on its own micro premises. Priem and Butler (2001) argued that the definition of resources is typically all-inclusive and poor at discriminating between those resources that managers can practically manipulate and those beyond their control. Paradoxically, most of the empirical research in the RBV tradition marginalizes the very activities, managerial or otherwise, that are central to its argument that the roots of superior performance lie in unique and hard to copy attributes of firms. Such attributes surely take the form of patterns of activities but there has been little empirical work that has explored just what form such activities take and how they contribute to the achievement of competitive advantage, if indeed they do. In so far as such work exists it relies heavily on the sort of abstract categorization of activities and practices we referred to earlier. Our focus on practices and activities is therefore potentially central to a RBV view of strategy.

There are other areas of theory that have become core to the strategy field for which much the same critique might be levelled. For example the debate about *dynamic capabilities* draws on evolutionary theory. Evolutionary theory has, at its roots, the importance of a variety of generating activities at the micro level that may have macro effects. Yet scholars rarely examine the roots of dynamic capabilities at such levels, relying instead on the more observable and often documented systematized routines or 'oversimplified behavioural foundations' (Gavetti 2005) of organizations that are actually themselves 'black boxes' of activities, the variations of which need to be understood at a more finely grained level (Feldman and Rafaeli 2002).

Institutional theorists acknowledge that they have tended to focus on 'the behavior of organizations as entities and the nature and effects of their formal and collective parts' (Tolbert and Zucker 1996: 75). The concern has tended to be on how individuals are captured within norms and rules, and the effects of that, as distinct from the role they play in creating such norms and rules. As Phillips (2003) has noted, this is regrettable since the acceptance by institutional theorists of a socially constructed world would suggest that institutional actors play a significant part in institutional processes. Indeed, so much is acknowledged by Barley and Tolbert (1997: 94): 'Actors create institutions through a history of negotiations that lead to "shared typifications" or generalised expectations and interpretations of behaviour.' Until recently, however, there has been a notable absence of studies that provide convincing explanations of the nature of such 'negotiations' or how they contribute to institutional change.[2]

The same need, to take more seriously what people do, is to be found in *empirical research* in relation to strategy. For example, in relation to the topic

---

[2] For exceptions see Johnson, Smith and Codling 2000; Seo and Creed 2002; Maguire, Hardy and Lawrence 2004.

of *corporate diversification*: 'After nearly half a century of research, the advice we academics can offer managers in designing and implementing their corporate strategies is tentative at best. More than a hundred academic studies have failed to determine if diversification enhances profitability or whether related diversification outperforms unrelated diversification' (Grant 2002: 91). From a Strategy as Practice perspective this is not surprising since we cannot or should not assume that apparent relationships judged to exist by researchers are really exploited in practice. It was long ago pointed out by researchers (Grant, Jammine and Thomas 1988) that progress in diversification research requires more small-sample, fine-grained investigations capable of capturing the activities of diversifying; in other words what people actually do in diversifying their firms.

Similarly research on *corporate structures* has failed to establish clear performance relationships, especially around the advantages of the multidivisional structure and its fit with various diversification strategies (Whittington 2002). Again there has been a reliance on large-scale statistical studies and measures that fail to differentiate between significant variations in structure, for instance between various types of multidivisional structures (Markides and Williamson 1996), and that are too static to pick up the continuous structural changes of contemporary business (Galunic and Eisenhardt 1994; Brown and Eisenhardt 1997). If structures are in near continuous motion, then we need a better appreciation of the activities involved in creating and implementing structures – or more accurately in the activities of structuring.

However we are also concerned about research on what has become known as *strategy process*. On the face of it this might seem strange. After all, surely processes are to do with what people do. Moreover, we acknowledge that strategy process research has opened up the 'black box' of the organization and recognized the importance of organizational politics (Pettigrew 1977) and organizational tensions (Normann 1977). However, such work tended to be at the fore in the 1980s and early 1990s. Increasingly 'process studies' have come to be concerned with the systems and processes of organizations as wholes as the units of analysis (Chakravarthy and Doz 1992; Chakravarthy and White 2002), neglecting the practice that is *inside* such processes (Brown and Duguid 2000).

For example *strategic planning* has long been seen as a central interest in process studies of strategy. Yet for decades the research focus here was the search for a relationship between the presence of such planning and performance outcomes of the firm (Miller and Cardinal 1994), neglecting almost entirely the detailed activities involved in such planning. It is hardly surprising that so many contradictory findings resulted. Only recently have there been signs of an interest in asking more detailed questions of the planning process in organizations (Grant 2003). (In chapter 2 we take strategic planning as an example of how different theoretical lenses might inform research on the topic.)

Within the process tradition, research in the 1970s offered us detailed insights into the activities involved in *strategic decision making* such as those provided by the longitudinal case studies on resource allocation process by Bower (1982), the politics of investment decisions by Pettigrew (1973) or the clinical dissection of comparative decision processes by Mintzberg and his co-researchers (Mintzberg, Raisinghani and Theoret 1976). Hand in hand with the plea for greater research 'rigour', with few exceptions (e.g. Perlow, Okhuysen and Repenning 2002), research on strategic decision making has migrated to cross-sectional studies with the aim of providing categories of decision making modes (e.g. Papadakis, Lioukas and Chambers 1998; Wally and Baum 1994), sacrificing attention to what people actually do, indeed often doing away with managers altogether in the name of research convenience such as the use of MBA students in experiments (e.g. Bettenhausen and Murnighan 1985). Again there have been exceptions to this and, interestingly, these are the ones that tend to be more highly cited and influential. So, for example, Burgelman's (2002) account of Intel's evolving strategy has extended the work of Bower (1972); and Eisenhardt's (Eisenhardt and Bourgeois 1988; Eisenhardt 1989a) comparative case approach has contextualized and grounded more abstract insight into decision making. But these remain the exception rather than the rule.

Within the 'process field' one response in the 1980s and 1990s that sought a more rigorous base of understanding the role of individuals with regard to strategy was work on *managerial cognition*. The underlying rationale here was that individuals did indeed play a key role in strategy development, and therefore that understanding the way they made sense of strategic issues was important. This gave rise to a whole research agenda usefully summarized by Walsh (1995) and Hodgkinson and Sparrow (2002). However, the problems such research faced and faces in relation to the management of strategy take us back to the reasons for the practice-based view that we take.

A good deal of the early work on managerial cognition attended to how managers made sense of strategic issues; it therefore tended to privilege the individual. There are several problems here. First, it cannot be assumed that, because an individual or individuals make sense of a situation or a problem in a given way, that can be taken as a sufficient explanation for what they do. There are strong arguments to suggest that how people engage with an uncertain and complex world is explained as much by their 'doing' as by their cognitive representations of the world (Taylor 1993); indeed that the two are intimately linked. Second, whilst it might be interesting to understand how individuals make sense of their strategic world, strategies are rarely developed by an individual; they are developed by groups of people. As Weick and Roberts (1993) pointed out, understanding the sensemaking of groups inevitably involves understanding the activities of groups in terms of what people do as they interact. Indeed many of those engaged in cognitive or sensemaking research now embrace the concern for understanding practice and the activities of people. In this respect, the study of cognition is moving closer to our interests.

There are, then, powerful economic, theoretical and empirical reasons for an attention to Strategy as Practice; but there is a further very practical reason. Much of the mainstream research on strategy, in taking an organizational-level focus, risks becoming more and more remote from managers. A strong instrumental reason for the importance of a view of strategy more closely concerned with activities is that managers manage activities. Much of the influential literature on strategy, important as it is, has left the manager bereft of insights, let alone guidelines for action, at this level.

A developing characteristic of Strategy as Practice: the need for plurality

So far we have considered the need for the study of Strategy as Practice in the context of how strategy has come to be studied over the last few decades. This contextualization of Strategy as Practice also helps identify further ways in which the field differs from that which has developed as 'mainstream' strategy research. Given our focus on the importance of people – the way they interact in the development of strategy – it follows that there is a need to shift the research agenda from a preoccupation with the firm and its performance to include a concern for people, the tools they use, and their practices and performance in the development of strategy. In so doing there are implications with regard to the need to move from the relatively unitary perspectives that have characterized strategy research in terms of levels of analysis, explanatory variables and theoretical perspectives, to greater plurality that distinguishes research in our field.

More plural levels of analysis

Strategy practice research may be concerned with different levels of analysis and, importantly, the relationship between them. It not only goes *beneath* organization-level processes to investigate what goes on inside organizations; it also goes *above* these processes to interrogate how the practices and tools originate from a wider business environment outside the firm (Molloy and Whittington 2005). Strategy practices such as strategic planning, strategy workshops or consultancy practices need to be understood as institutionalized phenomena that influence what organizational actors do and in turn how strategies develop in organizations. Within organizations we may also wish to build on the growing interest in routine aspects of organizations that contribute to dynamic capabilities, learning, experimentation and change. However, rather than just regarding these as systematized organizational level phenomena – the ostensive routines Feldman and Pentland (2003) refer to – we need to recognize them as malleable on the basis of how they are actually enacted – Feldman and Pentland's performative aspect of routines – and informal as well as formalized. We are also interested in the behaviour of individuals in so far as it influences strategic outcomes. Our interests therefore span levels, but with a common emphasis on understanding what people do both within and as an influence on institutional and organizational contexts: the next section of this chapter develops this point.

Plurality of actors

Traditional strategy research, in so far as it focuses on people at all, has tended to concern itself in the main with senior executives, and in particular chief executives. Indeed in much research the views or opinions of a senior executive are taken to be the strategic position of the firm or the rationale for the strategy (Hambrick and Mason 1984); or the CEO is regarded as *the* strategic decision maker. We have long known from much research into strategy process that this is a false picture; that strategy development is not so dependent on an individual or even a small group (Pettigrew 1973, 1985; Mintzberg et al. 1976; Johnson 1987). There are many influences, such as middle managers, consultants and even investment bankers. If we take the lessons from institutional theory, we know that organizations copy strategies and are therefore influenced by people outside their own organizations or people who cross institutional boundaries (Greenwood and Suddaby 2006). Emergent processes of strategy development involve multiple organizational actors across levels in the organization and from outside the organization. Indeed, it has been shown that to a greater extent in fast-moving, dynamic business environments, the role of senior executives may be more to do with discerning emerging strategies than with making strategy as such (Brown and Eisenhardt 1998).

All this may be inconvenient for those who wish to assume away such complexity for the purposes of an elegant and simplified set of research questions and research design, but here we argue that this plurality of strategic actors has to be accommodated if we are to research Strategy as Practice. The implication of this is that we have to take seriously the roles of multiple actors, build on theory that helps us to do so, and design research that engages with such complexity – challenges that are taken up in the chapters in this book.

Plurality of dependant variables

March and Sutton (1997) have argued cogently the dangers and limitations of studies, so typical of strategy research, that seek to explain organizational performance expressed in terms of unitary measures and assumed causally related explanatory variables. They also grant – though do not pursue – the argument that 'Organizational performance can . . . be considered at a disaggregated level' (698). We concur. It makes little sense to try and explain the performance of firms as wholes if we do not understand well the components of that performance. In effect the argument is that an extended notion of the 'dependent variable' of performance is required. Without the recognition of the importance of such disaggregation, we can be left with research findings that are at best partial, quite likely insubstantial and at worst misleading. Indeed the arguments made above about the insubstantiality of research in RBV, diversification and research on organizational structure illustrate the point. A Strategy as Practice perspective argues, in particular, for the value of explaining (and therefore helping to improve) the performance of people as they interact and enact institutional and organizational practices.

Such disaggregated 'dependent' variables might, for example, include the following.

- At the level of the individual, there is the ability of people to understand strategic issues and influence strategic decisions; and people's skills in particular strategic activities.
- Whilst recognizing the importance of individuals, however, it is likely that researchers will wish to embrace groups of people and their interaction. Here we may be concerned with the influence of group dynamics in relation to strategy development; with collective skills in strategic activities; with the levels and the dynamics of experimentation; and with sources and the dynamics of power relationships between groups.
- Also relevant is the extent to which, and how, analytic tools, planning systems or strategic episodes such as board meetings or strategy workshops

affect the development of strategies – intended or realized (Mintzberg and Waters 1985).

Ultimately our concern should be, not to understand these variables simply for their own sake, but to understand how they contribute to strategic outcomes. To build on an example given above: it may be spurious to attempt a correlation between the existence (or not) of a planning system and an overall organizational performance measure. However a focus on the explanatory variable of the skills of the actors in undertaking the planning might well contribute to a greater understanding of the role of strategic planning in strategy development.

Plurality of theories

Given these considerations, it is difficult to see how one theory can inform the sort of activities that interest us. This does not mean that we do not have an interest in theory, but it does mean that we may not wish to accept the dominant influence of the existing theoretical traditions in the strategy field. It may be that we have to search for and apply theories that better address practice and action. In so doing we need to ask if it is possible to understand the complexity with which we are concerned through singular theoretical lenses. We may need to employ multiple theoretical lenses. These are themes taken up in the next chapter.

Mapping the research domain

The previous section has given the background to the development and introduced some of the key characteristics of Strategy as Practice. This section builds on that discussion to position the many strands of Strategy as Practice in relation to some of the more widely established themes of strategy and management research.

As work on Strategy as Practice has grown, so it has seemed to go in many directions. For instance, some have been concerned with processes (Maitlis and Lawrence 2003; Regnér 2003), others with tools (Jarzabkowski 2004), others with people (Mantere 2005), others with the way people interact to make sense of strategy (Balogun and Johnson 2004), others with discourse, seeing managers' talk as practice and strategy as created through talk (Samra-Fredericks 2003). In the mêlée, it is sometimes hard to see the links from one part of the domain to another, and other possible directions may be in danger of getting lost altogether.

The structure of the domain

This section employs an exploded map of the strategic management discipline that shows the links between parts of the strategy field (see figure 1.1). Using this map we consider where our interest in strategy practice is located and so explore the opportunities and needs for research. A brief explanation of the map is needed first, however. Vertically it shows that there are 'micro' levels and more 'macro' levels of concern relevant to strategy. The figure then has six blocks with three levels, leaving aside the links between them that will motivate the discussion in what follows. In terms of these blocks, the middle level represents the central current orthodoxy of the strategic management discipline. As explained above, here the typical endeavour is to link organizational decisions and actions to organizational performance (Rumelt, Schendel and Teece 1994). Staying with this middle block, conventionally these organizational actions are categorized as either 'content' (the left-hand column) – what strategies are – or 'process' (the right-hand column), concerned with how strategy is achieved. On the content side, we give as an example diversification, but could also include the success of competitive strategies, acquisitions, internationalization or innovation. On the process side, we cite strategic change, but could also include strategic decision making, strategy implementation and the like.

The other two levels, whilst generally acknowledged as relevant in relation to organizational strategy, do not represent mainstream research in the strategy field. The top level is concerned with macro-level institutions and institutionalization. Here we are concerned with practices that take on legitimacy at the institutional level and which people in organizations encounter and with which they engage. Strategies themselves may become institutionalized: we give the 1960s pursuit of conglomeratization as an example but could have given the example of the espousal the e-business strategies of the late 1990s. Institutional strategy processes include strategic planning, as in the figure, but managing for shareholder value or business process re-engineering are other examples. Practices at this institutionalized level certainly influence organizational actions. Institutional theorists continually point to the mimetic behaviour of organizations (DiMaggio and Powell 1983) in terms of both strategies and strategy processes.

The conventional organizational level of strategy research and the institutionalized practices that inform it both assume the lower level of micro activities in figure 1.1 but traditionally do not enter it, at least explicitly. Here, however, we are concerned with this micro level: with the activities of those who enact, develop and deliver strategies; with the activities related to the *doing of strategy*. To take an example given in the figure, the organizational strategy of diversification involves people building relationships between organizational units. Strategic planning and strategic change processes both involve the debate of strategic issues. We argue that it is time to penetrate to this lower level in figure 1.1 and attend to such activities as they relate to both content and process.

The map presented as figure 1.1 reflects divisions that, through the practice lens, become less rigid. What people do in relation to strategy straddles all the categories. It is this capacity to cross the boundaries between content and process, micro and macro, that gives to Strategy as Practice such a rich and exciting research agenda. It is the broad outlines of this agenda that we will now consider.

A research agenda

If we retain at least for the purposes of this discussion the traditional notion of strategy as 'strategy content' and 'strategy process', the vertical links labelled V1–4 in figure 1.1 represent explanations that bridge the lower level of people's activities with the more macro levels of organizational and institutional practices. In so doing they help identify important research questions. What follows uses these vertical linkages in the figure as an organizing framework to discuss our research agenda in terms of both indicative existing work and future opportunities.

V1: Here we have the *link between people's activities and organizational level processes*, a link that can be addressed in two directions.

First, people's interactions inform and constitute organizational processes. The characteristic episodes of activity (Hendry and Seidl 2003) involved in the larger processes of organizational decision making or change include, for example, engaging consultants (Schwarz 2004), project team meetings (Blackler, Crump and MacDonald 2000), strategy workshops or away-days (Hodgkinson et al. 2006) and commonly held meetings in which strategic issues are discussed. Clearly the outcomes of such episodes are dependent on the activities within them. For example Hodgkinson and Wright's (2002) account of a failed strategy away-day shows how the detailed activities within that episode were fateful for the larger organizational processes of strategic change it was intended to support, and Samra-Fredericks' (2003) shows how the language used in a top management team debate influenced the strategic decisions of the meeting.

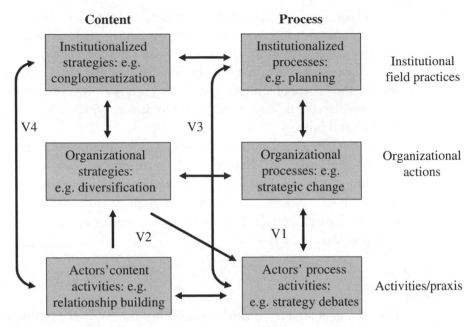

Fig. 1.1   An exploded map of strategic management

More widely, we can ask how the behaviour of people or the relationships between people influence the more formal systems and routines of organizations as they relate to the management of strategy. For example, work on dynamic capabilities has examined the role that formal systems, for example of mergers and acquisitions, has played in organizational learning (Zollo and Winter 2002; Zollo and Singh 2004). Though acknowledged as important, there is less research on how the more informal interaction between people, and the ensuing improvization and experimentation, are an important constituent of dynamic capabilities (Dougherty, Barnard and Dunne 2004). However, this interest in the relationship between formal organizational processes and the activities of people is exemplified in Burgelman's (2002) and Bower's work (Bower 1982; Noda and Bower 1996). Employing an evolutionary view of strategy development, they show how ill-defined technological or market forces may be communicated upward and how initiatives may be championed by front-line or middle managers in a political process of competition for scarce resources and top management attention.

The common theme here is that it is not just the formal systems of organizations that are important in research terms. How such systems are enacted and how that interaction leads to variation and experimentation are significant research questions. So too is how the more informal aspects of behaviour modify standard operating procedures, affect change processes in organizations or indeed enable an organization's more formal systems to out-perform those of other organizations.

Our concern is also with how organizational-level initiatives are pursued in terms of what people actually do. Figure 1.1 gives the example of strategic change. The literature on readiness for change (e.g. Miller, Johnson and Grau 1994; Jones, Jimmieson and Griffiths 2005) recognizes the importance of what people do to enact change and focuses on individuals' capacity or willingness to take on board planned change. Most of that literature, however, leans towards psychological explanations of readiness or unreadiness, largely avoid-ing activities, not least the politics, associated with change. Certainly, however, studies of strategic change do point to problems, rooted in the behaviours of people, in translating strategies into action (e.g. Pettigrew 1985; Harris and Ogbonna 2002) and Balogun and Johnson (2004, 2005) have shown the importance of sensemaking activities amongst middle managers in this regard. At this level of people's activities, work on strategic change initiatives remains a significant research opportunity.

The success of strategic change programmes is often attributed to leader-ship, on which there is certainly a good deal of research. However, it was many years ago that Burns (1978) argued that we know little about what leaders actually do and, with regard to academic research as distinct from populist books, this still remains the case. For example, much of the work on transfor-mational leadership is still leader-focused, often highlighting vague concepts such as 'charismatic' or 'inspirational' leadership and ignoring any exchange dimension to leadership or specific activities carried out by leaders (Barker 1997; Yukl 1999). Beneath such abstraction we know little about how leaders convert strategy into action in terms of their own skills in action (though for an exception see Gioia and Chittipeddi 1991, a paper summarized in this book). Again it is a significant research opportunity.

Research in the accounting, operations-management and organizational-behaviour traditions has also long shown the problems in aligning behaviours with the expectations and intentions assumed of such systems and how such systems have political as well as practical consequences (e.g. Ridgeway 1956; Argyris 1990). We know enough from these studies to see the problems that need to be explored further. We know there can be a disconnect between the intended strategy of organizations and the systems used to put them into operation. But we also know that the systems themselves often fail to impact on the activities of people in organizations. It is this breakdown between strategy, systems and the activities of people that surely provides a rich vein of potential research in our domain. Moreover it would be immensely useful to practitioners to understand this better.

In terms of V1, then, the research interest lies especially in the interrelationship of the effect of organizational processes and systems on what people do, and vice versa, how people's activities affect organizational processes and systems and in turn of the influence of these interrelationships on strategic outcomes.

V2: This is the link between activities within organizations and the strategies of those organizations. Given that a central focus of the strategic management discipline has been conventionally defined as improving the performance of the firm (Rumelt et al. 1994), this link to organizational strategies is not to be neglected lightly. The key question here is *how do people's activities underpin organizational strategies?*

Taking the example given in figure 1.1, a strategy of related diversification depends for its success on the ability to build relationships between businesses in a portfolio. Organizational routines of coordination necessary to support a strategy of diversification have been studied, for example (Eisenhardt and Martin 2000). However, building relatedness also depends on what people actually do in forging and sustaining relationships (Huxham and Vangen 2005) through active social networks. If this is to be studied it requires small-sample, fine-grained investigations capable of capturing both the subtlety of economically valuable relationships and their sensitivity to managerial action or inaction (Grant et al. 1988).

Similarly there are practices that underpin competitive strategies. These tend to be discussed in terms of how organizational routines and difficult to discern practices might bestow competitive advantage (Barney 1991; Peteraf 1993) or in terms of the dynamic capabilities that support particular strategies (Teece, Pisano and Shuen 1997). There have been attempts to study these bases of competitive advantage empirically, for example in terms of the kinds of innovation routines discussed by Lorenzoni and Lipparini (1999) and Zollo, Reuer and Singh (2002), or Salvato's (2003) study of the relationship of intraorganizational routines to innovation-based strategy. However, in these examples the interest is still in relatively formalized organizational routines. In terms of the interest in practice for which we argue, there is an opportunity to go further.

Fundamental to bases of competitive advantage as argued by resource-based theorists is that the resource characteristics (or capabilities) that lead to competitive advantage are those that are valuable, rare and difficult to imitate. Indeed Barney (1986) has argued that the capabilities most likely to bestow competitive advantage are those embedded in an organization's culture, rather than the formalized routines that can be readily discerned by competitors. However, with very few exceptions such as Ambrosini's (2003) study of the activities underpinning competitive advantage, there has been little work that has explored empirically the informal organizational routines and activities underpinning competitive strategies in anything like the level of detail required to evaluate the relevance of Barney's argument. This has formed the basis of a substantial critique of the resource-based view of the firm and its contribution to research in strategy (Priem and Butler 2001). After all, if researchers cannot or will not seek to identify the specific activities that drive competitive advantage in theory, RBV is of little use to practitioners and risks ending up as little more than a tautology; firms do better than others because they have (invisible) assets superior to those of their rivals.

These links between organizational strategies and the activities within organizations are, then, theoretically acknowledged to be important and central to much debate in the strategy field. There are, however, few studies that explore and explain such linkages. It is, arguably, a major opportunity for those seeking to make a contribution through research in Strategy as Practice.

This discussion of V2 has focused on the activities underpinning strategies. There is also, of course, the challenge of managing the implementation of an intended strategy. Mintzberg and Waters (1985) pointed out long ago that intended strategies often become unintended and we know anecdotally that managers themselves regard managing strategy implementation as a major challenge. In many respects this is the question that most closely links to the traditional Harvard question 'What would you do?' This is a 'process' issue in terms of figure 1.1 and raises the same sort of questions discussed in V1 above in relation to how strategic initiatives need to be studied in terms of people's activities (which is why the downward arrow from the organizational strategy box crosses diagonally to the process side of the map).

Overall V1 and V2 represent a rich research agenda with a great deal of potential to explain the missing links in strategic management research in ways that can directly inform and help managers. We have little to say to managers about what they can do to help make acquisitions work. We teach strategic management processes as though they are commonly followed in organizations but have little to say about differences in practice. How do managers influence top-team debates or board meetings? How do the actions of people in organizations influence and modify strategies? Are there patterns that can be discerned in the activities of people in organizations and how may these link to more formal processes that might account for competitive advantage? Can managers actually manage the routines and behaviours that underpin strategies or that change strategies? These questions, and more, depend on the pursuit of the sort of research agenda laid out here.

While the importance of activities was clearly signalled in the 2003 Special Issue, we gave less attention to the topmost level in figure 1.1, the supra-organizational or institutional. Here are the prevailing practices – legitimate strategies, discourses, tools and procedures – within the institutional field(s) in which organizations are embedded (Reckwitz 2002; Whittington 2006), and in which industry norms and recipes govern behaviour (Spender 1989). They might be professional, as in the kinds of communities of practices that often extend beyond particular organizations (Brown and Duguid 2000); they might be national, as in Whitley's (1999) notion of business systems; they might be supranational, as in the kinds of institutional fields that have been created by imperial power and international institutions described by Djelic (1998). In one sense, institutionalized practices provide the shared codes of behaviour, or scripts (Schank and Abelson 1977; Gioia and Poole 1984) which tell everybody how to go on. Without these codes, or in disregard of these codes, the activity collapses. In another sense these practices provide the rules and resources required for human agency. Following Giddens (1984), they provide legitimacy, discourse, authority, and expectations of appropriate behaviour that can both inform and empower institutionalized practice.

The relationship of institutionalized practices to the activities of people in organizations is certainly of strategic significance and worthy of study. The challenge for research that seeks to address this is to combine an intimate insight into micro-level activities with a continuous regard for the wider institutional context that informs and empowers such activities. This challenge of simultaneous embrace of lower and higher levels is something that we shall return to in discussing research methods.

V3: Here the concern is with *the relationship between institutionalized strategic management processes and people's activities within organizations.*

One of the papers summarized in this book examines the introduction of the strategic planning processes into Canadian museums (Oakes, Townley and Cooper 1998). The study shows that the success of museum directors in forcing strategic planning on to a recalcitrant sector relied upon novel discourses of strategy that had gained legitimacy in the wider social environment and which both guided their adherents and undermined their opponents. Such strategic planning processes are part of a wider movement that extends beyond any particular organization or the people in a particular organization. Without making these kinds of link to institutional practices, the success of the museum directors is inappropriately reduced to a purely organizational phenomenon.

There are other examples of research on institutionalized processes. Consulting interventions rely upon norms, expectations and reputations that are widely diffused within society, some negative and some positive (Clark 2004). Strategy tools, such as Porter's (1980) five forces, come to constitute institutionalized processes, so their actual use in particular episodes entails a translation from the upper level of institutions to the lower level of activity (Jarzabkowski 2004). There are institutionalized processes associated particularly with strategic planning cycles (Jarzabkowski 2003), project management (Molloy and Whittington 2005) and business process engineering that all influence people's activities in organizations.

Another question is how what people do informs or changes institutionalized processes? Institutional theorists have pointed out that there are 'carriers' of institutional norms and practices (Abrahamson 1996; Abrahamson and Fairchild 1999; Clark 2004). These include, for example, the activities of business schools or writers in disseminating 'best practice' (Whittington et al. 2003). Brunsson and Jacobsson (2000) argue that academic researchers are active 'standardizers' providing prescriptions for the best way managers should deal with different organizational matters. It is also what consultants set out to do, and there is an increasing interest in the activities of consultants in this respect (e.g. Clark and Fincham 2002). Presumably an extension of the interest in the way in which people amend organizational routines (Feldman and Pentland 2003) is the further question of the extent to which this may in time inform or change institutionalized processes. Again it has been argued theoretically that this does occur (Johnson, Smith and Codling 2000; Seo and Creed 2002), but there is little empirical work exploring it.

V4: Here the concern is with institutionalized strategies. It has been shown there are cycles of acquisitions and diversifications (Stearns and Allen 1996). Conglomeratization became common in the 1960s (Davis, Dieljam and Tinsley 1994); related diversification rather than unrelated diversification has more latterly become the norm (Rumelt 1974; Grant, Jammine and Thomas 1988). Managers generally talk about strategies of differentiation or low cost (Porter 1980, 1985). Our interest here is again the link between this macro level and people's activities. First, then, *how are institutionalized strategies actually pursued, not only at the organizational level, but in terms of people's activities within organizations?*

Institutional theorists themselves acknowledge the importance of micro explanations of institutional forms but have noted: 'There has been little effort to make neo-institutionalism's micro foundations explicit. Most institutionalists prefer to focus on the structural environments, macro to micro-level effects, and the analytic autonomy of macro structures' (DiMaggio and Powell 1991: 16). There have been insights here in terms of what are sometimes referred to as 'industry recipes' – in effect industry-wide institutionalized practice (Porac, Thomas, and Baden-Fuller 1989; Spender 1989; Hellgren and Melin 1991). The reconceptualization of the firm as a portfolio of assets embodied in the notion of the conglomerate also helped both to legitimate certain kinds of diversification strategy and, at the micro level, to define appropriate routines of internal coordination (Davis, Dieljam and Tinsley 1993). Other similar content practices include the discursive language surrounding the 'transnational' (Bartlett and Ghoshal 1989), which conveys particular meanings and the way people actually behave to enact such meanings.

Again, then, there is little empirical work and a potentially rich research opportunity here. Whilst we know they exist, we know little about how such institutionalized strategies are actually pursued by people in organizations or the consequences and effects of local deviations from institutionalized norms. We know that firms, whilst generally conforming to institutionalized strategies, occasionally deviate from them; Deephouse (1999) has discussed the consequences. Such deviations are presumably the result of activities within those firms, but to what extent such deviations are random or calculated or how they come to be enacted, in the face presumably of institutionally legitimized resistance, is much less clear.

This leads to a related question: *how do people's activities influence institutional strategies?* It is clear that institutionalized strategies are influenced by people and organizations, not least by the sort of deviations just highlighted. We need look no further than our own domain to see this. Prior to 1980 few managers discussed the bases of 'differentiation' or 'low-cost' strategies. What academics do has changed this. After the publication of Porter's books (1980, 1985) and the dissemination of these concepts through consultancy and business schools, they came to be on the agenda of strategy debates in countless organizations throughout the world. The same could be said for concepts such as 'competencies' (Hamel and Prahalad 1990), organizational learning (Argyris and Schon 1978), knowledge management (Nonaka and Takeuchi 1995) and so on. At least according to the popular management literature, there are also individuals in organizations whose activities have similar legacies. In the 1980s Percy Barnavik lived out Asea Brown Boveri's transnational strategy. In the 1990s Jack Welch embodied GE's boundarylessness (Ashkenas et al. 1995). Again what is not so clear is just how this happens and just how profound the effects are.

However there are signs that this constitutes a developing research agenda. There is increasing attention to the role of 'institutional entrepreneurs' (Fligstein 1997). For example Holm (1995) and Bacharach, Bamberger and Sonnenstuhl (1996) show how political processes may resolve competing 'logics of action' in transforming institutions; Maguire, Hardy and Lawrence (2004) show how the activities of AIDS workers influenced the institutionalization of AIDS treatment in Canada; and Suddaby and Greenwood (2005) examine the 'discursive struggle' between institutional actors that influenced change in the accounting profession. The extent to which and how the activities of people in organizations might have such profound impact is not only a fascinating academic question; again it surely has significant practical managerial – and indeed policy – implications.

Our suggestion is, then, that taking seriously and attending to people's activities as they relate to strategy offers an extensive and intriguing agenda. Moreover, we hope we have shown that this agenda is not an alternative to, but is complementary and additive to research in the mainstream strategy field; indeed to the increasing interest in institutionalized aspects of strategy. We conclude this part of our discussion by offering two general observations on the research agenda.

First, we believe that a focus on activities resolves a problem in the strategy field. The need to link strategy content and strategy process research has been an enduring refrain in the strategy field (e.g. Bowman, Singh and Thomas 2002). However here we have already hinted that we are uncomfortable with this divide. Scholars who have examined micro aspects of organizational processes explain them in terms of activities that are very similar to those of scholars (few as they are) who have sought to explain at the same level of analysis the basis of, for example, competitive strategies (Ambrosini 2003). What people *do* in terms of activities within organizations is the bedrock of both organizational processes and organizational strategies. In recognizing this the content/process divide becomes redundant at this level.

Second, we highlight a potential trap to avoid. Although our focal interests lie at a lower level of activities, it is nonetheless important to acknowledge the significance of the vertical relationships in informing our research agenda. Whilst recognizing that research that sets out to explain activities more fully can be insightful, there is a danger if our collective concern becomes absorbed in the details of strategy process activities alone. The neglect of the vertical

links may entrap us into strategic irrelevance on the one hand or decontextualized minutiae on the other. Many Strategy as Practice researchers so far have
concentrated on the activities at the micro level of strategy process. However,
an exclusive focus on this south-east corner of figure 1.1 will ultimately prove
unproductive because, without the links to other parts of the figure, what
happens inside it will be both hard to explain and empty of impact.

Defining concepts: practice and praxis

The discussion of the research agenda in the previous section makes clear
its multilayered nature. The focus is on what people do, but within their
organizational and institutional contexts. Given this multilayered nature, it
helps to be clear about the most basic concept employed, that of 'practice'.
This has been employed in different ways and it is helpful to distinguish
between them (Whittington 2006).

Practices as what people engage with

People's activity always relies on some wider context. Central to this context are
the institutionalized and organizational practices with which people engage in
order to carry out their strategy activity. There are a range of concepts which
refer to these kinds of practices. They include institutional procedures, systems
such as strategic planning, and tools and techniques of strategic analysis. They
also include *norms* or *scripted behaviour* (e.g. Barley and Tolbert 1997), such as
agenda-driven behaviour in meetings or boards. Characteristic s*trategy
episodes* (Hendry and Seidl 2003) such as board meetings themselves, strategy
away-days or temporal sequences in planning or budgeting are also of interest,
both as important organizational phenomena and as potential units of analysis in research. All these practices are common across organizations, but there
are also specific organizational *routines*, the 'repetitive, recognisable patterns of
interdependent actions carried out by multiple actors' (Feldman and Pentland
2003: 95) that come to guide strategy activity in particular organizations.
Feldman and Pentland explain such routines in two usefully complementary
ways. '*Ostensive routines*' are 'the ideal or schematic form of a routine . . . the
routine in principle' (101), for example the organization's project proposal
routine or selection routine as it is 'supposed to happen'. But there are also 'performative routines' and these take us to our next category.

Practice as what people do

As well as practice as what people engage with, there is practice as what people actually do in relation to strategy. In terms of routines, Feldman and Pentland describe these as *performative routines*: 'specific actions, by specific people in specific places and times' (Feldman and Pentland 2003: 101). This is close to what Whittington (2006) refers to as *praxis*, which connotes not only every-day activities, but the relationship between those activities and the context (societal, institutional or organizational) in which such activity occurs. Feldman and Pentland, in making their distinction, similarly make the point that the performative will affect and amend the ostensive. Thus in both the notion of performative routine and the notion of praxis there is an import-ant relationship between the actions and behaviour of people and the more formalized practices in terms of structures and, systems with which they engage. Praxis allows for non-routinized behaviour and the synthesis of new behaviour from old behaviours. To what extent, then, is strategic activity driven by or a function of routine, as distinct from being idiosyncratic? Or, to reconfigure the question, what role does the individual actor play in relation to institutionalized structures and routines? It is, of course, this influence of activity on wider structures that is the underlying theme of our research agenda.

An example might be in relation to the growing usage of the term *strate-gizing* (Whittington 2003; Whittington and Melin 2003) which has come to be used to describe *how people go about the process of making strategy*. As such it could be thought of and studied in terms of how people use institutionalized practices in organizations such as planning routines. But in so doing, a Strategy as Practice research agenda would be bound to address praxis. Just how are such routines actually employed and what are the effects of how they are actually employed. We are interested not solely in institutionalized prac-tices in their idealized sense but in the activities, the doing, that explain their role and impact.

The structure of the book

In the rest of Part I of the book there are two further chapters. The first, 'Practical theories', reviews bodies of theory that are relevant to and useful for the study of Strategy as Practice. The review is not exhaustive, but rather provides a conceptual framework by which to locate the central themes of different bodies of theory. The aim is to give a broad view of key theories, so that readers can more easily identify appropriate theoretical resources for their particular projects. The chapter is a starting point for deeper and more focused theoretical exploration.

This is followed by a discussion of methodological approaches to the study of Strategy as Practice, drawing on illustrative examples, some of which are presented more completely in Part II of this book. Thus chapter 3 identifies the types of research designs and methods that are compatible with the substantive and theoretical foci of the Strategy as Practice perspective as presented in chapters 1 and 2, and examines some of the challenges of this type of research. Issues addressed include the selection and bounding of appropriate units of analysis, sampling, access and ethics, appropriate data sources and ways of linking data to theory.

Part II then provides a number of abbreviated papers that illustrate key aspects of the study of Strategy as Practice. These are drawn from some of the best management journals in the world. They have been chosen because, in different ways, they exemplify characteristics we believe to be important in papers addressing Strategy as Practice. Papers have been selected not because they are by academics who see themselves as aligned with Strategy as Practice as it is developing, but because they have important lessons for scholars who aspire to be so aligned.

Each of the papers is abbreviated using verbatim sections, with linking summary explanations by ourselves as the authors of this book. This is intended not as a substitute for reading them in full, which we encourage readers to do, but as a means of highlighting key aspects of the papers and avoiding undue repetition across them. At the end of each one there is a commentary section by ourselves in which we summarize some of the key lessons from it as they relate to Strategy as Practice. This is not intended to be an exhaustive set of papers. There are others we could have included and others that readers might think we should have included. But our hope is that they will be a useful source of learning and inspiration for scholars of Strategy as Practice.

The final chapter in the book takes the form of an overall commentary on the future development of Strategy as Practice. It is, however, different from the rest of the book in that each of the authors expresses his or her views individually. Given the early stages of development of this research area, and the debates and different views in the community of interest around Strategy as Practice, it seems appropriate that individual views and emphases should be aired here. Indeed, our hope is that this will stimulate useful and constructive debate as Strategy as Practice moves forward.

2 Practical theories

Introduction

Strategy as Practice is a good place to be working. Chapter 1 has established it as a new domain, one with plenty of empirical opportunities. This chapter will introduce some of the abundant theoretical resources and models for research available to pursue these opportunities. Many of these resources and models come from outside the strategy discipline itself, for the perspective taken by Strategy as Practice research is already integral to a much wider turn towards practice within contemporary thinking (Schatzki, Knorr-Cetina and Von Savigny 2001; Egginton and Sandbothe 2004). Across the disciplines, people's ordinary practical activities are taking a central place in meta-theoretical discourse. Moreover, this meta-theoretical discourse is helping to drive parallel advances in more focused areas of theory, each with potential relevance for Strategy as Practice research. From studies of learning to research into science and technology, middle-range theorizing and empirical work are being done with direct relevance to Strategy as Practice. As they develop their new domain, researchers on Strategy as Practice can be sure both that they are participating in a broader shift in contemporary thought and that they have robust models from other disciplines to guide them as they pursue their own new directions.

This chapter, therefore, introduces some of the parallel traditions on which Strategy as Practice researchers might draw. It is a large-scale map intended to provide a general orientation. Its aim is not to give a detailed discussion of particular theories or a definitive account of what is 'in' or 'out' for Strategy as Practice research. Rather, it aims to help readers see how the field fits broadly together and the range of theoretical resources that are available to them. We hope that as readers identify particularly promising theoretical resources for their particular projects, they will be able to find enough pointers to allow them to explore more deeply according to their precise needs.

Thus the chapter starts by introducing the 'practice turn' in philosophy and the social sciences generally, focusing on three key types of question raised in this meta-theoretical discourse: the extent and nature of agency, the relationship between micro and macro levels of analysis, and the nature and status of practical implications. The chapter continues by discussing four more focused bodies of theory: first, those related to situated learning; second, the sense-making and organizational routine traditions stemming from the Carnegie School; third, those in the broad institutionalist tradition; and finally, those centred on actor-network theory. Comparing these bodies of theory along the two axes of content and process, micro and macro, introduced in figure 1.1 from chapter 1, this chapter will indicate their potential contributions specifically to Strategy as Practice research. The third section in this chapter illustrates the potential relevance of these broad bodies of theory for middle-range theorizing and research, taking strategic planning as the example. Our purpose here, as always in this book, is to underline the importance of translating theory into practical empirical inquiry. The title of this chapter affirms that theory should be useful.

Theoretical orientations

The growing research interest in the practice of strategy is no accident. It forms part of larger intellectual movements. Since the 1970s, the social sciences and humanities have been finally escaping the old Enlightenment faith in detached and abstract rationalism that had been so dominant for the preceding two centuries (Toulmin 1991, 2001). Social theory has seen a 'practice turn', with many strands but all sharing a common concern with what people actually do (Schatzki et al. 2001; Reckwitz 2002). Similarly philosophy has pursued its 'pragmatic turn', again in many ways, but typically involving a renewed respect for practical wisdom (Egginton and Sandbothe 2004).

For strategy researchers, consciousness of participation in larger intellectual movements is, of course, encouraging in a general sense. But the broad frameworks such movements offer can also point to important issues that researchers in any domain of activity, whether domestic, political or business, need to address. In this section, we shall highlight three issues: the degree and nature of agency attributable to actors; the relationship of 'micro' activity to 'macro' social phenomena; and the potential for practical influence that can be derived from the research. The kinds of approaches to these issues suggested by the broader practice turns in philosophy and social theory are, we shall see, potentially quite different from traditional approaches to process research.

The convergence of strategy research with broader intellectual movements is overdue. It is the strategy's discipline misfortune that its foundation in the 1960s stamped it so firmly with that period's lingering Enlightenment faith in scientific detachment and abstraction (Whittington 2004). In recent decades, strategy has been left behind. While philosophy has been recovering its submerged pragmatist tradition, and social theory has developed various theoretical frameworks for practice, strategy is only now beginning to throw off the narrow definitions of appropriate research set in its founding years. With Strategy as Practice, the strategy discipline is merely catching up with the progress of its sister disciplines. Here both philosophy's new pragmatism and social theory's rediscovery of activity have a great deal to offer.

Pragmatism

We start with the pragmatist tradition in philosophy not just because of the obvious resonance of its title with that of Strategy as Practice. As Richard Rorty (1999) suggests, pragmatism is part of a larger family of influential non-essentialist philosophies that include Derrida, Latour, Foucault and the later Wittgenstein. This non-essentialism implies a distrust of hard-and-fast dualisms, such as those between reality and appearance or subject and object. One implication of such a non-essentialist position is to accept that actors' awareness of the world is inescapably a product of their own language and activities, and to work with the consequences of this. We shall pick up some of these other family members in our discussion of social theories of practice. But in philosophy more strictly, it is pragmatism that is winning increasing attention (Egginton and Sandbothe 2004). While each of the other philosophical traditions offers relevant insights of their own, we shall therefore let pragmatism stand for at least some of the characteristic features of them all.

Pragmatism is in fact more than a century old. Its founders – Peirce, James and Dewey – proposed in various ways a philosophy that highlighted the importance of the practical. Knowledge was not an intellectual search for absolute truths, but was discovered in practical activity; its value was not established against abstract standards, but derived from its usefulness in guiding subsequent activity. Activity is at the same time the producer of knowledge and its measure. This broad perspective is exemplified by John Dewey's (1938) approach to educational and social reform. Dewey's politics emphasized less change in the larger structures of society, more the educational improvement of children as individuals. In this view, social change came through educating capable, active citizens, not by traditional formal didacticism in schools but by hands-on experience of practical skills.

For most of the twentieth century this reformist pragmatist current was submerged by the larger struggle between different economic systems in the world of politics, and by positivism and analytical philosophy in the academy. Only lately has pragmatism been revived by philosophers such as Rorty (1980) and Putnam (1995). Rorty, the more radical, proposes a view of knowledge far from the Enlightenment pursuit of absolute truths. For him, the test of knowledge is not its correspondence to some reality, but its contribution to coping better in everyday life and to sustaining better conversations in science. The pragmatist's criterion for knowledge is practical utility rather than ontological reality (Rorty 1998: 45). This is not necessarily a relativist point of view. Here Putnam (1995, 2004) takes a stronger position than Rorty. The findings of democratic, inclusive and transparent scientific inquiry can be trusted, for they are tested, rejected and improved through robust procedures in which the more useful will supersede the less. In judging utility, primacy is granted to the practising agent's point of view. Including practitioners in the research process itself is, then, not just a matter of ensuring relevance but a useful step to securing its very quality. There is no necessary trade-off between relevance and rigour.

The revival of pragmatism in philosophy is already finding its followers in management theory (Wicks and Freeman 1998; Powell 2002, 2003). It gives researchers at least three important guidelines. First, it values concrete action and experience. In pragmatist-orientated research, micro-activity takes the foreground; larger structures fade behind. Second, pragmatism places people at the centre of analysis. As for Dewey's school-children, people can be, but by no means necessarily are, active and creative agents, capable of using knowledge to shape the world and achieve their purposes. The pragmatist researcher must take people and their potential for agency seriously. Third, pragmatism emphasizes the importance of knowledge as practical, as making a difference, rather than striving vainly for correspondence with an elusive reality. Powell (2002: 979) writes: 'in a complex world, where facts are messy and disrespectful of our theories about them, we need not take the desperate course of constructing defences and pretences to "correspondence". Our truth is not correspondent, but *instrumental* – the better theory is the one that stimulates better research, better teaching, better learning, better practice.' Strategy research from a pragmatist perspective is not about creating abstract generalizations, but about getting close enough to actors and their activities in order to help them be more effective in the field. This kind of research can be aided, not encumbered, by involving practitioners directly in performing it. Pragmatism's three broad guidelines – valuing activity, agency and the practical – find frequent echoes in the more focused bodies of theory that follow later in this chapter.

The social theory of practice

The turn to practice in social theory shares pragmatism's concern for practical activity, but adds a greater focus on the relationship between this activity and the larger social systems or structures in which it is embedded. This turn reflects a broader recovery of practical reason within the sciences generally, challenging the detached scientific rationalism established by the Enlightenment (Tsoukas and Cummings 1997; Toulmin 2001). Seminal theorists of the practice turn in social theory include Pierre Bourdieu, Michel de Certeau, Michel Foucault and Anthony Giddens. Together, these theorists do not propose a grand theoretical 'system', in the mode of Talcott Parsons for instance. Rather, their work offers sensitizing vocabularies and frameworks that ground research in the practical activity and reason of human actors (Giddens 1984; Reckwitz 2002).

Practice perspectives differ in emphasis, but Schatzki (2001) synthesizes three core themes. First, practice perspectives are centrally concerned with activity of all kinds, not just the large and extraordinary but also the minute and the routine. This attention to the apparently banal is reflected in de Certeau's (1984) sociology of 'everyday life', Bourdieu's (1988: xi) ambition to exoticize the domestic and Giddens' (1987) claim for the importance of making remarkable the unremarked. De Certeau and his followers are concerned with all the minutiae of 'doing cooking' or 'doing shopping', and highlight the taken-for-granted understandings and artefacts that make these possible (1984, 1998).

Second, practice perspectives situate this activity within fields of social practice, in which human actors draw on the shared understandings, skills, language and technologies of the wider society. We find this in Bourdieu's (1990) notion of the habitus, Foucault's (1977) concern for discursive practices and de Certeau's (1984; de Certeau, Giard and Mayol 1998) attention to material artefacts. In Foucault (1977, 1978), it is the historical emergence of new discourses of madness or sexuality in Western society that makes some practices possible and visible, normal or abnormal. It is this recognition of the situatedness of activity in society that underpins practice theorists' essential claim to have transcended social theory's old divide: on the one hand, the micro-reductionism of individualist theoretical approaches, focused on the activities of individual people, and on the other, the macro-reifications of 'societists', strong believers in the power of abstract social structures and systems (Schatzki 2005). Practice theorists take seriously both micro activity and macro contexts.

The third core theme in the practice turn is a concern for actors and the kinds of skills and resources they bring to the ordinary activities of their daily lives. Here, actors should be seen not simply as programmed by social practice, but rather as potentially artful manipulators of the constraints and capital afforded by their social positions (de Certeau 1984; Bourdieu 1990). As particularly in Giddens' (1984) structuration theory, it is by such artful performance that actors reproduce and amend the stock of social rules and resources on which their activity relies. And, in so far as social scientific knowledge tends, in modern societies, to seep through its language and concepts into everyday performance, the social sciences directly or indirectly become a resource by which actors may develop their activity (Giddens 1987). Our research can make a difference to people's lives.

These social theorists of practice attend more to the mutual dependence of local activity and large structures than many pragmatist currents. At the same time, though, they manage to preserve the central common faith both in the potential for agency and in the capacity of increased understanding to support such agency. Especially through Giddens, this broad perspective is already influential in management and organization studies, particularly as encapsulated in 'processual' approaches (Whittington 1992; Pozzebon 2004). For processualists, the structurationist account of constrained but feasible agency provides a plausible theoretical motor for the difficult processes of organizational change (Pettigrew 1985). But the practice turn in social theory licenses at least three further concerns that together mark out a substantial difference from many established processual approaches.

First, as emphasized in chapter 1, the practice perspective is more fascinated by the practical activity of people. Whereas many processual approaches can be content with accounting for change at an organizational or even population level (van de Ven and Scott 2005), the theory of practice insists on attending to what people do in such change. In Brown and Duguid's (2000: 95) phrase, practice is 'the internal life of process': from this perspective, it is the busy activity of people within larger processes that ultimately matters. The second difference flows from this focus on people. The dependent variable in traditional strategy studies is the performance of the organizational unit as a whole (Barney 2002). A practice approach points more to the performance of the artful individuals that make up that organization. From there it is a short step to a Deweyan concern for helping these individuals through practical education. Strategy is not just about organizational performance; helping practitioners perform their jobs matters too. The third difference goes up a level or two. While processualists have always been attentive to economic or social context, this has typically been seen as 'external' (Pettigrew 1985). The practice perspective, on the other hand, tends to read economic and social 'context' as both essentially involved in the definition of actors and directly implicated in the possibility of their action (Whittington 2006). As in Foucauldian accounts particularly, even the smallest activity – for example, the possibility of soldiers marching in disciplined order – relies upon a much larger matrix of social and economic conditions. Social and economic context are not outside, but thoroughly internalized in everything that happens. In this sense, although some might resist these terms, the practice perspective both looks more deeply into the micro-activity inside organizational process and attends more seriously to the macro-context outside process.

In sum, pragmatism in philosophy and the practice turn in social theory orientate research in some clear broad directions. Together they insist on the importance of activity and experience; they offer the possibility of agency; they recognize the role of knowledge in supporting this agency. There are differences, of course. As a philosophical position, pragmatism is naturally more concerned with validity criteria, emphasizing practicality over the search for absolutes. As theories of society, practice theories have given greater weight to linking activity with the wider conditions that make it possible. Nevertheless, together pragmatism and practice theory offer a sensibility amply able to motivate and direct research into the doing of strategy.

Pragmatism and practice theory, then, set the broad directions for such research, but they are both ultimately meta-theoretical. The task for researchers, of course, is to translate these meta-theoretical orientations into practical research. This next section explores four areas of theory more closely attached to empirical research, each offering models to emulate.

Theoretical resources

This section examines four broad theoretical traditions that have directly engaged with the kinds of activity stressed by the practice turn and pragmatism. First, there is the Situated Learning tradition, associated with ideas such as tacit knowledge and communities of practice. Second, we put together the

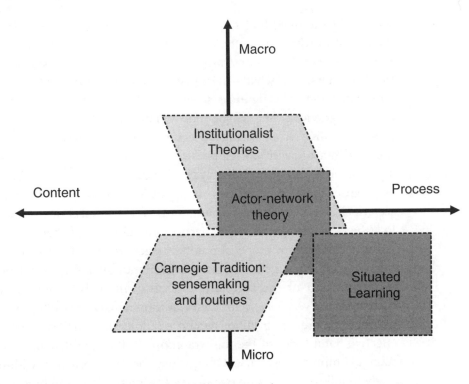

Fig. 2.1   Four theoretical resources for Strategy as Practice research

sensemaking and organizational routine perspectives, as both sharing the Carnegie School's emphasis on bounded rationality. Third, there are institutionalist perspectives, broadly conceived, both in their predominantly American Neoinstititutionalist form and in the more European Foucauldian variant. Last comes actor-network theory, challenging fundamental assumptions about micro and macro, content and process. In terms of orientations, concepts and empirical models, all of these areas of theory offer potentially powerful resources for strategy as practice research. They are not the only models available: for example, we shall touch on symbolic interactionism, ethnomethodology and dramaturgy in the final section. However, we highlight these four because they represent distinctive starting points and are already supported by intriguing empirical research.

We can map these traditions' distinctive starting points in terms of two axes. Figure 2.1 transforms figure 1.1 from chapter 1 along two continuous axes. Thus the vertical axis represents the relative emphasis on micro- or macro-level phenomena, a tension identified in our introductory chapter 1 and addressed also by the practice turn within social theory. At the bottom of the vertical axis is an exclusive concern with detailed activity; at the top is a focus on broad patterns or forces in society at large. The horizontal axis attends to the extent to which these theoretical resources focus predominantly on the process issue of 'how' – in strategy, strategic change or decision-making – or the content issue of 'what' – in strategy, issues such as diversification or internationalization. The figure is schematic. Positionings reflect the theories' centres of gravity rather than bounded domains. We deliberately represent the axes as continua, emphasizing degrees of relative emphasis, and we demarcate the shaded areas with dotted lines only, suggesting porosity in boundaries. There is the potential, and already some endeavour, to reach out beyond these boundaries to build bridges across the various quartiles. Indeed, as we have seen in chapter 1, an important ambition of Strategy as Practice research is to link the particular foci of each quartile more closely together.

But an important practical point emerges from figure 2.1: none of these theoretical traditions sits squarely across all four quartiles. Most tend towards the micro end of the spectrum, with institutionalist theories positioned highest on the vertical axis for their traditional macro orientation. Of course, the ideal theoretical tradition would straddle all quartiles equally, but the effective boundaries of the four traditions hint at the demands involved in such a comprehensive view. Often it may be more practical within a single study to follow a self-conscious strategy of 'methodological bracketing', concentrating on a subset of the quartiles, though ideally not one in isolation (Giddens 1979). Such a study should acknowledge what may have been 'bracketed', signalling what has been left out. But as studies cumulate in complementary quartiles, they should together finally build a more complete picture of activity involving both content and process, micro and macro.

We shall introduce the four main approaches, starting with the Situated Learning approach at the bottom right-hand corner of figure 2.1. We then continue clockwise through the sensemaking and organizational routines perspectives of the Carnegie School tradition, Institutionalist theories and finally actor-network theory, the most central because most challenging to the figure's extreme polarities.

Situated Learning

At first sight, learning might seem remote from the concerns of Strategy as Practice research. But the Situated Learning tradition in fact draws directly from pragmatists such as Dewey and practice theorists such as Bourdieu, focusing on how people learn in everyday activity. A situated approach values learning in the contexts of ordinary lives, rather than extracted to some place of formal education (Elsbach, Barr and Hargadon 2005). As we shall see, the 'Situated Learning' tradition is highly suggestive in terms of theoretical constructs, empirical method and even some of the core concepts of strategy.

Lave and Wenger's (1991) book *Situated Learning* established the main features of a research tradition that has since talked increasingly to issues in management. Although they were interested in a wide range of skills – from shoppers' use of maths in a supermarket to clerical workers in the office – their emphasis on learning as something that occurs socially and through activity has a direct resonance. Learning is done by people, not as individuals but as 'people-in-the-world'. Learning is about becoming members of 'communities of practice', for whom legitimacy may be at least as important as cognition. The social character of these communities of practice means that horizontal relationships may be at least as important as hierarchical ones. Practice involves command of a complete 'activity system', embracing communities, rules, artefacts, tools and signs (Engeström 2001). Many key skills are highly tacit, embedded in the minutiae of activity, and therefore to be learnt only through direct experience (Wenger 1998). Learning emerges through activity.

It is for this appreciation of the minutiae of activity that we position the Situated Learning approach in the bottom half of figure 2.1, with an emphasis on the micro. Communities of practice are, moreover, typically conceived of as small groups within particular organizations, for instance a group of photocopying engineers or insurance clerks (Orr 1996; Wenger 1998). A challenge for the approach is to take greater cognizance of macro-level effects, such as power in society and extra-organizational networks (Brown and Duguid 2000; Contu and Willmott 2003). Moreover, its concern for learning places it predominantly on the process side of the figure. A strong preconception of the Situated Learning approach is that knowledge should be seen not as something static, but as dynamically evolving through activity.

Nevertheless, the Situated Learning approach has potentially wide relevance to research on the doing of strategy, both theoretically and as a model for research. The emphasis on tacit knowledge has always been important in the resource-based view of the firm, conceptually at least (Ambrosini and Bowman 2001). Sympathy with emergent and horizontal models of behaviour resonates with Mintzbergian concepts of strategy formation. Orlikowski (2002) draws on Situated Learning concepts to transform Hamel and Prahalad's (1990) famous notion of 'core competence' from a property seen as fixed or given to something that is constituted everyday in the ongoing practices of an organization's members. What all these ideas reinforce is a distrust of claims to locate competitive advantage in the formal, the explicit and the large scale. The Situated Learning approach encourages us to engage directly and intimately with what people actually do inside organizations.

The Situated Learning approach moreover offers us both models and concepts for empirical research. The theoretical commitment to situatedness obliges researchers to immerse themselves deep inside the activity they are observing: Orr (1996) follows his photocopier engineers through their days, starting with their team breakfasts; Hutchins (1996) goes on to the ship's bridge to study his pilots; Wenger (1998) does the work of his clerical workers himself. Concepts such as activity system (Engeström 2001) and community of practice (Lave and Wenger 1991) emphasize the interdependent nature of activity, involving peers, local cultural rules and even the material artefacts upon which people rely to get things done. The actors of the Situated Learning tradition are far from the perfectly rational, isolated individuals of neoclassical economics. This distance from rational economic models of the actor is something developed also in the Carnegie School.

The Carnegie tradition: sensemaking and organizational routines

The Carnegie School, associated with the work of March and Simon (1958) and Cyert and March (1963), has spawned two important streams of work with potential relevance to research on doing strategy – that concerned with organizational sensemaking and that concerned with organizational routines and capabilities. The two streams are distinct, but they both stem from the Carnegie School's insistence on 'bounded rationality', as opposed to the 'perfect rationality' hitherto presumed in conventional neoclassical economics (Argote, McEviley and Reagans 2003). If actors are boundedly rational, their struggle to make sense of their worlds becomes a problematic and consequential process in itself. If actors are boundedly rational too, they are prone to rely upon past routines rather than *de novo* calculation in their activity. Some of these routines will develop an efficacy that others can only imperfectly imitate and thus become sources of competitive advantage. Because of their shared intellectual origins, and the similar positions they occupy at the micro end of figure 2.1, we shall treat sensemaking and organizational routines under the same heading as members of the Carnegie tradition.

For Strategy as Practice researchers, the value of the sensemaking tradition in particular is its insistence that cognition is shaped by action, especially interaction with others (Weick 1995). Thus the sensemaking tradition goes beyond the detached maps, proxy variables, simulations and experiments that have been characteristic of a good deal of Carnegie-inspired cognition research (Hodgkinson and Sparrow 2002). Sensemaking researchers have made major investments in direct observation of real interaction, using methods such as ethnography, participant observation, diary techniques and regular focus groups with research subjects over time (e.g. Gioia and Chittipeddi 1991; Weick and Roberts 1993; Balogun and Johnson 2004). Typically this sense-making tradition concentrates on interaction at the level of groups, treated as somewhat detached from the wider social environment – fire-fighting teams, aircraft carrier crews or top management groups, for example (Weick 1993; Weick and Roberts 1993; Maitlis 2005). It is very rare that group sensemaking is situated within societal structures. That there is potential to do so, however, is illustrated by Rouleau's (2005) study of how supplier–customer sensemak-ing links to the social structures of gender and language in the Quebec fashion industry. Being male or female, Francophone or Anglophone, makes a difference to local sensemaking and interaction. There is more to be done to move sensemaking from its present micro focus to a broader acknowledgement of societal structures.

The strength of the sensemaking tradition so far, however, belongs on the process side of the domain sketched out in figure 2.1. Sensemaking emerges as a potentially critical activity for strategy and change. Dutton and Dukerich (1991) use a sensemaking approach to follow the recognition and acting on of an emergent strategic issue – homelessness – for the New York Port Authority (cf. Dutton and Dukerich 2006). More recently, Maitlis' (2005) longitudinal study of three orchestras finds that distinct patterns of sensemaking (frag-mented, restricted, guided or minimal) around key issues can have important implications for the coherence of subsequent organizational actions and the sense that organizational actors make of them. In a classic study summarized later in this volume, Gioia and Chittipeddi (1991) use participant observation to uncover the related phenomenon of sensegiving, in which a university president embarked on change gives sense to his employees on what he intends and what he is achieving. Gioia and Chittipeddi (1991) remark on the role in sensegiving of concrete activities, such as meetings, presentations, appointments, employment of consultants and so on. However, in a telling difference between the interests of process and practice theorists, their account concentrates on the overall change processes as abstract stages (i.e. envisioning, signalling, re-visioning and energizing), rather than examining the concrete activities inside these processes as effortful and consequential accomplishments in themselves.

The other relevant perspective within the Carnegie School tradition is the growing research on routines and dynamic capabilities (Cohen et al. 1996; Teece, Pisano and Shuen 1997; Becker et al. 2005). Originating with Cyert and March's (1963) insight into how standard operating procedures develop over time to displace discrete decision making, these have now been integrated into the resource-based view of the firm as sources of potential advantage. Routines are standard behaviours, rules of thumb or even strategies that are used, consciously or not, in a largely repetitive fashion. Such routines might range from the actions of workers on a production line to such heuristics as 'always be number one or number two in all your markets' (Cohen et al. 1996). In Teece et al.'s (1997) classic definition, dynamic capabilities refer to an organization's ability to integrate, build and reconfigure such routines (or competences), particularly in innovative ways. Given the role of routines and capabilities as sources of organizational competitive advantage, this tradition of research has tended to focus on the micro- rather than macro-level forces: the predominant interest is in the differences between particular organizations, whether in terms of strategy content or strategy process. Indeed, the more micro the routines and capabilities are, the more valuable they are likely to become, because less easily descried and imitated by competitors.

Theoretically, then, the Carnegie approach to routines and capabilities strongly supports research attention to the detailed activities that go on inside organizations as wholes. However, a good deal of empirical work in this tradition remains semi-detached (Johnson et al. 2003). For example, Zollo and Singh (2004) uncover the role of routines such as project management and training manuals in acquisitions, a classic strategy content issue, but do so by means of a survey. This semi-detached approach to routines reinforces rather fixed notions, with little sense of interpretation or agency: in such an approach, routines or practices such as project management become objectified. Responding to this, Feldman and Pentland (2003) have recently built on Bourdieu, Giddens and Latour to develop a distinction between ostensive routines, in other words standard and ideal procedures, and performative routines, what is actually enacted. Following this logic, Howard-Greville's (2005) ethnographic study of technology 'roadmapping' as a strategy practice reveals the potential for considerable flexibility in the actual performance of even long-standing routines. The challenge for future Strategy as Practice research is to understand more about how routines are actually performed. As we shall see, this same problem of interpretation and agency is common to the kinds of macro-level phenomena emphasized in a good deal of institutional theory.

Institutional theories

The dominant form of institutional theory today is Neoinstitutional theory, drawing heavily on similar root assumptions to those of the Carnegie School, particularly in rejecting perfect economic rationality (Scott 2000). Where Neoinstitutional theory has traditionally differed is in swinging the focus up, towards the macro end of the spectrum in figure 2.1. In place of organizational routines, institutional theory emphasizes institutional rules or cultural norms in the wider environment that define how organizations should be (Meyer and Rowan 1977). In advanced societies today, one of the strongest norms is that organizations should be strategic (Nelson and Winter 1982; Knights and Morgan 1991).

The institutionalization of strategy as a general phenomenon in society is part of what Meyer and Rowan (1977) have identified as a secular trend towards increasing rationalization of organizations, under pressure from the professions, nation states and the media. Conforming to the dictates of rationality, or appearing to do so anyway, is driven at least as much by the need to be legitimate in the eyes of powerful external actors as by calculations of simple economic advantage. Researchers in this tradition have shown the influence of institutional environments in accounting for the spread throughout large organizational populations of strategies such as diversification (Fligstein 1990), structures such as the multidivisional (Palmer, Jennings and Zhou 1993), departments such as Human Resources (Baron, Dobbin and Jennings 1986), and positions such as Chief Financial Officer (Zorn 2004). As such, the balance of research so far has been on the content side of figure 2.1, although rationalistic practices such as financial reporting or Total Quality Management extend the institutionalists' terrain across to the process side (Young, Charns and Shortell 2001; Kostova and Roth 2002; Mezias 1990).

Typically these Neoinstitutional theorists have grasped their phenomena through large databases and surveys. Some of this is very useful: for Strategy as Practice researchers, knowing what people typically do can provide important contextual background in interpreting particular inter-actions. However, a great deal of institutional research has so far stayed at a level of aggregation in which the details of activity are hidden and the exercise of agency is smothered. A Strategy as Practice perspective would want to extend Neoinstitutional theory's insights at the macro level to detailed interactions at the micro level. Ethnographies of strategy practice can be more directly informed by institutionalist understandings of the appropriateness of strategy conventions in different contexts. For example, the legitimacy of certain standard MBA strategy practices varies over time and across national contexts. The task of the institutionalists is to inform the strategy ethnographer of the likely appropriateness of such MBA strategy practices in particular circumstances, whether a Chinese family business or a European hospital.

Institutional theorists of various kinds are already beginning to theorize and research this connection of the micro and the macro. Discourse analysis, script theory, structuration theory and dialectical notions are all being invoked in order to conceptualize the interdependence of micro-level activity and macro-level institutions (Johnson, Smith and Codling 2000; Seo and Creed 2002; Phillips, Lawrence and Hardy 2004). Barley's (1986) paper, summarized later, was an early endeavour of this type, using structuration theory to link macro-level competition between occupational groups to micro-struggles between hospital radiologists and technologists over who should control the new CT scanner technology. A more recent exemplary empirical exploration of this interdependence is Maguire et al.'s (2004) study of how AIDS activists acted as 'institutional entrepreneurs' in creating new practices in the Canadian political-medical arena. Using interviews, documents, correspondence and participant observation, these researchers are able to connect the detailed activities of concrete individuals to the institutionalization of a new national-level norm of cooperation between campaigning organizations and pharmaceutical companies.

Promising though these attempts to bridge the macro–micro divide may be, the Foucauldian perspective on institutions is altogether more radical. For Foucault (1977), integrating the two is something of a non-problem, for institutional effects are implicated in the very definition of actors as people. So far, this Foucauldian perspective on institutions has found little empirical application to strategy, although the paper by Oakes, Townley and Cooper (1998) summarized later in this volume takes a very similar perspective. Nonetheless, in a theoretical paper Knights and Morgan (1991) do draw explicitly on Foucault to offer suggestive insights on how the historical rise of strategy as a practice in advanced societies has transformed managers' self-understanding from bureaucratic administrators to strategic actors with an internalized responsibility for their own performance. In this way, the 'macro' become part of the 'micro', as institutional forces form actors' very essence and suffuse their least activities. This confounding of polarities is something that actor-network theory has developed still further.

Actor-network theory

Actor-network Theory (commonly abbreviated as ANT) has its origins in the sociology of science, but has now inspired studies extending from military aircraft (Law and Callon 1988) to intrauterine devices (Dugdale 1999). This breadth of application is clearly promising for a new field such as Strategy as Practice (Denis, Langley and Rouleau 2007). Moreover it challenges the dualities of figure 2.1 in a fashion that supports our aspiration for a more integrated approach to strategy. With regard to the horizontal axis, its concern with activity subverts the stable properties associated with strategy content, tending to render everything as process. As for the vertical axis, ANT distrusts the hierarchical distinction between 'micro' and 'macro', preferring 'flat ontologies' along the horizontal plane of networks (cf. Seidl 2006). All this makes ANT hard to place on figure 2.1. But ANT's very disregard for the figure's distinctions provides a useful reminder here. Strategy as Practice research is not to be confined to one corner: chapter 1 offered a deliberately exploded map of the strategy field; the promise of Strategy as Practice is to achieve a reintegration that reflects the coherence of reality.

Nevertheless, ANT's weighting towards the bottom part of figure 2.1 reflects its origins in micro studies of the work of scientists and technologists in their laboratories (Latour and Woolgar 1979; Knorr-Cetina 1995; Michael 1996). In a phrase anticipating Strategy as Practice, the characteristic concern of these studies was to understand 'what technologists actually *do*' (Law and Callon 1988: 288). ANT researchers began to tease out the kinds of work involved in producing scientific and technical knowledge, the kinds of people who did it, and the kinds of skills and tools they used. As they did so, they established a key methodological principle: 'follow the actor' (Latour 1987; Law and Callon 1988). In concentrating intensely on what people are actually doing, Latour (2005) praises the research quality of obsessive 'myopia'. Ethnography and photography are typical research methods (Latour and Woolgar 1979; Latour 1999).

ANT offers at least three insights destabilizing to conventional theoretical approaches. First, ANT is suspicious of social phenomena being treated as 'things'. For Latour (2005), such phenomena – whether groups, nations, markets or strategies – are always in the making and cease to exist as soon as people stop doing the work that makes them. Treating social phenomena as constantly in formation leads researchers backstage, uncovering the practitioner skills, knacks and contingency involved in keeping them going. Applying this principle to strategy subverts the stability assumed by the content pole of figure 2.1: ANT would claim relevance to strategy content issues, but treat them completely differently, as continuously precarious activities. The second insight is with regard to the potential importance of non-human actors. The progress of science and technology is profoundly shaped by the kinds of tools and materials available to its practitioners (Clark and Fujimoto 1992). Asking 'Where are the missing masses?', Latour (1992) extends the argument to actors of all kinds, proposing that non-human actors – even automatic doors and sleeping policemen – have an influence equivalent to that of human actors, though one that is somehow easily neglected. From the ANT perspective, tools and materials can have an impact on activity of their own.

ANT's third destabilizing insight is into the arguably arbitrary nature of macro and micro. Actor-network Theory does what it says: it keeps on following actors of all kinds across the flat network of connections required for action to take place. In the analysis of a military aircraft project, there is no need for an 'up' and 'down' or 'micro' and 'macro' to link aerodynamics, engineers, aircraft companies and the British state into a single network (Law and Callon 1988). 'Micro' studies should beware putting the 'macro' to one side. Latour (2005: 148) quotes the famous architect: 'As Rem Koolhaas said: "context stinks". It's simply a way of stopping the description when you are tired or too lazy to go on.'

A good deal of ANT appears somewhat exotic, but there has been some effort to integrate it into the management disciplines (e.g. MacLean and Hassard 2004) and the theory's proponents have themselves made direct links to strategy. For example, Akrich, Callon and Latour (2002) analyse innovation as an art involving the assembly of a network of human and non-human actors, whose elements are being continuously tested and reconfigured. Here innovation is not a thing, but a precarious and ongoing achievement (cf. Dougherty 1992). In a theoretical article, Callon and Law (1997: 178) describe an archetypal strategist ('Andrew') as embedded in a network of other human and non-human actors:

It is tempting to say that 'Andrew is a strategist'. But this is a shorthand that is dangerously misleading. For like all the other actors we have described, Andrew-the-strategist is a heterogeneous network: Andrew + fax + fellow managers + secretary + head office + trains to London + his PC + the work of scientists and engineers + the memos that circulate + the time slips filled in by employees – it is this combination that creates the possibility of strategic action.

In outlining here this heterogeneous network of humans and non-humans, ANT is pointing to an intriguingly extensive research agenda on what it takes for people actually to 'do strategy'. The actors of strategy are not just people, but include such stuff as computers, forms and even trains as well.

Strategic planning from four perspectives

The empirical agenda for Strategy as Practice can take from the theoretical discussion so far some common themes. From Dewey, through de Certeau, to the Situated Learning, sensemaking and ANT traditions, there is a strong focus on activity. In pragmatism, Situated Learning and ANT, though less strongly in Neoinstitutional theory or some accounts of routines, people are the central drivers of this activity. Time and again there is a strong emphasis on the significance of the 'micro', whether in Bourdieu's concern to exoticize the domestic, Wenger's attention to the minutiae of learning, the importance of opaque and inimitable routines or Latour's ambivalent 'myopia'. For de Certeau, Engeström and ANT, material tools and artefacts are a potentially critical part of this 'micro'. Neoinstitutional theory especially highlights the macro origins of these tools and artefacts, together with the rules and norms that govern their use. Indeed, the links between the micro and the macro are often stressed: for structuration theory and increasingly for Neoinstitutional theory, this is a central theme, even if ANT suspects the very categories themselves. Emphases differ, but what we can take from all these theoretical perspectives is this: that at the centre of Strategy as Practice are people, working with others and reliant on tools of all kinds, the success of whose activities depends both on mastery of the minutiae deep within their organizations and connection to the wider world outside.

The task now is to indicate how these kinds of insights can be translated into concrete research questions at a middle-range level (Bourgeois 1979). We shall illustrate some broad approaches by taking the example of formal strategic planning. Readers can mentally substitute their own phenomenon as they continue, but we choose strategic planning as an archetypal strategizing activity. Even if widely challenged (Mintzberg 1994), strategic planning remains, in some form or other, the most popular management technique (Rigby 2005). Certainly, strategic planning has been the subject of a long stream of research, focused on the traditional question of its relationship with performance, but this research has recently become increasingly inconclusive and frustrated (Brews and Hunt 1999). In its place, Strategy as Practice orientated research is already beginning to offer new and productive insights into strategic planning (Jarzabkowski 2005) and this section will explore how the four more focused bodies of theory introduced in the previous section could continue to develop this long-standing and important topic.

We shall start at the most 'macro' level – if ANT will still allow us this term. Here Neoinstitutional theory would offer the same kind of straightforward questions asked of other management practices. For example, it would ask about the rate at which strategic planning spread historically (Fligstein 1990); the evenness of diffusion patterns across sectors or countries (Whitley 1999); the characteristics of pioneering firms (Palmer et al. 1993); and the nature of its carriers – consultants, the media or mobile businesspeople (Abrahamson 1996; Whittington et al. 2003). These questions would approach the issue of strategic planning's performance from a different direction. Instead of simply testing the direct economic performance effects of strategic planning at the level of the firm, the Neoinstitutionalist approach would grasp its advantages and disadvantages more roundly. By probing the swiftness of diffusion, the evenness of acceptance and the character of pioneers, promoters and resisters, strategic planning would be explored as something that is pushed, practised and resisted for all kinds of reasons, going beyond economic performance (cf. Langley 1989; Oakes, Townley and Cooper 1998). Its overall success, or putative fall (Mintzberg 1994), could be assessed in terms of trends at a societal level. The Neoinstitutionalist perspective might thus widen our appreciation of the different rationales for strategic planning and deepen our understanding of its limits.

However, this institutionalist perspective could also offer a useful frame for more micro-level explorations of strategy activity. Here, following structuration theory and others, the institutionalized practices of strategic planning would be seen as potentially offering rules, resources, scripts or discourses for local strategizing (Giddens 1984; Johnson et al. 2000). The shape, participants and outcomes of particular episodes of strategy activity could be interpreted according to how formal planning practices were legitimate, contested or even absent in local arenas. Here a macro appreciation of strategic planning as a set of institutionalized practices would be directly informing micro-level analysis of strategy analysis. To take a brief illustration: the failure of a scenario planning exercise at a publishing company reported by Hodgkinson and Wright (2002) might be traced not just to the politics and competence of the participants, but to the local legitimacy of such planning practices and the academic consultants that introduced them (Whittington 2006).

At this micro level, both the Situated Learning and the sensemaking traditions also raise important questions for strategic planning. Given the large place occupied in strategic planning first by data collection and analysis, and then subsequently to communication of conclusions, sensemaking and sensegiving are clearly central elements. While Gioia and Chittipeddi (1991) outline broad processes, a sensemaking perspective on practice would be drawn to the intimate dynamics of interaction amongst planning teams, at particular times and particular places. By analogy with its focus on small groups under pressure (e.g. Weick and Roberts 1993), such a sensemaking approach might be particularly sensitive to the possible influence of tight timings in the planning cycle, or the exclusivity and secrecy of the planning team. A Situated Learning approach, on the other hand, would be more interested in how people become accepted as full and influential members of a strategic planning team in the first place. Here the planning team might be treated as a community of practice, in which legitimate participation may require not just simple nomination, but the kind of apprenticeship which allows acquisition of the subtle minutiae of appropriate local practice. In asking what it takes to become a planner, the Situated Learning approach would be true to the long pragmatist concern for the development of people above organizations. And, recalling Feldman and Pentland's (2003) distinction between the ostensive and the performative, one of the skills of an accomplished planner would be expected to lie in the ability to interpret local planning routines in an adaptive, creative way.

ANT would approach the making of a planner from an even more non-individualistic point of view than the Situated Learning tradition. Recalling 'Andrew-the-Strategist' (Callon and Law 1997), an ANT analysis would explore the network of people and technologies necessary for a planner to perform his or her job. Certainly there would be team members, but ANT might also trace links far outside the organization, to the network of consultants, former colleagues and business school teachers that furnish them with the basic conceptual apparatus of planning in the first place. ANT would be particularly alert too to the material technologies involved in planning: flip-charts, brown-paper, mobile phones, video-conferencing, laptops, and the spreadsheets and presentational software typically supplied by Microsoft. In an ANT analysis of any planning episode, the software engineers of Seattle would be actors alongside the planners themselves (Molloy and Whittington 2005).

Conclusion

Strategy as Practice is a new current, one that is distant from dominant forms of content research and distinctive even from traditional process approaches.

Yet the message of this chapter should be encouraging. Strategy as Practice is following the direction of contemporary movements in philosophy and social theory: in this sense, it is part of the mainstream, and traditional strategy research is out of step. Moreover, this participation in the broad currents of contemporary research furnishes Strategy as Practice researchers with rich theoretical resources as they tackle the new questions of their empirical domain.

This chapter has sought to identify some of the main contours of relevant contemporary theory. This is not an exhaustive set. As Stolte, Fine and Cook (2001) argue, sociology today offers many rich traditions of 'sociological miniaturism', each capable of illuminating in its own way aspects of detailed human activity relevant to strategy practice. For example, symbolic interactionism, dramaturgy, discourse analysis and ethnomethodology all offer potential also for Strategy as Practice research. The Meadian symbolic interactionist tradition might shape attention to the roles of culture, symbols and personal identity for strategists and strategizing groups, and Goffman's related dramaturgical approach has already been extensively used to explore more generally how managers 'perform' in an actorly sense their given roles, strategic or more administrative (Callero 2003; Mangham 2005). Discourse analysis (Fairclough 2005) allows for the deep exploration of language and discourse in strategy, sensitive to both micro and macro levels, with Vaara et al.'s (2004, 2005) studies of strategic alliances and mergers pointing a particularly promising way forward for more research on how managers practically use discourse in strategy and the subtle consequences this can have. A quite similar but even more detailed approach is the ethnomethodological tradition of conversation analysis, offering the prospect of deep understanding of the tricks and traps involved in bringing off particular episodes of strategy talk (Samra-Fredricks 2003; see also Lynch and Peyrot 1991). There is plenty of theory out there, and already some useful research capable of inspiring and guiding more.

In introducing the particular sets of theory that we have concentrated on here, however, our ambition has been simply to indicate the quality and range of theoretical resources and empirical traditions that are available to Strategy as Practice researchers. While readers may choose to explore some of these more deeply according to their particular needs, together they do provide some common orientations. At the base, philosophical pragmatism and practice theorists such as Bourdieu, de Certeau, Foucault and Giddens underpin a common sensibility, one that takes seriously the practical activity of people in their ordinary endeavours. Approaches such as Situated Learning, the sensemaking perspective and the notion of performative routines all promote a respect for the detail of these activities, appreciating the subtle skills required to carry them off. But institutional theories of one kind or another, and Actor-network theory too, encourage us not to become exclusively focused on the micro, reminding us of its location in a much wider set of relationships. De Certeau, Engeström's 'activity systems' and ANT also widen the gaze, to include the material technologies that too can make a difference to strategy practice. Overall, these theories tend to warn against fetishizing the strategy content and strategy process divide. Neoinstitutional theory and the Carnegie perspective on routines are equally at home in each of content and process, and ANT tends to subvert the two categories in the first place.

The key task, of course, is to translate these theoretical perspectives into empirical work. This chapter has taken formal strategic planning as an example of an important strategy practice that can be approached from the perspectives introduced here. They generate a wide range of research questions, from how societal institutions may shape the outcomes of micro-episodes of strategy making to the skills and technologies required to be an effective strategic planner. Readers may well have their own particular phenomena to address, but these questions should indicate how even such an apparently hackneyed territory as strategic planning can be refreshed from a Strategy as Practice perspective. The abundant empirical work that has already been undertaken within the various theoretical traditions discussed here offer tried-and-tested models for research in the field. It will be the task of the next chapter to explore methodological avenues for Strategy as Practice research still further.

3 Doing research on doing strategy

The previous chapters have argued for the importance of taking a closer look at strategy as it is practised in the day-to-day work of organization members. They have also examined some of the theoretical frameworks that might be mobilized to understand these activities. So far, however, we have provided little guidance as to how research based on such a perspective might proceed. How do we research strategy practice empirically?

The simple and most obvious answer to this question is that we must 'go out and look', i.e. find ways to capture such activity as it occurs so that it can be examined closely and understood.[1] Like many simple and obvious answers, however, this hides a multitude of complex issues that we attempt to explore and clarify in more depth in this chapter. To do so, we draw both on our own experience, on the methods literature, and on the illustrative papers that form the central core of this book.

We begin this exploration by arguing that in-depth and largely qualitative data are a central requirement for developing the Strategy as Practice perspective. Qualitative approaches are often recommended when relatively little is known about an area of study or when a fresh perspective is needed, as is certainly the case here (Eisenhardt 1989b). However, perhaps more importantly, the nature of the phenomenon itself – dynamic, complex, involving intense human interaction – demands an approach that can capture these features empirically (Patton 2002). Cross-sectional questionnaires and quantitative data bases based on *a priori* categories are not really up to the task, at least not on their own.[2] There is a need to get closer to the phenomenon. Amongst other things, this implies doing observations in organizations to capture the in-vivo experience of doing strategy, conducting interviews and other forms of interaction with organization members to understand the interpretations

---

[1] Similar to an approach that Mintzberg (1979) labelled 'direct research'.
[2] But surveys could be used to establish basic descriptive data such as the frequency, timing or location of certain phenomena, or the people involved, as a precursor to the type of study emphasized here.

that people place on these activities, and collecting the artefacts of strategizing such as minutes of meetings, reports, slide presentations, objects, etc. The empirical materials used will be mostly qualitative, often eclectic, and will tend to involve a small number of organizations or situations studied in some depth. The illustrative papers we have included in this volume all have this feature in common (although, as we shall see later, this does not mean that there is no role at all for quantification).

Having established this central premise, we now explore some of the specific choices and challenges that empirical researchers interested in the practice of strategy will face, and suggest some approaches to addressing them. Some of these challenges are similar to those faced by any researcher doing qualitative work. However, we do not wish this chapter to be a treatise on qualitative research and we assume that the reader has basic knowledge of it, or access to other sources on the philosophies, techniques and quality criteria typically associated with it (e.g. Lincoln and Guba 1985; Strauss and Corbin 1990; Patton 2002; Miles and Huberman 2003; Yin 2003). Instead, in the remainder of this chapter, we focus on the particular characteristics and dilemmas of doing research on strategizing.

We shall discuss the particular research choices and dilemmas associated with the study of the practice of strategy under four headings, organized in terms of an archetypal research sequence: 'Approaching Strategy as Practice', 'Bounding Strategy as Practice', 'Capturing Strategy as Practice' and 'Theorizing Strategy as Practice'. These sections deal respectively with epistemological choices and research strategies; sampling and research design; access and data collection; and analysis and theorizing.

Approaching Strategy as Practice: epistemological choices and research strategies

As we mentioned above, the set of papers included in this volume all rely heavily on qualitative data. Yet despite this common overall orientation, they adopt a range of different epistemological positions and research strategies. We shall draw on these illustrations to examine the main choices available and some of their implications.

Eisenhardt's (1989a) paper on 'Making fast decisions in high velocity environments' is an example of a study that takes what Guba and Lincoln (1994) would call a *post-positivist* position. It uses a comparative case study approach (Eisenhardt 1989b; Yin 2003) to develop middle-range theory relating decision speed to a series of decision strategies used by top management teams. The assumptions are that a unique reality exists and that the data collected (mainly through in-depth interviews) provide access to this reality. The theory developed takes the form of a set of causal relationships whose generalizability can be tested in further studies. The author distils the 'facts' about each case from multiple interview accounts by verifying different sources against one another and classifying responses into carefully constructed categories. She is then able to examine the correlations and chains of causality among these categories.

In contrast, the paper by Gioia and Chittipeddi (1991) adopts an *interpretivist* position and an ethnographic method to study strategy formation in a single organization over time. The authors were interested in how cognitive understandings of organizational participants evolved during the initiation of strategic change. Here, the assumption is that reality is socially constructed and the analysis focuses on the meanings attributed by organization members to ongoing events. The data collected are seen as representations rather than facts, and the researchers argue for the need for deep involvement in the cultural setting in order to reflect these representations fairly.

Beyond the classic epistemological distinction between positivism and interpretivism, the work of Gioia and Chittipeddi (1991) as well as that of Barley (1986) and Balogun and Johnson (2004) can be distinguished from that of Eisenhardt (1989a) on another important dimension: the attention given to tracing temporal dynamics or to understanding phenomena in *process* rather than *variance* terms (Mohr 1982; Langley 1999). This is another key choice for the researcher that has consequences for research design, data collection and theorizing. While variance theories explain phenomena such as strategic change in terms of causal variables, process theories explain them in terms of the activities, events and choices that constitute them over time. Both types of theories can contribute to improving understanding of Strategy as Practice. However, many of the theoretical resources introduced in the previous chapter (e.g. Situated Learning, actor-network theory, as well as broader meta-theories of practice) tend to favour process theorizing.[3]

Another set of illustrative articles differ from those mentioned above in the way they pay particular attention to language. In these cases, the data collected

---

[3] The reader should be aware that the term 'process' is used here to distinguish a specific type of theoretical form (involving sequences of events over time and temporal dynamics rather than relationships between variables (see Mohr 1982; van de Ven 1992). This is different from the usage in earlier chapters where 'strategy process' is used to distinguish a specific research tradition interested in strategic management processes rather than 'strategy content'.

through interviews, recorded observations and documents are treated by the authors not as approximations to truth (as in Eisenhardt's (1989a) study) nor even as pure interpretations of what is or was occurring (Gioia and Chittipeddi 1991), but rather as 'discourse' – talk or text that is consciously or unconsciously orientated towards an audience and serves a particular purpose. The task of the researcher in this case is to reveal the forces and purposes underlying this discourse and to examine its effects. For example, Samra-Fredericks' (2003) study draws on conversation analysis embedded in an organizational ethnography to examine the rhetorical devices used by strategists to convince their colleagues.

Oakes et al. (1998) also focus on the role of language, using documents and interviews to show how the introduction of the language of business planning subtly redefined who and what was important among the Alberta museum community (favouring a view of museums as serving customers in contrast to the traditional role of preserving artefacts). However, unlike most of the other papers presented in this volume, they explicitly adopt a *critical* paradigm in the sense that they attempt to unmask the latent power dynamics underlying what may on the surface be seen as normal, 'rational' and taken for granted.

Finally, another orientation towards research on strategy practice is 'action research', in which researchers intervene (sometimes as consultants) and attempt to learn systematically from the results of their own interventions. Studies by Hodgkinson and Wright (2002), Greiner and Bhambri (1989) and Bürgi, Jacobs and Roos (2005) (the last included in this volume) are examples of this type of work. Here, the qualitative data are often a by-product of an intervention or a strategic consultancy process. This approach has the advantage of providing closer access to strategy practice than is normally possible. However, the credibility of the conclusions may be problematic, given the close proximity between the observer and what is observed.

The various research orientations described above (post-positivist versus interpretivist versus critical; discourse analysis; action research; process versus variance theorizing) suggest a range of different ontological and epistemological choices that may drive research on Strategy as Practice. Clearly, a first decision that a researcher will need to make concerns where to position him or herself among these possibilities. This choice might be based on natural orientation or on a deliberate selection. But in any case, this choice will be related to the types of research questions that are being asked and will in turn determine the research designs, data sources and analysis techniques that are appropriate. The meanings attributable to the data (fact, representation or discourse?) and the types of conclusions that will be drawn will also depend on these choices. The key here is to achieve consistency between assumptions and methods.

For example, those interested in developing theories that relate particular strategic practices to outcomes in a positivist tradition (like Eisenhardt (1989a)) will tend to prefer a comparative case study approach and a method of summarizing data that allows the development of well-defined constructs that can be tabulated and compared. They will see a need for a reasonable sample size of cases (from four to ten is ideal according to Eisenhardt (1989b)) and will therefore tend to favour breadth over depth in qualitative data collection and analysis. In contrast, those interested in participants' interpretations, like Gioia and Chittipeddi (1991), will tend to prefer ethnography or in-depth interviewing as a research strategy and will be looking for depth, detail and nuance rather than convergence on well-defined constructs (Dyer and Wilkins 1991).

In turn, researchers interested in the development of process theories that capture temporal dynamics will tend to see longitudinal data collection as essential to capture the evolution of events over time. They may be more suspicious of retrospective reports than variance theorists (because of the potential distortion of time sequences) and will favour ethnography, historical analysis or real-time interviewing. However, depending on the focus of their theorizing (longer-term change processes or micro-processes that are more temporally bounded), they may be more or less concerned with fine-grained detail.

Those interested in the role of language in strategic practice will have different needs again. They will generally require access to naturally occurring talk and text. Here, the precise words people use will be particularly important. Thus, if documents are the object of analysis, there may be a need to collect not only final versions of reports but also their preceding drafts and other related documents. If people's utterances are the focus, electronic recording devices become essential. Because most discourse analysis methods are extremely time consuming, a high degree of selectivity is generally required. The trick is to pick precisely the pieces of data that offer the most useful insights.

Another key issue that researchers need to consider before proceeding to develop more detailed research designs is the degree of theoretical and conceptual framing needed before entering the field. Interestingly, many if not most of the illustrative papers in this volume appear to have a large inductive component. None is a hypothesis-testing piece in the traditional positivist sense. This does not mean that they are atheoretical (most have a strong theoretical orientation) or that there were not some concepts and ideas driving initial data collection. Some authors (e.g. Eisenhardt 1989a; Bürgi et al. 2005) clearly discovered their theoretical angles and particular research questions only after data collection was underway (for example see statement by Eisenhardt (1989b)). Others had clear research questions from the beginning (Langley 1989; Gioia and Chittipeddi 1991) but these were open-ended and could have led to a variety of responses and theoretical contributions. Finally, others began with sets of 'sensitizing concepts' derived from a general broad meta-theoretical scheme (for example symbolic interactionism for Barley (1986, 1990), and Bourdieu's (1990) theory of fields of production for Oakes et al. (1998)).

To some extent, this rather inductive orientation reflects the state of knowledge in the field. It also perhaps reflects our own bias for work that generates new insights in a field where quantitative survey research seems limited in its capacity to tap into the detailed micro-processes we are describing. It is true also that, whatever the starting point for a study, most qualitative research generates unexpected discoveries. Qualitative data have a multivocal character: they may speak to several different issues and may even take on different meanings when different epistemological assumptions are applied (see Alvesson and Sveningsson 2003). The creative researcher will be open to exploiting unexpected opportunities for learning as they occur.

That said, we recommend all researchers to enter the field with clear research questions and some conceptual handles with which to bound the focus of their study and to structure their data collection and analysis. (If a researcher is short of ideas for good research questions, strategy practitioners can undoubtedly contribute useful suggestions.) Some initial exploratory work may be desirable to get a feel for the feasibility of a full-scale project, but good qualitative studies have a logical design at their end, if not at their beginning. Most of us cannot afford to spend too much time in random exploration before converging towards that design. We address more explicitly the issue of design in the next section.

Bounding Strategy as Practice: sampling and research design

One of the thorny issues that immediately confronts any researcher interested in strategy practice is the identification of appropriate units of analysis, the definition of their boundaries, and the nature of the corresponding 'sample' to be studied. We consider these issues in this section.

Choosing units of analysis

The unit of analysis refers to the precise object of the research – the entity about which one is trying to draw conclusions (Patton 2002; Yin 2003). To illustrate the dilemma associated with this choice, consider what is and is not included in the idea of strategizing. How would one draw boundaries around an incident of strategizing? How would one construct a sample of such incidents? The concept itself is open-ended, and the more so if we adopt a perspective in which not only top managers but also other organizational members are seen to be contributing to the strategizing effort – a contention that has attracted several researchers to this approach (Westley 1990; Balogun and Johnson 2004; Rouleau 2005). To the extent that one adopts a definition of strategizing as including any activity that might contribute to the orientation of the organization (and not just the formal and explicit strategic planning process), the concept further spreads itself out over space and time (Pettigrew 1990) to the point where almost any organizational activity can be considered part of strategizing. The resource-based view of the firm indeed locates competitive advantage in organizational routines and dynamic capabilities that are both deeply embedded and widely distributed across the firm. Yet, to paraphrase Wildavsky (1973), if strategizing is everything, then maybe it's nothing.

Most researchers will want to avoid this extreme ambiguity. The emphasis on activities suggests a need to define units of analysis in micro terms. But how micro is micro enough? The focal unit of analysis could be very narrow (e.g. individual strategy retreats or workshops, individual managers, meetings, conversations, etc.) or it could be broader (strategic decisions, strategic issues). Among the illustrative papers in this volume, we actually see a variety of strategies. For example, at the broadest level, Eisenhardt (1989a) focuses on a set of strategic decisions, Gioia and Chittipeddi (1991) focus on an episode of strategic change initiation, Oakes et al. (1998) focus on a broad planning philosophy among a set of organizations and its implementation amongst them. At the narrowest and most micro level, Samra-Fredericks (2003) focuses on small strips of conversation within the broader setting of meetings among strategists. Clearly, there are myriad possible choices, related to the research questions being tackled.

Drawing on Luhmann's (1995) social systems theory, Hendry and Seidl (2003) introduce the notion of a 'strategic episode' as a particularly attractive unit of analysis for research on Strategy as Practice. An 'episode' in Luhmann's theory is a 'sequence of events structured in terms of a beginning and an ending' between which 'the normal constraints of communicative practice are suspended and alternative communicative practices are explored' (Hendry and Seidl 2003: 180). The idea put forward by Hendry and Seidl is that most organizational activity is structured around operational routines that are reproduced in patterned ways. Over time, random variations may occur in this stream of activity as patterns are imperfectly reproduced. However, unless the structures of communication change, these shifts will not necessarily be 'goal directed' or have any strategic significance. The creation of 'strategic episodes', in the form of strategy reviews, retreats or other kinds of meetings, etc., can be seen as the setting aside of certain specific times and places within which different rules apply and in which the structure of communication may be changed in such a way as to permit reflexive thought about the operational organizational routines that lie outside the episode. From this viewpoint, it is within these episodes that 'strategizing' is really taking place, because it is here that there is potential for altering the strategic trajectory. Hendry and Seidl (2003) propose taking these strategic episodes as a unit of analysis.

Luhmann's (1995) theory provides a number of indications for the types of features of these episodes that need to be examined if their role in the practice of strategy is to be understood. For example, the way in which the episode is initiated so that it is decoupled from operational routines that lie outside it may be important, as will the way the findings, reflexions and practices developed during the episode will be recoupled to those routines afterwards. Finally, the degree to which space is allowed to develop a new and different communication structure within the episode may determine its usefulness. The notion of strategic episodes as developed by Hendry and Seidl (2003) is thus an intriguing theoretically grounded way of defining units of analysis for the study of Strategy as Practice. Clearly there is room for the development of other ways of thinking about units of analysis for strategy practice research.

Defining and bounding units of analysis

Even when a clear logic for the choice of units of analysis exists, operationally defining them in an empirical study may still be challenging. Langley's (1986) doctoral thesis (from which the paper reproduced in this volume was developed) illustrates this problem and the tactics that may be used to handle it. Langley was interested in the role of formal analysis in strategic decision making and confronted an initial difficulty of defining the two main units of analysis: what was actually meant by 'an analysis' and by a 'strategic decision'? How would these units be recognized?

As described in Langley (1989), formal analysis was eventually defined as 'a written document reporting the results of a systematic study of an issue'. This sounds simple on first reading but, in tracking down her sample, the author was forced to develop some ways to deal with the ambiguity surrounding its meaning while capturing what was most important (Langley 1986). The first tactic involved a fairly long and explicit list of exclusion criteria. These were used to avoid consideration of descriptive reports, multiple drafts of the same document and so on. This might be called an 'isolation tactic'. This can only work to the extent that it is truly possible to develop objective criteria that allow such radical separation. The second tactic was to admit variation in the nature of the sample chosen and to capture it explicitly within the research design itself. Thus, all the documents collected were coded according to a series of criteria that measured their degree of analytical content. This became a control variable in the study.

Bounding what may be considered to be a 'strategic decision' was equally challenging. Decisions in real life are not so easy to pin down – they are made and unmade sometimes without any visible traces, they string themselves together and generate sub-decisions on similar and related issues (Langley et al. 1995). Langley eventually decided to change the unit of analysis from 'strategic decision' to 'strategic issue' because it seemed that organizational agendas were structured much more strongly around issues than decisions. Even here, however, it appeared that many strategic issues were interrelated in the organizations studied. To get around this ambiguity, the second tactic mentioned above was reused: variation was recognized and an explicit portrait of the extent to which different issues were related was included in the report (Langley 1986).

In summary, even once the main unit of analysis has been chosen, bounding it sufficiently to enable systematic empirical research is not always simple. Tactics for dealing with this may vary from reductionism (isolation tactics characterized by a focus on narrowly defined objects that exclude ambiguities) to the deliberate maintenance of ambiguity. Those adopting a positivist perspective will tend to prefer the first tactic while those adopting an ethnographic or interpretive perspective may prefer the latter tactic believing that, as Van Maanen (1995: 139) indicated, 'to be determinate, we must be indeterminate': the research itself must reflect the ambiguity present in the empirical situation, even including the ambiguity in its object. A middle-range tactic, and we believe a useful one, is the one emphasized by Langley (1986): explicitly admitting variation and mobilizing it within the research design.

Sampling

The issue of defining units of analysis is of course related to the issue of sampling. Once the main units of analysis have been defined (a decision, a company, a strategic episode, a strategy, etc.), the question becomes how many units to study, which ones, where to find them and how to obtain information on them. Three general principles seem to be important for sampling in qualitative research (Patton 2002; Miles and Huberman 2003). The first principle is that the sampling of the major units of analysis should be 'purposeful' rather than probabilistic or random. Given that the overall sample size is likely to be small, the sample should be chosen deliberately and consciously to maximize the value of the information obtained in terms of the types of inferences or insights that can be drawn from it. Of course, convenience is bound to be a factor in this type of research. However, not just any available unit or site will do. The collection of units chosen should normally have some logic behind it.

For example, if one has enough resources to study in-depth episodes such as strategic retreats or away-days in, say, four organizations, those four might be chosen in a variety of different ways. One way would be simply to take cases as they come (and given possible access issues, this might be the easiest choice). However, a more interesting and potentially useful way might be deliberately to take two cases of strategy retreats that occur with a new CEO, and two that occur in a situation of continuing leadership, or perhaps alternatively two that involve consultants and two that do not. Following on from the discussion of strategy episodes above, such choices would enable a consideration of how the initiating context for the event might influence what goes on within it, and in particular the capacity of the managerial group to engage in reflexive activity that questions previous strategies. In addition, there might be some interest in ensuring that the four organizations chosen are as similar as possible on other salient dimensions (industry turbulence, size, etc.) to control for the effects of these factors.

The general idea is that the theoretical purposes of the research will determine which dimensions should be dominant in sample selection. The 2×2 design suggested here (four cases chosen to replicate a comparison along a single dimension) can be particularly powerful in terms of bang for buck. The contrasting dimension may enable some propositions to be developed about the role of this dimension, while the fact that this is replicated in another pair of similar cases adds credibility to the conclusions and paves the way for possible generalization. (Yin (2003) would describe this as combining literal and theoretical replication.) If the four cases had been chosen without some guiding frame, the potential for clear inferences would be less certain.

Patton (2002) provides a useful list of purposeful sampling strategies and their possible strengths and weaknesses. These include sampling for exceptional cases that might offer special insights, sampling for maximum variation to ensure that any conclusions are likely to be valid for a wide spectrum of organizations, and sampling typical cases that are likely to be representative of many others. The overall point is not that any particular design is best, but rather that samples should be chosen thoughtfully and deliberately as a function of the potential for inference they offer.

A second principle important for sampling in qualitative research is 'saturation'. The idea here is that once the sample of main units of analysis or cases has been established, an effort should be made to collect information from as many sources as possible and as completely as possible on that unit to ensure that it is fully understood. Thus, sampling of data sources *within* cases tends to follow a somewhat different rule from the sampling of the cases themselves. To achieve saturation, the researcher generally continues data collection until he or she reaches the point where additional sources (another interview, another observation, etc.) do not appear to add new understanding or perspectives on that particular case.

Finally, a third principle related in some ways to the first is the need to design for 'comparison'. Comparison allows the recognition of both repetitive patterns and intriguing contrasts. It forces theorization and stimulates insight and understanding. While this insistence on the need for comparison may be seen as controversial by some who prefer to emphasize the richness and insight obtainable from particularistic stories (Dyer and Wilkins 1991), we would argue with Eisenhardt (1991) that the best research stories (of strategy practice or of other phenomena) are rich and insightful at least partly because they embed comparisons of some kind. For example, in their paper illustrated in this volume, Gioia and Chittipeddi (1991) explicitly refer to the 'constant comparison' method of grounded theorizing put forward by Glaser and Strauss (1967) as the basis for their empirical and theoretical storytelling about strategizing in a university.

The grounds for comparison to be considered in designing the empirical research are thus multiple. One comparative strategy that can function particularly well with a single case study is to compare empirical data with theory. This approach is adopted among others by Oakes et al. (1998) in this volume, who compare their empirical observations with Bourdieu's (1990, 1991) theories of regimes of production. The most obvious comparative strategy is to compare different cases as wholes. This is observed in Eisenhardt's (1989a) work, where companies with faster and slower decision making processes are compared. Cases may also be decomposed into smaller units which are compared among themselves, as in Langley's (1989) work in which a large set of 'formal analysis studies' are compared in terms of their purposes and the interactive contexts within which they are carried out. Time may also serve as a unit of comparison, as in Gioia and Chittipeddi's (1991) study and most notably in Barley's (1986) work. Finally, comparison may be on the basis of small incidents within a larger case, as in Samra-Fredericks' (2003) selection of strips of conversation and in Gioia and Chittipeddi's (1991) work as mentioned above.

Barley's (1986) study summarized in this volume provides an extraordinary example of a qualitative research design that combines the principles of purposefulness, saturation and comparison to maximize the potential for the generation of useful insights from a relatively small number of cases (see figure 3.1 and the comments on the paper itself later in this book).

Barley's (1990) design includes several levels of analysis and dimensions of comparison. Barley was interested in how the introduction of a new technology (in this case new radiological imaging technology) comes to influence organizational structure. He defined structure as an emergent quality reflected in the way in which people interact. He deliberately chose a particular technology (CT scanning) as the focus of his research and analysed how it influenced interactions over time, beginning from the moment of its introduction and continuing over several months. He included several levels of comparison within the study. To detect the differences between how people interacted around older and newer more sophisticated technologies, he compared operations surrounding these technologies at the beginning of the study ('synchronic' analysis). This analysis served as a baseline for the subsequent 'diachronic' analysis, in which he compared interactions around the CT scanner at different periods in time separated by personnel and structural changes. Finally, to determine how differences in the starting conditions and other choices might affect emerging structures, he conducted a 'parallel' analysis between two organizations introducing the same new technology.

A remarkable quality of this design not shown in the diagram, however, is the use of smaller units of analysis to build up knowledge of the larger ones. Essentially, Barley based his understanding of each phase of introduction of the new technology on an analysis of the conversations that took place between technicians and radiologists during radiology examinations. He

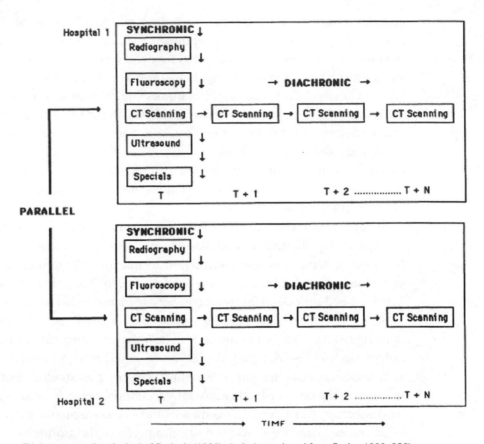

Fig. 3.1   'Triple comparative design' of Barley's (1986) study (reproduced from Barley 1990: 226)

generated a typology of 'scripts' associated with the content and sequence of exchanges among the protagonists during these examinations and was able not only to characterize the scripts but to estimate their relative frequency within each phase of development. Thus, to capture fully the pattern of inter-actions taking place, he had to work with a sample of radiology examinations. The 'saturation' principle obviously applies at this smaller, more micro level. The richness of detail and saturation here was necessary to describe fully what was going on in each phase and at the same time to understand how and why evolution to a new phase occurred. This research design was developed in a particular context and for a particular purpose. However, future research on strategy as practice could certainly learn from the way in which he empirically linked micro-processes to more macro-organizational issues (see the later summary and editorial comments) and from the elegance of his research design for achieving this. Using the language of our introduction, we urge researchers to 'go out and look' but nevertheless to bring a few tools with them (compass, map) to help them find their way.

Capturing Strategy as Practice: access, data collection and ethics

So far, we have established the importance of obtaining first-hand knowledge of the practice of strategy and we have looked at some overall research approaches and design principles for achieving this. However, we have not addressed three crucial questions that researchers who take these ideas seriously are almost bound to encounter. First, how does one obtain access to undertake empirical research on a topic that is almost by definition sensitive and confidential? Second, what data sources are most suitable for capturing strategy practice and how can such data be obtained? Third, what particular ethical issues are raised by this type of research? We will address these issues in this section.

Access and proximity trade-offs

The question of accessing strategy phenomena is clearly challenging. It is perhaps no accident that some of the papers presented in this volume are based on data from the public sector, where anxiety about competitive position and concerns about confidentiality may be less intense (e.g. Gioia and Chittipeddi 1991; Oakes et al. 1998; Langley 1989). Nevertheless the exemplars do include several studies of private businesses (Balogun and Johnson 2004; Eisenhardt 1989a; Bürgi et al. 2005), and all of the studies presented in this volume clearly involved a good degree of access, indicating that the challenges can be met. However, only a few provide hints on how this was achieved and on the precise nature of the relationship that was developed between researchers and organization members.

Clearly, access to such sensitive processes, often at the top levels of organizations, will not normally be obtained without some form of reciprocity between the organization and the research team (Pettigrew 1990, 1992a) and without the creation of a certain level of trust. At a minimum, organization members will hope to learn something from the research and will expect useful feedback. Obtaining an outsider's view of organizational events may be sufficient to stimulate interest when managers are intellectually curious, have a good relationship with the researcher from previous contacts, and see participation in research as part of a contribution that they can make to society (a more frequent stance than might perhaps be imagined). However, for some organizations and in some cultural contexts, access will only be granted when more substantive benefits can be offered.

Reciprocally, for many researchers, the benefits that can be returned to the organization are not simply a price of access, but also an important responsibility given the time and effort required from organization members and the relevance of the knowledge base that academics may have acquired in previous research and consulting ventures. For example, action researchers Bate, Khan and Pye (2000) have argued that researchers should not step back from helping the organizations that they are studying when they see that they have problems for which researchers may have workable solutions. However, it is clear that subsequent research observations do not have the same status as those that would have been obtained if the researcher had not been directly involved.

Still other researchers argue that research should ideally be collaborative: that neither researchers nor organization members have a monopoly on the development of knowledge and that, particularly in the case of the study of micro-practices such as those associated with strategy, practitioners have a clear advantage (Balogun et al. 2003). Their practical knowledge can only be made explicit for the joint benefit of both the researchers and the organization when both participate as equals (Reason 1994; Balogun et al. 2003). Such a stance promotes close access but allows organization members a greater role in defining and answering research questions than is usual in most research projects.

Finally, the question of access is also mixed up with the question of financial sponsorship and/or consulting. Clearly, research in which the organization pays to support the research may increase the quality of access (at least to some parts of organizational activity though perhaps not to others), but alters the obligations of the researcher, the capacity to make independent judgements and consequently the nature of the knowledge generated (see, for example, the paper by Bürgi in this volume and the comments included on it).

All this suggests that there is some kind of trade-off between close proximity to the practice of strategy that can be acquired from participative research and direct involvement and the independence usually expected from academic researchers. Figure 3.2 represents this trade-off. Close proximity enables access to situations that would not be available to other researchers with potentially very positive effects on the quality of the data collected. On the other hand, it involves at least three risks: first that the actions of the researcher may change the nature of what he or she is studying (contamination); second

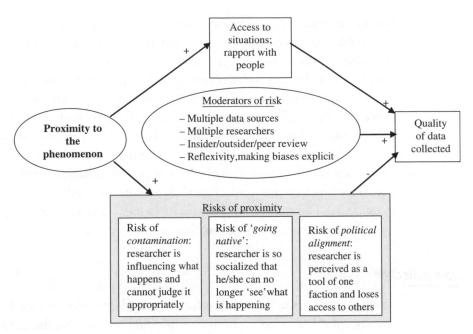

Fig. 3.2   Access trade-offs in research on strategy practice

that the researcher will become so socialized into organizational perspectives that he or she may be unable to see them clearly ('going native'); third that the researcher will become politically aligned with one or other group within the organization and therefore have difficulty in presenting a balanced perspective.

A researcher who maintains too much distance and declines to provide feedback or input will rapidly find him or herself missing out on important information. On the other hand, excessive proximity can compromise the quality of the research in other ways. However, since close access is so valuable to obtaining data on micro-processes, figure 3.2 suggests some strategies for mitigating the risks.

Multiple data sources and the involvement of multiple researchers can clearly assist in moderating potential biases. This is underlined in several of the papers presented in this volume. A particularly interesting strategy for mitigating the risks of proximity is that used by Gioia and Chittipeddi (1991). One of the researchers (the 'insider') held a position within the organizational structure close to the strategy making process, although not at a senior level. He thus had access to strategy meetings and other strategy-relevant events and was able to make detailed observations with the knowledge of the top management team. The other researcher (the 'outsider') was a faculty member within the same organization, but not involved directly in the events described. The combination of their different perspectives contributes to the credibility of this research. Finally, it is important in this type of study that researchers are honest with themselves and their readers about the conditions of access to research sites and about the role that their own backgrounds and biases may play in the research results. Such reflexivity is often missing in published research. From this viewpoint, Barley's (1990) companion piece to the study presented in this volume (Barley, 1986) is particularly refreshing. It takes the form of a 'confessional tale' that describes Barley's personal experience in conducting that study, including references to all the issues presented in figure 3.2. Oakes et al.'s (1998) paper (see later) is also more explicit than most research articles concerning these issues.

Data collection

Moving beyond the issues of access and to data collection itself, we have already noted the importance of multiple data sources and the different roles that each can play. A good deal of past research on strategy practice has relied extensively on interviews as the principal data source (including many studies in this volume). Interviews will remain an important source as they are unbeatable for capturing individuals' feelings about events. However, they are not so good at capturing the micro-behaviours and interactions that are the stuff of strategy practice. We would argue that in-vivo observations are an underused source of data and are particularly important for advancing understanding of strategizing. In different ways, the studies by Gioia and Chittipeddi (1991), Samra-Fredericks (2003) and Barley (1986) illustrate the types of insights that can be developed from this type of research material that is unavailable from interviewing.

Balogun and Johnson's (2004) study presented in this volume also offers some creative and interesting alternatives and complements to interviewing. These authors made extensive use of middle managers' diaries and focus groups to collect data on the roll-out of a strategic change across a large organization. Diaries have at least two major advantages as a tool for data collection on the practice of strategy (see also Balogun et al. 2003). First, they enable the collection of data across a wide range of individuals involved in strategy. This can be particularly important when the focus of the research lies beyond the top management team. Second, they are temporally embedded, allowing the collection of data on how people's perceptions evolve over time. The use of focus groups or group interviews (Morgan 1997) has some of the same advantages but also others. Focus groups are economical in researcher time in a context where many people are involved in strategizing. Also, as a data collection approach midway between interviews and observations, they also allow the researcher to see how people interact around issues and they can permit the confrontation of opinion directly (Balogun et al. 2003; Balogun and Johnson 2004). The systematic use of these strategies along with others produced a particularly rich database for the study of the implementation of a strategic orientation among middle managers. Of course, one could ask how the fact of participating in focus groups and/or writing diaries might have affected what occurred in the organization, given the enforced reflexivity these activities involved. Yet the same questions might be posed of individual interviewing also. The researchers' presence can never be entirely neutral, which again brings us back to the trade-offs described in figure 3.2.

Another innovative data collection strategy is suggested by Stronz's (2005) work on an implementation team in an insurance company. She videotaped naturally occurring strategy implementation team meetings over a period of several months. Using an action science framework (Argyris, Putnam and McLain Smith, 1985), she then chose excerpts from these meetings to present to implementation team members individually, questioning them about their goals during the meeting, their action strategies, what they felt they could have done differently and how they viewed the results of these meetings. This approach seems a particularly useful way both to capture strategizing as it occurs, but also to aid recall from interviewees as they review their reactions to the strategizing processes. To the extent that this interviewing process occurs at the end of the period of data collection, this approach may also enable the researcher to provide constructive feedback to organization members and contribute both to academic knowledge and to organizational learning without involving the researcher in a formal intervention role.

Finally, while researchers often use documentation as a complementary source of data, there has been relatively little attention given to the role of physical artefacts or objects in strategy practice as such (for an exception, see Molloy and Whittington 2005). Strategic plans are often promulgated in the form of text, and the process of producing, diffusing and implementing them generates a large number of other artefacts (such as powerpoint presentations, flip-charts, etc.) as well as other texts. 'Wordsmithing' can be an important part of the process of producing workable strategic documents in a context involving multiple participants. Emerging strategies can change their meaning as texts are rewritten: they may become more focused and explicit or alternatively more open and ambiguous. The emphasis placed on different orientations may shift significantly. Some earlier drafts of texts may be completely ignored. Others may be appropriated extensively. The way in which strategic texts are produced, reproduced and diffused is an important part of strategizing that merits closer empirical attention. The multiple versions of strategic plans and the other texts and artefacts that feed into them and follow them are a worthy object of detailed analysis in and of themselves, placing documents not as a peripheral data source but as central to understanding. Ideally, the study of series of interrelated strategy documents would need to be placed in context using other data sources such as interviews and observations.

Photographs are another underused research tool that may be of particular value in studies of strategy practices because they can capture the details of strategizing work that might otherwise escape attention. For example, in a study of reorganizing practices, Molloy and Whittington (2005) used photographs of scenes from away-days to focus attention on the symbols of strategy (objects, binders, diagrams, etc.), and on the everyday tools of strategizing such as post-it notes, computers, overhead projectors and powerpoint slides, and to examine the physical arrangements of people during these events (for example junior and senior consultants, senior managers, other participants). While such details may seem banal at first sight, these elements and the way they are manipulated and organized may have important symbolic and substantive implications in terms of the success of these events and the meaning they have for participants. For example, Hodgkinson and Wright (2002: 961), in a study of a strategy consultancy intervention, describe how the CEO undermined the intervention in subtle ways – by positioning herself in the room to be physically remote from other members and by the way she 'physically seized control of the marker pen' to redraw the diagrams on the white board, while other participants 'looked down at the carpet'. Photography can capture and freeze such meaningful scenes for richer and more detailed analysis than may be possible with verbal reporting (Collier and Collier 1986).

Ethical issues

In concluding this section, it is worth drawing attention to some ethical issues associated with intensive data collection in a small number of organizations. Researchers often have access to sensitive materials and to people who are quite easily identifiable by others in their organization even if the research report anonymizes organization names and individuals' names. In order to obtain this access, researchers must provide a certain degree of confidentiality and protection for their respondents. And yet, as researchers, their duty is also to report on what they see to the extent that it can improve learning about the phenomenon studied. This almost inevitably leads to dilemmas. What can one do with a wonderfully juicy and revealing quotation if the respondent who made it subsequently refuses to allow it to be used?

An exchange about just such an incident occurred on the 'Strategy as Practice' email discussion list. The researcher involved had sent back a fully transcribed interview to the informant for validation (based on an audio-tape). The informant insisted on changing parts of the interview. The discussion on the listserv was interesting for the variety of opinions expressed about what the researcher could and should do. Some suggested that in the spirit of informed consent, the researcher was obliged to accept the changes and not to use the original material. Others urged the researcher to use both the original material and the changes proposed to it as data, and further to question the respondent about the reason for the changes and use that as data also! Although this suggestion may appear seductive, it is clearly not consistent with generally accepted ethics guidelines (at least, not unless the informant gives his or her informed consent for this!). In the interests of both accurate research reporting and respect of respondents, a better approach on the part of the researcher might have been not to send the transcript back to the respondent but rather allow him or her to review the final research report. Even here, however, there are bound to be certain areas of disagreement.

Clearly, researchers cannot substantially change their interpretations to please organization members if they believe those interpretations are important and accurate. One way of dealing with disagreement is to indicate explicitly in the research reporting that respondents did not necessarily share all of the researchers' interpretations (an approach used by Oakes et al. (1998) in this volume). Another creative way for dealing with this that we have seen is to allow a dissident manager to present his/her own case in a companion text (Hafsi and Demers 1989). Ultimately though, it is inevitable that research reporting is to some extent affected by the need for confidentiality, and most importantly by the commitment to avoid harm to people who willingly and trustingly gave their time to the researchers. The conscientious researcher will thus tell the truth and nothing but the truth as he or she sees it, but not always (if we are honest among ourselves about this) the whole truth.

Understanding Strategy as Practice: analysis and theorizing[4]

So far in this chapter, we have emphasized the importance of close attention to the practice of strategy in order to develop a better understanding of it. However, the use of small but intensely studied samples generates a need to find ways to reconnect the material manifestations of strategizing in highly specific contexts to the more general research endeavour of developing knowledge that is of value beyond them. This is not an obvious undertaking (see also Langley 1999). Achieving it demands both strong empirical research designs (as we have argued above) and a preoccupation with theory. A risk of the empirical approach that we have advocated is that it may produce only local descriptive knowledge. In this section, we will look at the different types of contributions that this type of research can make (moving from simpler to more complex ones) and we will examine some strategies for increasing the credibility of its conclusions and its potential usefulness beyond the specific sites studied.

Descriptive contributions

Armed with a complex qualitative dataset, what are the kinds of contributions a researcher can make to a general understanding of doing strategy? A first type of contribution is a deliberately descriptive one. To the extent that there are few descriptive narrative presentations of how strategy is produced, the availability of detailed accounts will have value. Even here, however, the researcher will need to explain why the account is interesting and what one may learn from it. One way to underline the value of the descriptive account is to contrast it with the 'received view', i.e. with the normative accounts promulgated in practitioner sources and business school teaching. For example, Mintzberg and colleagues' work on strategy formation in a variety of different contexts – for example entrepreneurial firms (Mintzberg and Waters 1982); a

---

[4] Qualitative data analysis techniques appropriate for doing research on strategizing are fundamentally little different from those appropriate to qualitative research of other research objects. We have thus avoided devoting a great deal of space here to technical questions of content analysis, coding and computer software. We refer readers to other sources for detailed advice on these (Strauss and Corbin 1990; Miles and Huberman 1994). Specific techniques may be required by those interested in discourse analysis approaches (e.g. Mann and Thompson 1992; Fairclough 1995; Phillips and Hardy 2002). Rather than elaborate on these techniques, we prefer in this section of the chapter to highlight the broader challenge of mobilizing data to generate valuable theory about strategy practice, illustrating several ways in which this might be done drawing on some of the illustrations included in this book.

public sector film production agency (Mintzberg and McHugh 1985); a university (Hardy et al. 1984; Mintzberg and Rose 2003) – successfully debunked rational strategic planning as the only way that strategy could be promulgated. The study of the National Film Board (Mintzberg and McHugh 1985) was particularly productive in the way in which it illuminated within an extreme case the concept of 'emergent strategy'.

The scope for this type of contribution is, however, limited. Once it has been pointed out that the emperor has no clothes (for example, strategy is not necessarily produced through formal planning), other forms of contribution that deepen this insight are needed (by asking, for example, by what other means strategy is generated).

Although it is much more theoretically driven, the study by Bürgi et al. in this volume has some of the same qualities as the work of Mintzberg and colleagues. It illustrates with a very powerful example the possible role of tactile processes in strategy making, drawing both on theory and on an experiential case to make its points. The introduction of this idea into the domain of strategy is surprising and novel. It contrasts sharply with the received view, and the contribution of the paper lies very much in this element of surprise.

Another type of possible research contribution that remains descriptive, but that may have more conceptual content than a narrative account, is the generation of typologies. Typologies or taxonomies can play a particularly useful role in pinning down the different kinds of phenomena or practices that are involved in strategy practice and showing how they work. For example, the paper by Langley (1989) in this volume develops a typology of the kinds of roles played by formal analysis in organizations, relating these to the context in which they are initiated. The typology of effective rhetorical strategies developed by Samra-Fredericks (2003) is another interesting example.

The theoretical status of typologies and taxonomies is controversial, with some arguing that these descriptive devices do not add significantly to knowledge (Bacharach 1989). However, we would argue that they do constitute valuable building blocks for developing that knowledge. Typologies of micropractices (such as the uses of formal analysis) that can be useful in further research may also be developed, based on a relatively small number of organizational settings, provided that the practices that are examined can be observed across these settings and that the settings themselves incorporate a sufficiently wide range of variation. Finally, empirically developed categories increase in value if they can be systematically linked to existing theoretical frames, or if they can be further used to develop relationships with contexts or with outcomes.

Variance theorizing

This brings us to a second kind of contribution from this type of research, the development of mid-range theories that link strategic practices to some form of outcome. The outcomes likely to be relevant for studies of micro-strategy will tend to remain at a micro or meso level. The causes of corporate perform-ance are multiple, and lie in external and internal factors that may not all be captured in micro-level research. The study by Eisenhardt (1989a) is a fine exemplar of this approach. She shows how decision making strategies among top teams can be related to decision speed, an intermediate outcome.[5]

In considering Eisenhardt's study, it is worth looking in more detail at how she succeeds in generating a credible mid-range theory of decision speed from a limited number of cases (eight in her paper). Her data analysis and theoriz-ing strategies are particularly interesting. Eisenhardt identifies five main deci-sion process patterns that are related to decision speed, each of these presented in a tightly formulated proposition. These process patterns were derived inductively from comparisons among the cases and the subsequent develop-ment of coherent constructs that mobilize both quantitative and qualitative indicators to describe the relative presence of these patterns. The evidence supporting each proposition is presented in the paper in four separate stages. First, Eisenhardt shows the quantitative and tabular evidence, illustrating the correlation between the decision process pattern considered and decision speed across the eight cases. We see here how the use of quantitative indica-tors within the case study is particularly powerful in increasing the credibility of the results. Second, Eisenhardt presents qualitative examples of fast and slow decision makers, introducing numerous short quotations that add depth to the tabular presentation. In a third and crucially important step, Eisenhardt asks the question: 'why?' Why would there be a relationship between the given process pattern and decision speed? She goes on to theorize these relation-ships, drawing on both her qualitative data and the literature to generate a series of three mediating variables which together serve to explain the empir-ical relationships uncovered. In a fourth and final step, she reconsiders her observations in the light of previous literature on decision speed, showing that her propositions, while sometimes counterintuitive, can be reconciled with prior knowledge in the area.

One cannot lay claim to statistical generalizability on the basis of eight cases. However, in the systematic way she replicates the findings across the

---

[5] While Eisenhardt's (1989a) study goes on to relate decision speed to corporate performance as well, this is not the strongest part of her work.

eight cases, and in particular through the emphasis on understanding *why* these findings might occur, Eisenhardt provides a strong basis for a credible theory of decision speed that has what Yin (2003) calls analytical generalizability in the sense that the integrated theory has been shown to be valid in multiple contexts. This theory has subsequently been replicated in other research efforts using experimental and survey methodologies (Judge and Miller 1991). The systematic comparative analysis and theoretical logic exemplified in this study have obvious potential for theory development on a variety of other issues related to the doing of strategy. In addition to relating strategic practices to outcomes, there is also room for other nomothetically driven work that relates practices to their context.

Process theorizing

A third type of research output somewhat different from those described above concerns the development of 'process' rather than 'variance' theory – a distinction that we mentioned in an earlier section. Process theorizing is concerned with developing explanations for phenomena based on an understanding of temporal evolution: it is concerned with sequences of events, activities and choices over time rather than with relationships between variables. Variance theorizing tends to be static. Process theorizing reintroduces dynamism, and as such holds strong resonance with a practice perspective. Tsoukas and Chia's (2002) description of change as 'organizational becoming' rather than a measurable difference between time 1 and time 2 reflects this view. Because of their emphasis on 'becoming', process theorists are less preoccupied with establishing precise final outcomes. From a process perspective, organizational performance is an extremely transitory phenomenon, a cause as much as an effect. For example, it may be seen as a piece of data that organization members struggle with or it may be an objective that they hold on to and attempt to influence or manipulate through their actions. Furthermore, in practice and process theorizing, the very word 'performance' also has a somewhat different meaning. For example, for Feldman (2003), performance means achieving or enacting a particular practice or routine. This does not mean that process theorists have no interest at all in outcomes. However, it does mean that they do not necessarily see outcomes as all-important. Outcomes are way-stations in a series of ongoing events. They may be the result of previous events but they are also the starting points for subsequent activity.

If it does not necessarily focus on outcomes, how can process theorizing contribute? We believe that its contribution is mainly in increasing the level of theoretical understanding. Two process-based contributions in this volume seem particularly useful in this regard: the work by Gioia and Chittipeddi (1991) and that by Barley (1986). Both of these contributions are also of interest for their very systematic data analysis approaches based this time on the coding of events and incidents rather than on the development of variables.

We have already noted the interest of Barley's (1986) research design. The particular contribution of his study is precisely to reach beyond correlational relationships between technologies and structures to show how new technology is incorporated into an ongoing organization over time. The study reveals in minute detail the way in which individuals act on the technology as it is introduced. Micro-interactions cumulate over time to stimulate changes in structure. In turn, changes in structure result in shifts to micro-interactions that lead to further alterations in structure until some kind of stability is achieved. Parallels could easily be developed between what Barley observed and the practice of strategy at other levels. For example, what happens when a new CEO is introduced into an existing top management team? How do interactions evolve, generating changes in structure and strategy, and then how do these new structures and strategies affect subsequent interactions? Just such a process was the focus of a study by Denis, Langley and Pineault (2000). Barley's study is also exemplary for its analytical approach, which we have described partly above. He used a form of temporal bracketing (Langley 1999) to decompose his data into comparable time periods and then systematically coded micro-events within each of these periods for comparative purposes. As in the case of Eisenhardt (1989a) but in a different context, we also see how the use of quantification within a qualitative study may enhance the credibility of the results. This issue is explored in more depth in the editorial comments on this paper presented later.

Theory testing

A final type of research output from micro-strategy work concerns some form of mobilization of pre-existing theory either for illustrative or for theory testing purposes. Barley (1986) actually does this quite explicitly, drawing on structuration theory (Giddens 1984) and negotiated order theory (Strauss 1978) to develop his analysis. Pre-existing theory also inspired Oakes et al. (1998). We believe that there is room for more extensive use of pre-existing theory, including many of the perspectives offered in the previous chapter in developing future work. There is also room for the confrontation of different theoretical frames for understanding micro-strategy processes within the same study (Allison 1971; Langley 1999). The trick however in mobilizing these theoretical resources is to use them constructively to develop insights into issues of strategy practice. The epistemological problem is that many social theories (structuration, political theory, actor-network theory) are quite difficult to refute because their concepts are easily malleable. The challenge for the researcher is to show how the interpretations that they generate are powerful as a means for understanding the particular phenomenon under study – an understanding that would not be obtainable otherwise.

Conclusions: doing research on doing strategy

In this chapter, we have reviewed the major issues and choices that researchers are likely to face in doing research on doing strategy. We have drawn on the illustrative papers presented in this book to develop the discussion of these issues. In this final section, we shall briefly return to three more generic issues that underlie some of the previous discussion: the role of quantification, the role of practitioners, and the role of creativity in doing research on the practice of strategy.

The role of quantification

We have argued at the beginning of this chapter that qualitative data that capture strategy practices in detail are essential to developing a better understanding of the 'doing' of strategy. We maintain that position in this conclusion, believing that a return to studies based on purely quantitative indicators or perceptions will drive researchers back towards the decontextualized abstractions that led to a need to open up the current research stream in the first place.

However, this does not mean that there is no role for quantification. Indeed, several of the illustrative papers in this book draw on quantitative indicators and various forms of counting to complement qualitative data. Quantification is particularly useful when there is a need to categorize or summarize qualitative observations (Barley 1986; Langley 1989), when there is a need to confirm and triangulate qualitative judgements (Eisenhardt 1989a), and when there is a need to compare cases, time periods or other units of analysis in order to propose possible generalizations. Numbers are also highly strategy-relevant organizational artefacts in themselves. To the extent that they are mobilized in strategy practice or are relevant to strategy practice, they become de facto a part of the in-depth description (for example financial numbers, sales figures, etc.). Finally, quantification may also help legitimize qualitative work for certain types of publications.

However, whenever it is used, it is important that quantification should elucidate rather than hide the detailed understanding acquired about the doing of strategy. One of the authors recalls reviewing an otherwise interesting paper in which observed and recorded strategic conversations were reported purely in terms of quantitative scales. This level of abstraction made it impossible to link the arguments to any substantive real-life experience. Quantify by all means for any or all of the reasons suggested above, but do not throw away the richness that lies behind it.

The role of strategy practitioners

Doing research on the practice of strategy almost inevitably engages strategy practitioners in some way or other. They are in fact the primary 'research subjects'. We have already addressed in earlier sections some of the dilemmas generated by the need for access to top-level and sometimes sensitive discussions: notably the need for reciprocity, potential biases, and ethical questions associated with disclosure and confidentiality. These questions remain. However, in this section we draw attention to other roles that practitioners may play.

For practitioners – at least experienced ones – are not only 'research subjects' that academics can observe, but also in a strong sense 'experts': they possess a rich store of tacit knowledge about strategy practice that the Strategy as Practice perspective aims in part to make explicit. If we take the practice turn in its most literal sense, we need to consider the possibility that in-depth knowledge of a practice can only be properly acquired by participating in it. This at least would be the position of the Situated Learning perspective described in chapter 2. This argument leads us to consider whether the best way to capture such knowledge might actually be to become a practitioner.

Of course, some academics are also strategy consultants. Yet, when this happens, their writings tend to emphasize formal techniques and not the everyday experience of doing strategy. The other problem, of course, is that as soon as a strategy practitioner becomes an expert, the tacit knowledge involved in the practice may become quite unconscious (Polanyi 1966). The people perhaps the most able to render the tacit explicit are 'apprentice-novices', those who learn the practice through experience in close contact with experts and yet are still able to articulate that learning. All this suggests that one potentially valuable approach to developing knowledge on practice is actually to find a 'master' (recognized strategy practitioner expert or consultant) and to become an 'apprentice' – a particularly demanding form of participant observation! Naturally, the access, confidentiality, credibility and ethical issues can be exacerbated with this form of research. However, this does in some sense represent the logical conclusion of accepting a strong-form practice-based view of strategy.

A final point about the role of practitioners is that they are not only both subjects and experts, but also potentially beneficiaries of the Strategy as Practice research stream. Yet it is not entirely certain that they will be able to capture the potential benefits from reading the traditional published research papers likely to emerge from the types of studies described here. Other ways need to be found to share and communicate the relevant knowledge. For example, there is a need for teaching case development as well as the creation of various kinds of experience-based pedagogical tools. It is also here that different forms of collaborative research such as that of Balogun and Johnson (2004) and Stronz (2005) may be relevant. The capacity to engage practitioners in productive reflection on their own practice (using diaries and focus groups in the case of Balogun and Johnson and videos in the case of Stronz) creatively combines data collection with constructive learning opportunities for those involved in the research.

The role of creativity

This brings us to our final point: that the Strategy as Practice perspective offers great scope for methodological innovation. We have pointed out some of the ways in which previous researchers, and especially those featured in this book, have met the challenges associated with this research topic and we have hinted at some other untapped possibilities. But the field is not yet saturated: we invite creative and interested researchers to invent new and better ways to capture and understand these phenomena.

Part II

Illustrative papers

Introduction

In this part of the book we present eight abbreviated papers that illustrate key aspects of the study of Strategy as Practice. The papers, earlier published in leading management journals, have been chosen because, in different ways, they exemplify well characteristics we believe to be important in papers addressing Strategy as Practice. They provide useful examples of different research methods, of the use of different theoretical lenses, of how research might address and explain the role of actors and activities in organizations, and of how more detailed activities might relate to strategic outcomes or organizational consequences. Given that Strategy as Practice is a newly developing research domain, few of the authors of these papers would identify themselves with that domain, at least when they wrote them. The papers have been selected because all of them have important lessons for scholars who aspire to give future contributions to Strategy as Practice.

Each abbreviated paper has the same structure, starting with the original *abstract* of the paper, followed by a short *editors' introduction* by the authors of this book, where we present the main reason(s) why the paper has been chosen for inclusion in this book about Strategy as Practice. Then follows the *paper summary*, using verbatim sections of the paper with linking summaries by ourselves highlighting key aspects of the paper. Finally, at the end of each of the abbreviated papers is an *editors' commentary* in which we summarize some of the key lessons from each paper as they relate to Strategy as Practice. Following the aim of this part of the book illustrating good research practice of relevance for Strategy as Practice, it is natural that our commentaries focus on the strengths of the papers, but we will also hint at some possible limitations of each one. To conclude, we hope it will be clear for the reader why each has been chosen and what it illustrates particularly well. The papers are presented in chronological order, starting with the oldest, the very interesting paper by Barley, published in 1986.

The eight papers chosen for abbreviated presentations are not an exhaustive set. But our hope is that they will be a useful source of learning and inspiration for scholars of Strategy as Practice. In the last part of the book we will return to these eight papers, applying a more comparative view on the whole set, summarizing their research questions, the theoretical resources they have mobilized and the type of methods they have used.

4 Technology as an occasion for structuring: evidence from observations of CT scanners and the social order of radiology departments

(*Administrative Science Quarterly*, 31 (1986): 78–108)

Stephen R. Barley

Abstract

New medical imaging devices, such as the CT scanner, have begun to challenge traditional role relations among radiologists and radiological technologists. Under some conditions, these technologies may actually alter the organizational and occupational structure of radio-logical work. However, current theories of technology and organizational form are insensitive to the potential number of structural variations implicit in role-based change. This paper expands recent sociological thought on the link between institution and action to outline a theory of how technology might occasion different organizational structures by altering insti-tutionalized roles and patterns of interaction. In so doing, technology is treated as a social rather than a physical object, and structure is conceptualized as a process rather than an entity. The implications of the theory are illustrated by showing how identical CT scanners occasioned similar structuring processes in two radiology departments and yet led to diver-gent forms of organization. The data suggest that to understand how technologies alter orga-nizational structures researchers may need to integrate the study of social action and the study of social form.

Editors' introduction

This is not a paper that claims to be about strategy, but it is highly relevant to this book for three reasons. First it is an extremely well designed piece of micro-level research. Second it is a rare example of the links in figure 1.1 in chapter 1, both of the interrelationship of institutional forces and activities (V3) and also of how activities influence organizational outcomes (V1). Third, it is a truly exemplar paper in terms of its style and structure.

Here we focus on four key features of the paper: (1) the initial set up of the argument and research questions; (2) the research design and methodology; (3) the use of comparative case analysis in showing the findings; and (4) the use of quantitative analysis to underpin the findings from the qualitative analysis.

Paper summary

The paper begins by arguing that it is generally accepted by scholars that technology changes both societies and organizational structure but the evidence as to just how this is the case is not clear, indeed is 'confusing and contradictory'. However, Barley argues that rather than seeking to resolve such contradictions we need to accept that technology's impact on organizational structure may be inconsistent and seek to understand how and why that is so.

There follows a wonderfully succinct set up to the paper that critiques organizational-level and cross-sectional analyses, makes the case for a concern for the two-way links (duality in Giddens' terms) between what people do and technology as an exogenous force, and establishes his theoretical position crisply.

Technology and the structuring of structure

Most students of technology and organization have used the term structure to denote abstract, format relations that constrain day-to-day action in social settings. When structure has been treated as an autonomous, formal constraint, three other presumptions have typically followed: that technology is a material cause, that relations between technology and structure are orderly, and that these relations hold regardless of context. Moreover, since relations are usually held to transcend contexts, researchers have tended to study technology's influence on structure at organizational levels of analysis. That such a notion of structure and its corollaries undergird organizational research on technology is substantiated not only by the prevalence of cross-sectional research designs but by the determinism that haunts the literature in such phrases as the 'technological imperative' (e.g., Khandwalla, 1974; Fry, 1982).

In contrast to this dominant notion of structure, organizational theorists such as Silverman (1971), Weick (1979), Van Maanen (1977, 1979), and Manning (1977) have advocated an alternate formulation that views structure as patterned action, interaction, behavior, and cognition. Unlike in the first usage, in which structure stands outside of and prior to human endeavor, in the second, structure is understood as an emergent property of ongoing action. The contrast reflects the essential difference between those sociological traditions that portray structure as a template for action and those that treat structure as a contour of human behavior (see Burrell and Morgan, 1979; Salaman and Thompson, 1980). Although this alternate conception of structure legitimates the probability of multiple outcomes, it has yet to seriously penetrate the study of technology.

Taken alone, however, neither conception may adequately represent the way technology influences the structure of a workplace. As Goffman [1983] was fond of observing, in everyday life
actors are simultaneously the marks as well as the shills [*sic*] of social order. While it is difficult to see how social structure can arise except out of the actions of people, people's actions
are also surely shaped by forces beyond their control and outside their immediate present. A
full account of structural change therefore appears to require a synthetic view of structure as
both a product of and a constraint on human endeavor.

Negotiated-order theory and structuration theory represent two recent attempts to forge such
a synthesis. As articulated by Strauss (1978, 1982), negotiated-order theory derives from symbolic interactionism and takes as its point of departure the events of everyday life. In contrast,
structuration theory attempts to broach functionalist and phenomenological notions of social
order at the level of social theory (Giddens, 1976, 1979). But while the two approaches differ
substantially in scope and detail, both share the premise that adequate theories must treat
structure as both process and form.

In theoretical terms Barley argues that there is a similarity between the structurationist position of Giddens and the negotiated-order approach of Strauss:
'structures consist of sets of rules that specify parameters of acceptable
conduct, but structures are also modified by the actions they inform, just as
languages are altered over time by everyday speech' (80). He therefore argues
that our research attention should be focused on the processes in such structures and such conduct. In so doing he notes the relevance of institutional
theory since 'actors draw on institutional patterns of signification, domination and legitimation to construct roles and to interpret persons/objects and
events in their environment (Giddens 1979:82)'. However, he argues that in
so doing there occurs what he calls 'slippage'. Institutional norms are not perfectly replicated in the activities of daily life, particularly at times when there
are exogenous shocks which might include new technology. Such slippages
persist and become replicated patterns, and they in turn affect institutional
structures.

In these circumstances he suggests that there are some imperatives for
organizational research. First, since this involves a temporal process, a longitudinal as well as cross-sectional perspective is required. Second, the context
has to be taken seriously rather than assuming the same effects will occur for
very different sorts of organizations. And third is the requirement to study
how technology is incorporated into the everyday life of an organization's
members.

All this means that the very notion that technology itself triggers changes
in organizational structures has to be questioned. Rather, technologies are
better viewed as 'occasions which trigger social dynamics which, in turn,
modify or maintain an organisation's contours' (81).

Mapping the evolution of structure

Barley then translates this theoretical position into a sequential model that informs his analysis, both explaining it and showing it in a figure. 'The two realms of social organization, action and institution, are depicted as parallel horizontal arrows signifying contiguous flows through time' (82). Time periods are identified in terms of 'changes in circumstances recognized as significant by an organization's members and brought about by exogenous events or shifts in organizational strategy' (82).

This approach informs empirical inquiry in a number of ways. It is necessary to understand the traditional patterns of behaviour, interaction and interpretation before the technology arrives, and then how such interpretations, behaviours and interactions change as new technology is introduced. To do so requires participant observation since retrospective accounts and archival data are insufficient in such circumstances. In doing so, Barley employs the construct of scripts that he defines as 'recurrent patterns of interaction that define, in observable and behavioural terms, the essence of actors' roles (Schank and Abelson, 1977)' (83). He argues that 'actors' identities are replaced by the positions they play, their behaviours and speech are reduced to generic form and content, and the action unfolding is charted as a sequence of terms composed of typical acts' (83). The influence of new technologies therefore depends on the way in which they disturb and amend scripts. If this is so, then it can be understood why the same technologies lead to different outcomes given that 'technology is but one among many elements of social context that influence patterns of action' (84).

Barley's study was conducted in two community hospitals in Massachusetts; he calls them Urban and Suburban. In both of these the new technology of CT scanning was introduced into their radiology departments. He undertook observation and secondary data collection before these scanners began to operate, focusing on the activities and procedures in the two core technologies of radiology: radiography and fluoroscopy. He explains his methodology as follows:

. . . I gathered data by attending individual examinations in their entirety. The occurrence and timing of events were recorded chronologically during the course of each exam in small spiral notebooks to create behavioral records for every procedure observed. Conversations between participants were either taped or written in a shorthand devised for the purpose of documenting setting-specific argots. In addition to behavioral records. I also sought and recorded participants' interpretations of events at the time they occurred or shortly thereafter.

Once the scanners went on-line in late September, observation shifted from the x-ray areas to the two newly created CT areas. However, the method of observing and recording detailed behavioral information remained constant. Over the course of the study approximately 400 complete radiological examinations, including 96 CT scans, were observed. With the exception of a six-week hiatus during the Christmas holidays, data were collected at the two sites on alternate working days for a period of a year. The text of field notes and tape recordings collected during observation of the two CT scanners provided raw data for the analysis.

Analysis began by identifying breakpoints to define phases of structuring at each site. Mapping phases before scripts avoided temporal distinctions based on knowledge of the scripts themselves. To have used distributions of scripts to locate breakpoints would have asked theoretically propitious, but historically spurious, partitionings by maximizing the homogeneity and heterogeneity of scripts within and between phases. As indicated in the discussion of the sequential model of structuring, phases should start with significant exogeneous events or shifts in organizational strategy, as judged by insiders. Aside from the arrival of the scanners themselves, alterations in the scanner's staffing pattern were uniformly viewed by members of both departments as crucial disjunctures. Consequently, such shifts were taken to mark the temporal boundaries of structuring's phases at each site. Field notes revealed that, by this criterion, Suburban experienced two and Urban four phases of structuring.

The second step in the analysis entailed recursive scrutiny of the interactions that took place between radiologists and technologists, to isolate scripts characteristic of each area's interaction order. All recorded interactions between radiologists and CT technologists were called from the field notes and were arranged by site in chronological order. Each episode was then reduced to an initial plot, using the approach described in the previous section. Generic plot statements were refined by comparing episodes, and each plot's frequency was tabulated across the phases of structuring at each site. By examining the relative frequency of the plots in each hospital over time, I identified scripts characteristic of interaction in each CT area during each phase of its structuring. The scripts' content and form provided a basis for comparing role relations in the two CT areas with their analogues in the x-ray areas, while the scripts' temporal distributions traced the scanners' evolving interaction orders.

The third and final stage of analysis linked the scripted parameters of the two interaction orders to properties of each CT area's formal structure. Centralization was deemed particularly relevant for both substantive and empirical reasons. As is explained more fully below, prescribed distributions of discretion and authority lie at the core of radiology's traditional division of labor. Moreover, data were available for constructing measures of centralization that were independent of the scripts and the interactions from which they were derived. Consequently, by focusing on centralization it was possible to examine the link between the two interaction orders and one of radiology's fundamental institutions by using data independent of the scripts.

Measures of centralization were constructed by coding instances of routine decision making found in the field notes. Regardless of hospital, all CT scans were punctuated by nine operational decisions: (1) when to start a new patient, (2) where to start scanning, (3) how far to scan, (4) what techniques to use, (5) whether to reposition the patient, (6) whether to inject contrast, (7) what windows and centers to use, (8) whether the radiologist should view the scans, and (9) when to end the exam. Since each decision was made as a scan unfolded and since each resulted in overt action, as part of my observational regimen I routinely recorded the identity of the decision maker. My field notes documented CT scans in sufficient detail to determine whether the radiologist who was nominally in charge or a technologist had made each decision. Thus, the percentage of decisions made by a radiologist during the course of a scan constituted the index of centralization. Plots of the indices over time were interpreted as a department's centralization profile.

If institution and action in the CT areas were in fact linked via the structuring process, then the shape of each department's centralization profile should parallel trends revealed by a chronological analysis of scripts. This hypothesis was tested by regressing each department's centralization scores on the day of operation on which the scans took place, as well as the square of that value, to test for linear and curvilinear trends suggested by the analysis of the scripts. Day of operation was measured as an interval variable from the start of each department's scanning operations. The centralization scores were also used to validate the adequacy of the phases defined for each department's structuring. If phases were identified correctly, then a scatterplot of each department's centralization indices should evidence similar periodicity. To examine the adequacy of the phasing, each department's centralization scores were regressed on a series of dummy vectors that defined a two-stage and a four-stage model for Suburban and Urban, respectively. Each scan was assigned to a stage by the date on which it was performed. If phasing was accurate, one would expect a model constructed from the combined phases to predict Suburban's and Urban's data no better than the two-phase and the four-phase model, respectively.

Radiology's institutional context and traditions

Radiology in hospitals had become a 'professional monopoly', according to Barley. Radiologists, alone, interpreted images resulting from medical radiography, excluding others, including physicians, and controlling the work of the technologists who worked with them. The technologists knew how to operate equipment, manage patients and produce films for radiologists, but it was the radiologists who undertook the diagnosis. However, they too operated X-ray equipment, thus reinforcing hierarchy within which 'radiologists knew what technologists knew, but not the reverse' (87).

Barley observed the ways the two groups worked. In both hospitals interaction largely consisted of radiologists giving instructions in the form of imperatives to technologists, usually without justification or explanation and rarely seeking technologists' advice or opinion. In turn technologists waited on radiologists' directions, even if they knew what action would be required. Radiologists also avoided discussing patients' conditions with the technologists. In all these ways, authority was centralized on the radiologists.

The radiologists were able to keep apace of the technology of radiology because it had developed incrementally. However, the new technology of CT scanning was quite different and 'created a completely new system of diagnostic signs that radiologists have had to master' (88). For both hospitals the introduction to the new technology for both radiologists and technologists consisted of only a four-day programme that primarily addressed routine operations, with little time spent on the interpretation of data or how the scanner worked. It was, then, a major disruption to the traditional expertise in balance between radiologists and technologists.

The structuring of Suburban's CT operation

Barley reports his empirical findings in the form of a comparative case analysis (see chapter 3). He identifies temporal stages, employing both his own narrative and verbatim quotes to show their significance. Here we summarize but provide Barley's account in full of one of the episodes.

First, Suburban's handling of the arrival of CT technology. Given the lack of experience and expertise with regard to such technology, Suburban decided to hire new staff to deal with it. They appointed a sixth radiologist who was qualified to deal with such operations and two new technologists who also had CT experience. Together with two of the inexperienced technologists this made up the scanner team. Barley then reports the initial stage of adoption as:

Phase 1 Negotiation of discretion

Since none of the personnel had operated this particular machine or worked together, the initial stage was very much about clarifying roles. Barley identifies different forms of interaction.

Unsought validation

A different script emerged in the early days: (1) the technologists frequently took action without consulting the radiologist; (2) the radiologist might question what they did, usually asking for information or a rationale; (3) the technologists then provided the justification for their action; and (4) the radiologist typically confirmed their action and complemented them on what they had done.

Barley provides a verbatim example of how this took place, and argues that, in effect, the radiologist was recognizing the technologists, competence to make decisions about how scans would be conducted. Although nominally the radiologist retained the dominant role, the script confirmed both parties' expertise.

Anticipatory questioning

Technologists also conferred with the radiologist before taking action, and this gave rise to anticipatory questioning: '(1) a technologist asked the radiologist a direct question, (2) the radiologist provided the technologist with a direct answer, (3) the technologist made a statement about his/her next course of action, and (4) the radiologist confirmed the technologist's stated plan as appropriate' (90). In this context this questioning appeared rhetorical, implying that the technologists knew the appropriate reason. The effect was that 'anticipatory questions validated tech's expertise whilst preserving the radiologist's status' (90).

Preference stating

Despite their experience, technologists deferred to the radiologist's knowledge of disease, anatomy and diagnosis. Not surprisingly the radiologist also expressed preferences but, in so doing, provided a rationale for those preferences. On this basis the technologists were happy to comply with these references. This typically 'involved lengthy conversations about disease and interpretation that were uncharacteristic to the x-ray area' (91). They also served to establish the radiologist's credibility whilst treating the technologists as deserving of reasoned explanation.

'Through these interactions of unsought validation, anticipatory questioning and preference stating, the radiologist's traditional authority and expertise were confirmed, but it also ratified the technologists' claim to occupational knowledge' (91). Within three weeks they had developed a joint problem solving mode of working, with the radiologist becoming less involved in the routine and the technologists taking on more and more responsibility. Barley notes, for example, that the highly symbolic event began of technologists administering injections.

Barley then moves on to explain the second phase in the adoption of the new technology.

Phase 2 Usurping autonomy

In the early stages of scanning, the inexperienced radiologists, whilst in attendance, deferred to the experienced radiologist, but did not usually raise questions or interact with the experienced technologist. However, in the fourth week, the experienced radiologist decided he would not attend all the scans, which left the inexperienced radiologists together with the experienced technologists. The former interaction patterns then shifted in a number of ways.

Clandestine teaching

The inexperienced radiologists sought to follow the scripted behaviour that was their norm. They too stated their preferences. However, they did not have the knowledge and experience to carry this through and, inevitably, this led to exchanges in which the technologists' responses were, in effect, an attempt to teach the radiologists without appearing to do so. For example 'the technologists typically responded to the radiologist with a question or statement which tangentially supplied information necessary for the radiologist to reformulate his presentation of self as a knowledgeable partner to the interchange' (92). The radiologist could then adjust what he had said. This was, of course, a reverse of the traditional roles, since traditionally radiologists taught technologists. In turn this began to take form in more open role reversal.

Role reversals

In the past, diagnosis always flowed from radiologist to technologist. The most marked role reversal was when the radiologists began to ask the technologists for diagnostic interpretation. And this began to happen especially when radiologists were pressed for urgent information by physicians. Again Barley provides an example of a verbatim encounter for such an incident. Whilst this very clearly reversed traditional roles, it also gave rise to anxiety amongst both the radiologists and the technologists.

Blaming the technologist

Of all the interaction patterns that arose in the second period of structuring, none was more indicative of how the interaction order had changed than the tendency for radiologists to mistake machine problems for a technologist's incompetence. On such occasions, the radiologist (1) stated or questioned a perceived problem, (2) insinuated or directly claimed that the problem was the technologist's fault, and (3) rejected the technologist's claim that the nature of the problem lay with the technology. The following typifies the script:

Rad: *(Brusquely)* This is pretty bad. The films on the last patient are pretty dark. Can you do anything about it?

Tech: Don't know.

Rad: What do you mean you don't know?

Tech: The problem is either in the processor or the camera there. I don't know how to set them. Dr. X knows how to set the camera. Maybe we should get him to come over and set the camera and I'll rematrix them.

Rad: *(Pointing to diagonal lines through the basal portion of the brain in a head scan)* Is this all artifact here?

Tech: Yes. There's nothing you can do about it.

Rad: Why not? You mean there's nothing *you* can do about it?

Tech: I believe it's all bone artifact. [Bone artifact in the basal brain was a chronic problem with all Technicare 2060's.]

As role reversals, clandestine teaching, and incidents of blaming the technologist gradually defined a new interaction order, the radiologists' moral authority tarnished and the technologists began to regard the inexperienced radiologists with disdain. To account for the new interaction patterns, the technologists formulated the view that the radiologists knew less than they rightfully should and that their ignorance created unnecessary work and kept the CT operation from running smoothly. The radiologists were also uncomfortable with the situation. The result was that radiologists began to express hostility towards technologists.

As anxiety and hostility increased, both parties sought to reduce it. The technologists tentatively began to take unilateral responsibility for routine operations without consulting a radiologist and, with no negative responses from radiologists forthcoming, this came to be the norm. In turn the radiologists withdrew from such routines, remaining in their offices, often behind closed doors.

So it was that Suburban CT technologists came to gain a large amount of autonomy in their work.

The structuring of Urban's CT operation

Barley then provides an account of what happened at Urban, again identifying similar phases.

Phase 1 Negotiating dependence

Urban dealt with CT technology differently. They recruited a knowledgeable radiologist to work alongside another radiologist who was a long-term member of the department and, although having no direct experience, had followed the literature on body scanning. They also assembled a group of eight technologists currently working at Urban. Again Barley identifies several categories of interaction to characterize this first phase.

Direction giving

At Urban the technologists needed to learn technical competence and the training fell to the radiologists. They were not trained teachers and had to do training on the job as situations arose. In these circumstances the developing script became: (1) a radiologist telling a technologist what to do; and (2) the technologist doing what he/she was told, often without question.

A verbatim quote illustrates this, where Barley explains the consequences (followed by the presentation of the second interaction category in this phase):

Direction giving differed from preference stating in that the experienced radiologists offered no justification for their suggestions. The script's success as a training strategy therefore hinged on the technologist's ability to form habits and abstract rules of action. That the excerpt above occurred over a month after the scanner came on-line, and that a more routine aspect of CT scanning could scarcely be found, casts doubt on the script's effectiveness. Direction giving failed as a training strategy because it was predicated on one-way communication in which the radiologist assumed the role of conceiver-of-action and the technologist the role of executor-of-action. Consequently, the interaction pattern not only failed to train, it reaffirmed the radiologists' professional dominance by extending their authority to such mundane matters as when to push what button. Even in the x-ray area a radiologist's directions were rarely so detailed.

Countermands.That technologists were unable to infer rules from radiologists' directions was partially explained by a second common interaction pattern whose script also consisted of an order-act sequence but whose context differed from direction giving. Simple direction giving presumed that radiologists would communicate preferences before technologists acted. But the radiologists did not always formulate orders prospectively. On numerous occasions radiologists recognized only in retrospect that an alternate course of action would have been more desirable. When such realizations struck, they typically redirected the exam, regardless of whether they thereby contradicted earlier directions. Order-act sequences that invalidated previous directions composed the script of a countermand.

There were many countermands, for diagnostic reasons but also because of 'radiologists' personal proclivities and rivalries' as well as the experienced radiologists experimenting with the new technology. There was also disagreement between the two radiologists, as a result of which they countermanded each other. Reasons for these countermands where not made known to the technologists and therefore appeared 'capricious'. The result was that the technologists had no basis upon which to take independent action and had to rely on following the radiologists' orders.

Usurping the controls

At Urban the experienced radiologists also took hands-on control of the scanning, often without any verbal exchange. The technologists regarded this as a 'disregard for their role and disdain for their abilities' (96), initially objecting but eventually accepting it as routine.

Direction seeking

Technologists also requested guidance from radiologists, resulting in straightforward direction giving, that is (1) the request was made, (2) the radiologist answered, and (3) the technologist acted. Whilst this was initially to do with learning, as it persisted it came to be a part of the social order.

All three developing scripts affirmed the dominance of the radiologists. The technologists came to seek directions from radiologists first because they did not know what to do, but also because they saw the radiologists' instructions as arbitrary. In so doing, the impression given to the radiologists was that the technologists were not attempting to learn or show initiative, which led to the radiologists exerting even greater control.

Phases 2 and 3 Constructing and ensuring ineptitude

In an attempt to overcome what the radiologists saw as a lack of learning, job scheduling was changed so that each technologist would run a scanner on a staggered two-week shift rather than rotating daily. The radiologists themselves also decided to spend more time in their offices, thinking this would break the technologists' dependency.

Unexpected criticisms

There was no increase in the technologists' confidence, but they were now distanced from the radiologists. Nonetheless they still chose to consult. However, since the radiologists were in their offices this required the technologists to visit them. Since radiologists were usually busy doing something else, this seemed like even greater dependence and led to irritation and sarcastic remarks by the radiologists. It also often led to the radiologists reverting to previous patterns of hands-on control on the scanners.

Accusatory questions

Eventually the radiologists came to see the technologists as incompetent, leading to accusatory questioning insinuating such incompetence: and again Barley gives an example of this. After forty days the radiologists had resumed responsibility for hands-on control of the scanners.

Phase 4 Towards independence

After sixteen weeks four technologists deemed to be least competent were transferred to other responsibilities. The more experienced radiologists then took up duties in other areas of radiology so as to give CT experience to inexperienced radiologists, triggering interaction patterns reminiscent of those at Suburban.

Technical consultation

Just as at Suburban, the inexperienced radiologists turned to the technologists for help. But, whereas at Suburban this was done openly, at Urban it was done clandestinely. Nonetheless it had the same effect, inverting Urban's earlier structuring as the script developed such that: '1) the radiologist enquired about an appropriate course of action and 2) the technologist provided the radiologist with an answer' (99).

Mutual execution

Unlike Suburban, at Urban the consultations between radiologists and technologists were restricted to technical information. The radiologists retained their role of diagnostic interpretation. Nor did they withdraw from daily operation of the scanners. However, in this role they were reliant on the technical competence of the technologists. The result was 'mutual execution of the CT scanning procedures in CT scanning' (99). Through this demonstration of technologists' expertise, confirmed by radiologists, roles became 'less rigid', with each partly recognizing that they 'possessed valuable, complementary skills'.

The sedimentation of alternate organizational forms

Barley then employs quantitative data to show that the categories and patterns explained so far in the paper are substantiated across the time period of the study in both locations. A figure in the paper shows the number of times the emerging scripts explained in the previous section appear in the field notes for each of the phases identified (even if they were discussed earlier as unique to that from one hospital). It also highlights the different responses to the same technology in the two locations and allows Barley to show quantitatively the magnitude of differences.

For example Barley shows that, whilst 'preference stating' was found in both locations and appeared more often in Urban's first phase than in Suburban's first phase, its greater significance at Suburban could be seen when examined in relation to other scripts. Specifically, 'the ratio of preference stating to direction giving was 1:1.7 during Suburban's first phase. The same ratio was 1:4.7 for Urban's initial phase' (102), thus reinforcing the perceived dominance of radiologists at Urban and the greater collegiality at Suburban.

Such numerical exposition of the data also allows other patterns to be corroborated. But the overall message that comes through is that there is an evolving pattern of interaction in which the impact of identical technologies led to different organizational structures. However, Barley makes the point that, for this to happen: 'it is insufficient for two interaction orders to be composed at different scripts. The scripts in each interaction order must also consistently embody overarching properties that differentiate the two systems' (102). Both in his descriptive and qualitative explanation of the differences and in his quantification, he shows how these 'two interaction orders coherently and consistently display quite different formal patterns. Suburban scripts indicate the structuring progressed from an interaction order characterised by mutual exchange to an interaction order in which technologists became the senders and radiologists the recipients of most information. In contrast, Urban's structuring moved from an interaction order in which radiologists possessed and sent all information to an interaction order marked by a more balanced sharing of information' (102–3). Overall, the emerging pattern at Suburban was more decentralized and more radically different from tradition than at Urban. However, Barley further demonstrates, again quantitatively, the greater decentralization at Suburban by plotting the proportion of decisions made by radiologists at the two hospitals. In this way he shows the different pace of decentralization of decision making at the two hospitals. He also further tests these visual plots by 'regressing the proportion of routine decisions made by a radiologist first on a linear model specified by the day of operation on which the scan was conducted and then on a quadratic model constructed by adding the square of that value' (104). He shows the results of both quantitative analyses and discusses how they link to and support both the graphical plot and the qualitative findings.

He then further uses quantitative analysis to test his findings on the phasing with regard to decentralization of decisions:

To determine if the centralization scores support each site's alleged phasing, the proportion of decisions radiologists made at each site was first regressed on a series of dummy variables that coded each scan's date in terms of the phase during which it allegedly occurred. Since Suburban was said to have experienced two phases and Urban four. Suburban's data were regressed on one dummy variable representing the first phase of structuring while Urban's data were regressed on three variables representing Urban's first three phases. Each site's data were then regressed on all four dummy variables in a combined analysis. If each site's phasing was adequately defined then the combined model should predict radiologists' involvement no better than the model constructed to depict the site's own phases of structuring. Table 2, which presents the regression analysis, shows such a pattern of results: in neither case did the combined model substantially increase the proportion of variance explained by the hospital's own model. Consequently, the data are consistent with the claim that Suburban evolved through two phases of structuring while Urban experienced four.

Table 2. Adequacy of Each Department's Own Model of Structuring for Predicting the Proportion of Operational Decisions Involving Radiologists*

Hospital	Model	Intercept	Suburban Phase 1	Urban Phase 2	Urban Phase 2	Urban Phase 3	R^2	Df	F
Suburban	Suburban	0.17	0.50						
		[7.46]**	[9.96]**				0.67**		
	Combined	0.13	0.53	0.01	0.07	0.14			
		[3.99]**	[6.91]**	(0.21)	[1.31]	(2.12)*	0.71**	[3.44]	1.43
Urban	Suburban	0.47		0.36	−0.04	22			
		[8.20]**		(4.77)**	[0.39]	(2.90)**	0.45**		
	Combined	0.47	0.22	0.21	−0.04	0.22			
		[8.66]**	[2.34]*	(2.19)*	[0.41]	[3.06]**	0.52**	[3.37]	1.54

* $p < 0.05$, ** $p < 0.01$.

* Numbers in parentheses are t-tests for corresponding parameters.

Conclusions

Those who would highlight management choice – what Barley calls a 'voluntaristic theory' – might conclude that it was the decision makers who determined the structures since it was the radiologists making the staffing decisions. But Barley shows that outcomes of such decisions were largely unintended. On the other hand, those who would privilege institutional structures would highlight the inevitable complexity of uncertainty introduced by the new technology.

Barley's conclusion is, however, that 'identical technologies can occasion similar dynamics and yet lead to different structural outcomes' (105). He argues that this would not have been evident from cross-sectional studies with large sample sizes that tend to ignore contextual dynamics. Differences in formal structures identified would tend to cancel each other out. The real significance of the technological changes needs to be understood, not simply in terms of the complexity and uncertainty they introduced, but in the context of the way in which this is made sense of in the social system. Nor is this simply to do with roles and hierarchies, but rather to do with the modes of interaction between the actors involved: in other words what they actually did.

Editors' Commentary

You will recall that chapter 1 argued that our role, ambitiously, is to be able to link the activities of strategy – what people do – to levels of outcome. This paper, perhaps uniquely, traces through the interaction between technological forces at an institutional level, how people behave towards that technology and in turn their influence on how organizations structure their response to such technologies – a significant strategic outcome. Barley was, of course, not writing as a strategist and, given that the paper was published in 1986, could not know of the discussions in this book. However, we can see it as a rare example of a study that addresses the interaction between all of the levels in figure 1.1 in chapter 1. Moreover it traces through in fine detail just how this happens.

In many respects the paper presents a traditional US management research design. Research methods are carefully thought through in terms of what it is seeking to understand; data are triangulated; it employs comparative cases; it controls for explanatory variables; whilst it employs an essentially grounded mode of analysis it examines the findings that emerge by means of quantitative analysis too. As illustrated in chapter 3, this allows Barley to draw out patterns of similarity; to trace through fine detail into significant outcomes; to allow for the collection of data in such a way as to allow both description and quantification; and to collect data on both observable action and what people say.

It is easy to get carried away here with the richness of the descriptive data in a way that unfolds to tell a story. But the elegance of the upfront positioning in the paper is especially worthy of comment. The research problem is crisply and quite clearly presented in terms of both the practical issues and the theoretical issues involved. The theoretical framework for the paper is explained clearly but relatively briefly and relative extant literature is covered, again without it becoming overwhelming. It is a model introduction to an empirical paper. It shows that when the author is clear about what he is trying to explain, there is no need for extensive literature reviews with an overinclusive coverage. Reverse this and the danger is clear. In the absence of a clear theoretical position, the risk is that the author is left trying to explain everything that might be relevant to the study. The outcome is, of course, usually the reverse: a lack of clarity on just what the paper is about.

It is, however, interesting to note how Barley himself explains the role of theory in the research project: 'To be sure theoretical concerns play a background role in so far as they provided a frame of reference and a set of sensitising concepts . . . However, like most ethnographers I embarked on the project with little more than a handful of general questions and no strongly articulated hypotheses' (Barley 1990: 220–1). The study was inductive in nature. The theoretical framework explained upfront in the paper emerged and developed as the work went on. It is, however, presented coherently in the paper as a way of framing the argument and is particularly effective in doing so.

The choice of the data presented also makes the case very convincing. It is clear from the accounts provided by Barley that his fieldwork notes must have been extremely extensive. The data presented here must represent a minute proportion of those, yet they are coherent as a whole and convincing. It is often the case that researchers claim that they cannot represent their data meaningfully within the constraints of an academic paper. This paper shows that they can but that it requires skills both in the choice and in the narration of that material to do so. It is much the same point as was made above with regard to theory. In this paper Barley is quite clear what he is trying to explore. It may not have all been as pre-planned as in a hypothesis testing paper: but it is clear in terms of his research question and his theoretical stance. Given that, it makes the task of data presentation the easier. He is not, here, trying to show the expanse of data he has: he is using the data to show his findings; and in scope of the findings are theoretically informed. Again, the reverse holds as a problem. In the absence of such clarity the researcher/author has problems choosing which data to present and often ends up presenting a confusing array.

In this respect this paper moves as close as any to the challenge that many of us face: to be able to use micro-level vignettes and stories in order to show the importance of the micro in relation to major inputs and outputs to those activities. It is rather like reading Geertzian ethnography. It is the ability to show how the minute intricacies of everyday life are in fact the fabric of major institutional forces and, indeed, potentially organizational, even institutional change.

The stories themselves are convincing. But the quantification of the data goes beyond stories to show in more summary terms the patterns that emerge. Moreover, Barley uses that quantification to 'test' his own emerging findings and, in so doing, renders his emerging account more convincing to the reader. Many qualitative researchers would question whether this quantification is necessary. It is worth the debate, but it is questionable if this paper would have had the impact that it has had on the diversity of academic communities without that analysis. It helps give the paper a wider audience than it might otherwise have had. However, it seems likely that Barley was seriously concerned to examine critically his own qualitative findings: do the patterns that emerge stand up to quantitative scrutiny? Again, the question has to be asked as to why so few researchers interested in qualitative data do not themselves design research that allows for such quantitative re-examination.

It is not much considered in the paper itself, but there are also signficant implications for practice here. The paper shows how decisions about staffing can have important but unintended consequences; how lack of training can impact on organizational effectiveness. It shows well and raises questions about the interaction of professional specialists. It also raises questions and produces insights about the management of technology.

If we are to be critical of the paper, it would, perhaps, be in the conclusions. Barley's main concern here is to discuss the implications of his findings with regard to the interaction of individuals' behaviour and the structuring effect of technology. However in this paper he does not return to discuss the wider implications of the theoretical model he introduces at the beginning of the paper and which informs his study. It was much later that, together with Tolbert (Barley and Tolbert 1997), this was developed more fully and has subsequently had a significant impact on theorizing and research on the interaction between the realm of action and the realm of institutionalized structure.

5   Making fast strategic decisions in high-velocity environments

(*Academy of Management Journal*, 32, 3 (1989): 5430–76)

Kathleen M. Eisenhardt

Abstract

How do executive teams make rapid decisions in the high-velocity microcomputer industry? This inductive study of eight microcomputer firms led to propositions exploring that question. Fast decision makers use more, not less, information than do slow decision makers. The former also develop more, not fewer, alternatives, and use a two-tiered advice process. Conflict resolution and integration among strategic decisions and tactical plans are also critical to the pace of decision making. Finally, fast decisions based on this pattern of behaviors lead to superior performance.

Editors' introduction

This illustrative paper contributed, for the time (1989), some new and surprising findings on the practice of strategic decision making. It is also selected because of its systematic use of an inductive case study methodology to generate a number of propositions about conditions, characteristics and drivers of fast strategic decisions. The paper is illustrating good research practice in its whole design, with its use of multiple case analyses to make inferences, its use of empirical accounts as illustrations and evidence of the propositions presented, its way of making use of theory to deepen the propositions, and its explicit connection to strategic outcome.

The findings presented in the paper are interesting because they are in total contrast to the perspectives on rapid strategic decision making then current. This paper concludes that fast decision makers use more, not less, information; they develop more, not fewer, alternatives. Furthermore, integration among strategic decisions and with tactical plans speeds, not slows, decision making.

However, the results reported in this paper are based on a very specific empirical context, the microcomputer industry in the United States in the mid-1980s, and are therefore limited in generalizability to a specific type of competitive context, here termed high-velocity environments. This leads to an important implication: the paper illustrates in quite a powerful way that theory is contextually dependent, an issue that we will come back to in our commentary after the summary of this interesting paper.

Paper summary

With a focus on fast-paced environments, characterized by radical technical change, this paper explores the speed of strategic decision making. More specifically the paper aims to answer two research questions: first a process question about *how* fast strategic decisions are actually made by executive teams, and second a cause/effect question about how the speed of decisions *links* to performance. The microcomputer industry studied is defined as a high-velocity industry, which means both rapid and discontinuous change not only in technology but also in demand and competition. The findings of the paper show that fast decision makers use more information and develop more alternatives than slow decision makers. Furthermore, conflict resolution is critical to decision speed, and integration among decisions speeds the decision making. Importantly fast decision making allows executives to keep pace with external change and is also linked to strong(er) performance. The results are reported as a set of propositions, where the theoretical point of departure is the challenging of three streams of research on rapid decision making. These streams argue that a high level of comprehensiveness slows decision making, limited participation and centralised power speed decision making, and limited conflict speeds decision making. Eisenhardt argues that earlier research avoided two key realities in focus in the study reported in this paper and expressed in the following two questions: How does the strategic decision maker overcome an inclination to procrastinate because of anxiety when facing high uncertainty? How does the decision maker maintain decision quality while moving fast?

Both questions imply that earlier research in fact describes rapid decision making in an inaccurate way. Furthermore there is a very limited research base on fast strategic decision making that in turn becomes an argument for the inductive research strategy reported in this paper. The multiple case design with its combination of several data sources is described in detail in the following section.

Methods

The study used a multiple case design that allowed a replication logic, that is, a series of cases is treated as a series of experiments, each case serving to confirm or disconfirm the inferences drawn from the others (Yin, 1984). Table 1 describes the eight microcomputer firms studied.

The study also employed an embedded design, that is, multiple levels of analysis, focusing on each firm at three levels: (1) top management team, (2) strategic decision, and (3) firm performance. Although an embedded design is complex, it permits induction of rich and reliable models (Yin, 1984).

Data Sources

Members of the research group conducted interviews with every member of the top management team of each firm, including CEOs and their immediate subordinates. The teams typically included the CEO and the heads of such major functions as sales, finance, and engineering.

There were four data sources: (1) initial CEO interviews, (2) semistructured interviews with each member of a firm's top management team, (3) questionnaires completed by each member of the team, and (4) secondary sources.

CEO interviews. An entry interview, using a semistructured format, was conducted with the CEO of each firm. The interview began by asking the CEO to describe the firm's competitive strategy. The CEO was then asked to describe the distinctive competencies of the firm, major competitors, and their performance. Each CEO then identified several recent or ongoing major decisions. The decision or decisions to study in depth in subsequent interviews with each member of the top management team were then chosen. The choices were based on criteria similar to those other researchers have used for defining strategic decisions (Hickson et al., 1986; Mintzberg et al., 1976).[2] To be chosen, a decision had to (1) involve strategic positioning, (2) have high stakes, (3) involve as many of the functions of the firm as possible, and (4) be considered representative of the process by which major decisions are made at the firm.

Top manager interviews. After the initial CEO interview, semistructured interviews with every executive in the top management team, including the CEO, were conducted. The interview consisted of 16 open-ended questions. Following the methods of inductive research, these questions were supplemented with ones that seemed fruitful to pursue during the interview. The interviews were typically from 90 minutes to two hours long but occasionally took as long as four hours.

The interview began with a request for a description of the firm's competitive strategy. Each executive then described the functional strategy of his or her area, other members of the top management team, the frequency and nature of interaction with each other member of the team, and routine decision-making meetings. Thus, a general view of the strategic decision process within the firm emerged.

In the second portion of the interview, the story of each strategic decision identified in the CEO entry interview was traced. This yielded a view of specific decision processes within the firm. The perspective of every member of the top management team was traced using standard interview questions. The questions concentrated on facts and events, rather than on respondents' interpretations, through the use of courtroom procedure (e.g., When did this first become an issue? What did you do? When?).

Two investigators conducted each interview with one responsible for the interview and the other for taking notes. Immediately after the interview, the investigators cross-checked facts and impressions. Several rules were followed. The '24-hour rule' required that detailed interview notes and impressions be completed within one day of the interview. A second rule was to include all data, regardless of their apparent importance at the time of the interview. A third rule was to end the interview notes with ongoing impressions of each company.

The combination of multiple informants, courtroom-style questioning, and tandem interviewing addresses some previous criticisms of research relying on executives' recollections (Schwenk, 1985). Moreover, previous research (Huber, 1985; Mintzberg et al., 1976) has indicated high temporal stability in executives' recollection of important decisions, especially for major recent decisions.

[2] Ideally, many strategic decisions would have been studied in each firm. However, doing so was almost impossible because strategic decisions are infrequent events. The approach here was to triangulate insights from one or two decisions with evidence on the overall approach to strategic decision making within the firm. The validity of this approach is enhanced by previous research indicating that firms make decisions in a consistent pattern (Fredrickson & Iaquinto, 1987; Miles & Snow, 1978; Nystrom & Starbuck, 1984), even when the top management team experiences turnover in individual positions (Weick, 1979).

In each of the firms studied five to nine informants were interviewed, all members of the top management teams in these firms. The eight microcomputer firms were Zap, Forefront, Promise, Triumph, Omicron, Neutron, Alpha and Presidential (all pseudonyms), varying in size, in terms of number of employees, between 50 and 500.

The two types of interview data were supplemented with

secondary sources, such as industry reports and internal documents, and financial performance data

questionnaires, resulting in quantitative data. The questions covered mainly a number of variables, such as power and conflicts, suggested by prior decision making research.

Data analysis

For the quantitative data, mainly from the questionnaire, team-level scores were calculated for conflict and power. For all the qualitative data from the interviews and other data sources the following analyses were done:

The qualitative responses were combined using profiles of the decision climates and of each executive from the descriptions each member of the top management teams had given. Traits mentioned by more than one executive were included in the profiles. For example, three of his four colleagues described the president of Alpha as 'impatient.' This trait was included in his profile, but other traits mentioned by only one person were dropped.

Decision stories were developed by combining the accounts of each executive into a time line that included all events. There was typically high agreement among respondents around the critical issues of when a decision began, when the decision was made, and how it was made. Again using Alpha as an example, the executives all agreed that the impetus for the decision studied was a specific board meeting, that the CEO made the decision alone, and that he did so just before the annual planning conference. Although they were few, conflicting reports were preserved in the stories. These usually concerned one person's assumptions about another's motives or opinions, not observable actions and events.

Once preliminary analyses had been developed from the respective data sets, I combined the analyses and induced propositions using methods for building theory from case studies (Eisenhardt, 1989[b]; Glaser & Strauss, 1967). The search for propositions was assisted by selecting pairs of firms and listing similarities and differences between each pair and by categorizing firms according to variables of interest, such as the presence or absence of a counselor to the CEO. From these lists and comparisons, I induced tentative propositions. After the development of these tentative propositions, each case was revisited to see if the data confirmed the proposed relationship, and if they did, to use the cases to improve understanding of the underlying dynamics. After many iterations between data and propositions, I used existing literature to sharpen the insights yielded by the inductive process. What emerged were propositions linking information, alternatives, advice, conflict resolution, and integration with decision speed and performance. As in deductive research, the propositions fit the evidence but did not perfectly explain the cases (Sutton & Callahan, 1987).

How are fast strategic decisions made?

The core of the paper is the presentation of the findings on five characteristics of how fast strategic decisions are actually made. Each finding, expressed as a proposition, is based on the combination of inductive and deductive stages in the research process. In this summary we will give a more detailed, and largely verbatim, description of the first proposition, including the type of reasoning, empirical evidence and illustrations that Eisenhardt provides for all five propositions. The remaining four propositions are briefly summarized.

Speed, planning and real-time information

Prior research has suggested that comprehensiveness slows the strategic decision-making process (Fredrickson & Mitchell, 1984). Consideration of few alternatives, obtaining inputs from few sources of expertise, and limited analysis shorten the strategic decision process (Janis, 1982; Mintzberg et al., 1976; Nutt, 1976). This perspective implies that the greater the use of information, the slower the strategic decision process.

The data from this research indicate a different view. Executive teams making fast decisions used extensive information – often more information than the slower decision makers used. However, that information was not forecasted information. Rather, it was *real-time information*, especially on a firm's competitive environment and operations. Real-time information is defined as information about a firm's operations or environment for which there is little or no time lag between occurrence and reporting. In formal terms,

Proposition 1: The greater the use of real-time information, the greater the speed of the strategic decision process.

The author then summarizes the empirical evidence on the speed of decision making where she assessed the overall speed based on the interview and story data.

Table 2. Speed of Strategic Decision Making

Firm	Examples[a]	Decisions and Key Questions	Decision Durations in Months
Zap	'We try to be the first.' (VP, engineering) 'If we get bogged down, he [CEO] kicks ass.' (VP, marketing) 'The worst decision is no decision at all.' (CEO)	Alliance: Should we form a strategic alliance or go public?	3
Forefront	'We're aggressive. We make things happen,' (director of marketing) 'Big opportunities go by if you don't act quickly.' (VP, sales)	New product: Should we develop a new product?	2
Promise	'I like quick decisions.' (CEO) 'We make decisions fast.' (VP, systems development)	Strategy: Do we need a new strategic direction?	4
Triumph	'Decision making at Triumph is much faster.' (VP, finance) 'He [CEO] listens, makes up his mind, and does it. He's made the decision process shorter.' (VP, sales) 'Do something, don't just sit around worrying.' (CEO)	Strategy: Do we need a new strategic direction? New product: What should our next product be?	1.5 1.5
Omicron	'Slow moving.' (VP, manufacturing) 'There was a frustrating amount of decorum. Consensus was very important.' (VP, sales) 'We did what we intended, but took, longer than we should have.' (CEO)	Strategy: Do we need a new strategic direction? Strategy: What should our new strategy be?	12 6

Table 2. (continued)

Firm	Examples[a]	Decisions and Key Questions	Decision Durations in Months
Neutron	'We were late.' (VP, finance)	Alliance: Should we form a strategic alliance?	12
Alpha	'We never did anything concentrated . . . no particular dedicated time . . . things kind of evolved.' (VP, sales) 'We were kind of casting around.' (VP, finance)	New product: Should we develop an IBM-compatible product?	12
Presidential	'Presidential was unfocused. We weren't concentrated.' (EVP) 'Lots of arguments – no decisions.' (VP, manufacturing) 'There was no structure . . . nothing got accomplished.' (VP, R&D) 'Nothing happened . . . It was so hard to get ideas through.' (EVP)	New product: Should we develop a new product?	18

[a] VP = vice president; EVP = executive vice president.

The qualitative analysis was then corroborated with measurements of the total duration of each strategic decision. In this measurement starting time was indicated by the first reference to a deliberate action (e.g. scheduling a meeting or seeking information), while the ending time of a strategic decision process was indicated by the situation where a commitment to act was made.

As Table 2 indicates, there was high variation in the speed of decision making. The first four firms listed – Zap, Forefront, Promise, and Triumph – made the decisions that were studied in less than 4 months, and substantial evidence from the interviews and stories corroborated that such a fast pace was typical. For example, most Promise executives mentioned without prompting that they made decisions 'quickly,' and their making a decision on strategic direction in 4 months is consistent with the data. Throughout this article, those four firms are referred to as fast. The second four firms – Omicron, Neutron, Alpha, and Presidential – spent at least 6 months, and typically more than 12 months, making the decisions that were studied, and the qualitative evidence (see Table 2) corroborated that this slower pace was typical. Thus, I refer to those firms as slow.

Table 3 summarizes the evidence for the use of real-time information, which was assessed by (1) executive responses to interview questions regarding the regular review of performance measures and targets, (2) a count of the number of meetings regularly scheduled to review current operations, (3) the presence of a vice president (VP) of finance – typically the key provider of real-time information in firms like those studied – and (4) the orientation of a firm's CEO toward information. Executives' preferences for various communication media and the use of real-time information in the making of the strategic decisions studied in each firm were also noted.

The data shown in Tables 2 and 3 indicate that fast strategic decision making is associated with extensive use of real-time information. Executives making fast decisions routinely paid close attention to quantitative indicators such as daily and weekly tracking of bookings, scrap, inventory, cash flow, engineering milestones, and competitors' moves. They preferred these operational indicators to more refined accounting data such as profit. These executives averaged 2.5 regularly scheduled operations meetings per week and indicated a preference for real-time communication via face-to-face conversation or electronic mail rather than through time-delayed media like memos.

The Zap case illustrates the linkage between the use of real-time information and decision speed. Zap executives claimed to 'measure everything.' Without prompting, the CEO described exact targets for gross margin and expenses for R&D, sales, and administration. Executives reviewed bookings daily. Engineering schedules were reviewed weekly. The VP of finance ran a computer model of firm operations weekly. The VP of marketing monitored the environment continuously. As she told us, 'I keep an eye on the market [and] funnel the information back.' The R&D VP told us that he monitored the technology 'grapevine' through his extensive network of friends. Monthly, the executive team reviewed a wide range of quantitative indicators, including revenue per employee, margins, backlog, scrap, cash, and inventory. This is a much more comprehensive set of indicators than the teams making the slower decisions used. Zap's CEO told us: 'We have very strong controls. We over M.B.A. it.' Zap executives also reported interacting continually through face-to-face communication and electronic mail. They avoided memos. For example, one executive described her communication with the CEO and several other VPs as 'constant.' Finally, the decision to forge a strategic alliance that was studied was triggered by the team's cash projection model, which predicted an upcoming cash shortfall. Zap executives made this decision in three months. A Zap executive claimed: 'The worst decision is no decision at all.'

The Triumph case also indicates the link between use of real-time information and rapid strategic decisions. For example, the first employee hired by the current CEO was a data-base manager whose job was to track new product development projects, the lifeblood of microcomputer firms. Firm members described the CEO as 'quantitative,' and he claimed to 'have lists for everything.' Interviewees described the weekly staff meetings at Triumph as 'a must.' One executive said, 'No one travels on Mondays.' My own visit revealed that the Monday meetings were intense. The day began with a four-hour meeting that '[covered] what's happening this week – what's happening with sales, engineering schedules, and releases.' In the afternoon, Triumph executives attended quality assurance and new-product progress meetings. The executives also conducted regular 'round table' forums at which lower-level employees gave feedback to senior executives. Triumph executives made the decision on whether to redirect their strategy in six weeks and also made a major product decision in six weeks. One executive advised: 'Do something, don't just worry about decisions.'

Table 3. Real-Time Information

Firm	Vice President for Finance?	Routine Quantitative Targets and Measures	Number of Weekly Operations Meetings	CEO's Information Orientation	Examples
Zap	Yes	Cash Bookings Scrap Inventory Margins Revenue/ employee Plus others	3	'Numbers guy'	'We have very strong controls. We over M.B.A. it. . . . We measure everything.' (CEO)
Forefront	Yes	Bookings Backlog Billings Receivables Customer service Plus others	2	'Short-term focused'	'Any company that is faced with long development can't know how things will evolve. You can only monitor the outside world and direct the evolving strategy at what you see.' (VP, finance)
Promise	Yes	Cash Bookings Inventory Cost Plus others	2	'Numbers guy' 'Very action- oriented' 'Pragmatic'	'We have the constant pulse of how the company is doing.' (VP, finance)
Triumph	Yes	Cash Bookings Engineering milestones Sales Quality assurance Plus others	3	'Quantitative' 'Focused'	'I keep lists for everything.' (CEO)
Omicron	Yes, but an engineer who was 'weak' on finance	None mentioned	2	'Visionary' 'Detached'	'Our business plan calls for certain business levels, but nothing specific. . . . My own [targets] are subjective.' (CEO)

Table 3. (continued)

Firm	Vice President for Finance?	Routine Quantitative Targets and Measures	Number of Weekly Operations Meetings	CEO's Information Orientation	Examples
Neutron	Yes	None mentioned	1	'Visionary'	'My role is to critique from a detached point of view. . . . I protect funds and assets for the board and investors.' (VP, finance)
Alpha	Yes	Sales Profit	1	'Always racing'	'We were not getting a lot of information.' (VP, manufacturing)
Presidential	No	Sales Profit gross margin	0	'Visionary' 'Detached'	'Management by rambling conversation.' (VP, manufacturing)

In contrast, there was little mention of real-time information from the teams making the slower decisions. What was mentioned suggested that such information was not particularly germane to their decision processes.

The author continues with illustrative evidence from the four firms with slower decision making. Based on the findings from all eight firms, three reasons are identified to why the use of real-time information results in faster pace of strategic decisions:

Real-time information speeds the issue identification, which means that problems and opportunities are spotted sooner by executives.

Executives who continuously attend real-time information are developing their intuition, which means that they can react more quickly and accurately to changes in the firm or the environment. (This reason, supported by quite limited evidence, builds on the literature about artificial intelligence and intuition; Hayes, 1981; Simon, 1987.)

Executive teams that have constant attention to real-time information gain useful experience in responding as a group, resulting in routines to respond rapidly when the situation requires fast actions.

The conclusion on the role of information for the speed of strategic decision making is that real-time information gives executives intimate knowledge of their business which may speed decision making. On the other hand, planning information which attempts to predict the future does not speed strategic decisions.

Speed, timing and number of alternatives

The decision making literature (Fredrickson and Mitchell 1984; and others) has concluded that generation and evaluation of multiple alternatives are likely to slow the strategic decision process. In contrast, the data from Eisenhardt's study suggest that consideration of more, not fewer, alternatives results in faster decision making. This leads to the following proposition:

> *Proposition 2: The greater the number of alternatives considered simultaneously, the greater the speed of the strategic decision making.*

Interview data with decision stories were combined with quantitative measurements of the number of decision alternatives to support the above proposition that multiple simultaneous alternatives are associated with fast decisions. The timing of initiation and discarding of each alternative was also determined. Decision makers in the faster teams maintained multiple options during the decision making process while the slower teams were considering few alternatives and searched for a new alternative first when an alternative was no longer feasible. The author gives three reasons for why the results do not support the view that considering many alternatives simultaneously is time-consuming:

Decision alternatives are difficult to assess in isolation. When comparing alternatives it is easier for the decision makers to ascertain strengths and weaknesses of the alternatives.

With simultaneous alternatives the escalation of commitment to any one alternative is reduced, and decision makers can quickly shift between options based on new information on any of them.

When considering several alternatives they are also analysed more quickly.

Speed, power and the role of the counsellor

Political factors influence the speed of decisions. Earlier studies (e.g. Mintzberg et al. 1976; Hickson et al. 1986) concluded that centralized power should quicken decision making. Again the findings of this study contrast with earlier findings as no clear pattern was found of how power centralization influenced decision speed. Instead the fast decision making processes were characterized by involvement of advice to the CEO from other experienced members of the top management team, supporting for the proposition:

> *Proposition 3: The greater the use of experienced counsellors, the greater the speed of the strategic decision process.*

Slower teams had no counsellors in the team or less experienced executives filling the counselling role, while all top management teams making rapid decisions had at least one experienced counsellor giving influential advice to the CEO.

Two arguments are presented for why experienced counsellors speed decision making:

Often being a long-time associate of the CEO, the experienced counsellor is a trustworthy and enabling executive who provides useful advice and helps hasten the development of decision making alternatives.

The experienced counsellor helps the team deal with the ambiguity that characterizes high-stakes decision making in fast-changing environments.

Furthermore, power centralization that gives the CEO authority to decide does not help overcome information and psychological barriers to difficult decisions. Here the experienced counsellor can play an important role.

Speed, conflict and resolution

Earlier research (e.g. Hickson et al. 1986) showed that conflicts influence the length of the strategic decision making, meaning that increasing conflict slows the pace of strategic decisions. The study reported in this paper found no evidence that decision speed was linked to any level of conflict. Instead conflict resolution was crucial. Fast decision making teams actively dealt with conflicts, resolving them, while teams making slow decisions had problems with conflict resolution. So it was not the level of conflict that mattered but rather the capacity to resolve upcoming conflicts:

> *Proposition 4: The greater the use of active conflict resolution, the greater the speed of the strategic decision process.*

Speed, fragments and decision integration

The fifth characteristic that was found to distinguish fast strategic decisions from slow decisions is about the integration of a strategic decision with both other strategic decisions and more tactical decisions:

Proposition 5: The greater the integration among decisions, the greater the speed of the strategic decision process.

The decisions studied were examined in relation to the degree of integration with other strategic decisions and with tactical plans like budgeting. All teams making faster decisions integrated those with other important strategic decisions and more tactical decisions. On the other hand slow teams treated each decision as a discrete process.

When explaining why more decision integration is linked to faster decision making, Eisenhardt presents the following reasons:

Integration of different decisions helps top managers to analyse the viability of a specific alternative more quickly.

Decision integration helps top managers to cope better with the ambiguity of important strategic decisions, where ties with other strategic decisions and their details mitigate the anxiety executives experience in high-stakes decisions.

Decision integration limits the risks for discontinuities between decisions and for dealing with the strategic decision at an abstract level.

How does strategic decisions speed link to performance

The second main finding in this paper is about how the speed of strategic decision making relates to performance, where the performance of the eight studied firms was assessed by:

each CEO's numerical self-report of company effectiveness

comparison of this self-rating with each CEO's rating of major competitors

figures of growth and profitability (both before and after the study)

the author's assessment of the decision regarding the support from the executive team for a made decision and the implementation of the decision.

Table 7 summarizes these data.

The data support the proposition that faster decision making is associated with better performance. Admittedly, the evidence is tenuous, because performance can depend upon many factors, including those described in earlier studies (Bourgeois & Eisenhardt, 1988; Eisenhardt & Bourgeois, 1988). Also, fast decision making using a different style than shown in these cases might lead to different results. For example, snap decision making by an impulsive CEO might lead to fatal errors. However, the proposition is presented because the performance differences were substantial and the data strongly suggested underlying dynamics that support the relationship. In formal terms,

Proposition 6: The greater the speed of the strategic decision process, the greater the performance in high-velocity environments.

Table 7. Performance

Firm	Decision Performance	1984 Sales[a]	1983–84 Sales Trend	1984 After-Tax Return on Sales[b]	Examples	1985 Performance[c]
Zap	'I'm happy with the decision.' (VP, sales)	50,000	Up	8%	'Right on the money.' (VP, sales)	Strong: 50 percent sales increase, initial public offering.
Forefront	'So far, I like what I see.' (VP, sales)	30,000	Up	9	'We are right on plan.' (President)	Strong: Initial public offering.
Promise	'Yes. I'm happy with the decision. Our strategy is now better articulated.' (VP, software)	1,000	Up	−1,280	'Struggling to be great.' (VP, finance)	Promising: 500 percent sales increase, losses trimmed.
Triumph	'Sure, I'm happy with the decision. It worked well.' (VP, finance)	10,000	Up	−33	'The slope is in the right direction. We have a shot at being a remarkable company.' (CEO)	Promising: 50 percent sales increase, break-even profits, initial public offering announced.
Omicron	'I wish it had been done in half the time. Sooner.' (VP, corporate development). 'Time is passing by.' (VP, human relations)	30,000	Flat	−9	'It's put up or shut up time.' (VP, human relations)	Turnaround: New CEO hired, 50 percent sales increase, profitability up to 5.9 percent.
Neutron	'We were late.' (VP, finance)	30,000	Flat	−31	'Puberty has been rough.' (VP, marketing)	Dead: Chapter 11.
Alpha	'The decision was used as a means of group focus (VP, manufacturing)	10,000	Down	−1	'Disappointing.' (VP, operations)	Mixed: Sales dropped 1 percent, profitability up to 3.5 percent.

Table 7. (continued)

Firm	Decision Performance	1984 Sales[a]	1983–84 Sales Trend	1984 After-Tax Return on Sales[b]	Examples	1985 Performance[c]
Presidential	'The only problem was that the decision took too long to make.' (EVP)	50,000	Flat	−20	'We didn't bring the technology to market as we should have. (EVP)	Down: Sales dropped 30 percent, continued to lose money.

[a] The sales figures are × $1,000 and rounded to preserve anonymity.

[b] After-tax profits ÷ sales.

[c] This is post-study performance.

For example, Zap's performance has been spectacular, with sales growing at 25 to 100 percent per quarter. Zap executives considered the alliance decision to have been successful and have since executed other similar decisions. Forefront's executives also positively evaluated their decision. One stated: 'So far, I like what I see.' Another said: 'The verdict so far is favorable.' Forefront has been a strong performer, with sales tripling and after-tax profits running at 9 percent during the year after the study. Similarly, the Triumph and Promise executives assessed their decisions positively. For example, one VP at Promise said, 'Yes, I'm happy with the decision. Our strategy is now better articulated.' Another at Triumph said, 'Sure, I'm happy with the decision. It worked well.' At the time of the study, both firms were struggling. Promise was an early venture just getting started, and Triumph had recently replaced its CEO. Since the study, sales at Promise have soared 500 percent, and Triumph has become one of only two survivors in its niche and has announced plans to go public.

By contrast, slow decision making was associated with poor performance. For example, Presidential executives viewed their new product decision as good, but too slow. As one VP told us: 'The only problem was that it took too long to make the decision.' Another said: 'Our products were too late and they were too expensive.' As the firm fell behind its competitors, sales tumbled 30 percent in the year after this study, and the firm continued to lose money. The delay at Neutron proved costly as well. The market opportunity was missed, and the firm went bankrupt a year after the study. At Alpha, the executives expressed relief that the CEO's original alternative was shelved. However, the firm continued to drift, with stagnant sales and profits.

Why is slow decision making problematic? One reason may be learning. Executives learn by making decisions, but if they make few decisions, as slow decision makers do, they learn very little. So they are likely to make mistakes. A second reason is that, in fast-paced environments, opportunities move quickly, and once a firm is behind, it is difficult to catch up. The qualitative data were particularly supportive of this point. For example, a Presidential VP said: 'We tried to use consensus, but it gave everybody veto power and we ended up doing a random walk. Our products were too late and they were too expensive.' Presidential still has not caught its competitors. Neutron executives echoed this view. For example, the VP of finance observed:

'The big players [customers and distributors] were already corralled by the competition. We were late.' The firm never regained its early momentum and went bankrupt.

The strong performers emphasized the importance of keeping pace with the fast-changing environment. Some quotes from executives in the group of firms with fast decision making may summarize the perspective representative for high-performers:

- 'If you don't innovate, someone else will.'
- 'You've got to catch the big opportunities.'
- 'Do something, don't just sit around worrying about decisions.'
- 'No advantage is long-term because our industry isn't static. The only competitive advantage is in moving quickly.'

Towards a model of the speed of strategic decision making

The research reported in this paper represents the dynamics in high-velocity environments that are characterized by poor information and difficulties to recover from missed opportunities. The fast-paced and technology-driven industry that is in focus is the type of setting that rewards fast, high-quality decision making. The findings have been presented above as a set of propositions. When summarizing these in a model (see figure 1) Eisenhardt includes her explanation of three mediating processes that explain decision speed.

Several of the propositions focus on how executives making fast decisions accelerate their cognitive processing. For example, these executives immerse themselves in real-time information on their environment and firm operations (Proposition 1). The result is a deep personal knowledge of the enterprise that allows them to access and interpret information rapidly when major decisions arise. In contrast, the slow executives have a less firm grasp on their business. So, when strategic decisions occur, they grope about, try to plan, and have trouble focusing on key information. The executives making fast decisions also use tactics to accelerate analysis of information and alternatives during the decision process. For example, they examine several alternatives simultaneously (Proposition 2). The comparison process speeds their analysis of the strengths and weaknesses of the options. They also gather advice from everyone but focus their attention on the most experienced executives, who are likely to have the most useful advice (Proposition 3). Finally, they integrate key decisions and tactical planning within the decision process (Proposition 5). Doing so quickens executives' assessment of the viability of alternatives. Overall, the executives making fast decisions accelerate their cognitive processing by using efficient problem-solving strategies that maximize information and analysis within time constraints (Hayes, 1981; Payne et al., 1988). These strategies are neither comprehensive nor noncomprehensive, but rather a mix of both.

Second, several of the propositions describe how executives making fast strategic decisions create a smooth group process. For example, constant perusal of real-time information allows

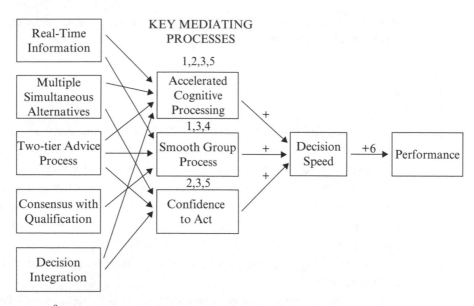

Numbers correspond to propositions in the text.

Fig. 1   A Model of Strategic Decision Speed in High-Velocity Environments[a]

executives to rehearse their performance routines with one another (Proposition 1). The result is a team conditioned to work together successfully in turbulent situations. Similarly, although the consensus-with-qualification approach emphasizes the roles of executives in their own areas, it also rests on participation by the entire team (Proposition 4). The data suggest that executives favor this approach. They want a voice but do not necessarily want to make choices, except in their own arenas. Finally, the fast teams use a two-tier advice process (Proposition 3). This advice process emphasizes the role of counselors, but all are consulted and can participate if they choose. In sum, the fast decision makers create a smooth group process through rehearsal and participation. In particular, these behaviors yield fast decisions because they combine participation and decisiveness in a way that is popular with executives.

Several propositions also converge on the importance of confidence in high-stakes decision making. Anxiety can cripple decision makers in such situations (George, 1980). The teams making fast decisions engage in behaviors to cope with this anxiety and build confidence. One tactic is to rely on the counsel of experienced executives, who impart confidence and a sense of stability (Proposition 3). A second tactic is to seek multiple alternatives (Proposition 2). Doing so gives decision makers the confidence that they have surveyed most of the likely options, leaving 'no stone unturned.' Most important, the fast executives tie together strategic decisions and concrete operating plans (Proposition 5). This attention to day-to-day detail and linkage across major decisions gives a sense of mastery and control that imparts the confidence to act and creates a structure within which action is possible (Gal & Lazarus, 1975; Langer, 1975).

Finally, the findings corroborate an earlier study by Bourgeois and Eisenhardt (1988) linking fast decision making with effective performance (Proposition 6). The findings suggest a configuration of cognitive, political, and emotional processes that is associated with rapid closure on major decisions.

Conclusions

The results, linking fast decisions to five factors such as use of real-time information and multiple alternatives, challenge traditional thinking about strategic decision processes. This new perspective stresses the importance of the top management team and the continuous interaction among the executive team members. The perspective implies a complex view on cognition beyond the dichotomy of rational versus incremental decision making. Managers are boundedly rational but they are also capable of using sensible problem solving strategies that compensate for such limitations.

Finally, the perspective means an emphasis of the role of emotions in decision making. An earlier paper (Eisenhardt and Bourgeois 1988) showed that emotions such as frustration and distrust shaped politics of decision making, and this paper identifies that confidence and anxiety influence the pace of decision making.

Editors' commentary

This paper illustrates good and interesting research practice mainly because of its systematic and thorough research design. Being a comparative case study within a positivist tradition, the paper shows many strengths (see also several comments on this paper in chapter 3). Starting from two research questions – one process-orientated question about how fast strategic decisions are made and one cause-and-effect question about how decision speed links to performance – the study results in a middle-range theory about decision speed. Here the focus is on both the process outcome in terms of decision speed, and the performance outcome on the organizational level in terms of financial performance.

The process outcome is explained as the result of five types of strategic practices, i.e. five different decision process characteristics, or patterns of strategic decision processes, that were derived inductively from cross-case analyses. The causal relationship between process characteristics and decision speed is expressed in five propositions. As shown in the summary above, the major part of the paper is the presentation of these propositions where each section is structured in the same systematic way, making the evidence behind each proposition as explicit as possible. The structure in each of these five sections entails the following steps for describing and explaining each process characteristic and proposition:

1 short summary of main findings
2 translating findings into a clear proposition
3 careful description of how evidence for the proposition was found in the comparative case studies through the author's systematic analyses of
   (a) interview responses from executives,
   (b) story data indicating the specific approach taken in each decision process studied,
   (c) specific measures for the decision characteristic in focus (e.g. measurement of degree of consensus in the executive teams when making the strategic decision)
4 presentation of tables, with both qualitative and quantitative data, presenting evidence from all cases in a novel way
5 rich illustrations of each proposition taken from decision stories and quotes from interviews
6 propositions all related to existing theory and challenging the predominant views on decision making at that time (late 1980s).

Finally the author successfully manages to summarize her findings in a neat and quite complete model.

As already emphasized in chapter 3, the comparative case study approach demonstrated in this paper still stands as a role model for (mid-range) theorizing based on case studies. The paper is a typical example of Yin's meaning of analytical generalization. As the author notes, this type of generalization does not imply that the findings hold for other empirical contexts beyond the high-velocity environment and more precisely the studies of eight small and medium-sized companies in the American microcomputer industry in the mid-1980s. In discussions about generalization there is often a predominant view that there is one truth, meaning that a new theory should replace the old one. However this paper shows that theories are highly contextually dependent, while there is a scholarly tendency to regard theories as universal. Maybe both the old theories on strategic decision making challenged in this paper and the theoretical contributions presented in this paper are valid, but in totally different empirical contexts. For example, the study by Hickson et al. (1986) of strategic decision processes was based on empiricial observations from European, mainly big and mature organizations where characteristics like negative consequences of politicking naturally came out much stronger than in Eisenhardt's study.

To conclude, a few critical comments on the methodological approach, seen in the light of the Strategy as Practice perspective argued for in this book. First, Eisenhardt has argued that the case study approach requires a reasonable number of cases ('four to ten'; Eisenhardt 1989b). Here is a difficult trade off, as case studies imply depth and richness. This paper is based on studies of mainly just one strategic decision in each case company. With analyses of more decisions within each case company, the design would have allowed for more depth in the empirical accounts of the decision process patterns in each case company, still allowing for the powerful comparative case method that the paper demonstrates. Furthermore, such an approach would have allowed both within-case comparisons and cross-case comparisons, making the results still more robust.

The paper is certainly about the practice of strategy. However, the cases are analysed as wholes rather than as a number of overlapping and ongoing decision processes built up by a continuous series of activities. Interesting though the decision process insights are, a more micro approach would provide further understanding and insight; i.e. the approach we advocate would add to the findings of her study.

Finally a comment on the finding expressed through the first proposition that stresses the importance of real-time information used by decision makers to increase the speed of decision making. In a study of environments characterized by rapid changes, it is surprising to note that the type of real-time information mainly used by executive teams in companies with greater decision speed is internal performance measures. One could expect that fast strategic decision making in such turbulent environments also requires external information on competitors and customer markets.

However, these remarks do not reduce the importance of this excellent paper regarding its influence on how to conduct comparative case studies and its many challenging findings on fast strategic decision making.

6

In search of rationality: the purposes behind the use of formal analysis in organizations

(*Administrative Science Quarterly*, 34 (1989): 598–631)

Ann Langley

Abstract

This paper describes the results of a study that examines how formal analysis is actually used in practice in three different organizations. Four main groups of purposes for formal analysis – information, communication, direction and control, and symbolic purposes – are identified and related to the nature of the social and hierarchical relationships between those who initiate analysis, those who do it, and those who receive it. It is concluded that, far from being antithetical as often assumed, formal analysis and social interaction are inextricably linked in organizational decision making and that different structural configurations may generate different patterns of use of analysis.

Editors' introduction

This paper focuses on a key aspect of strategy practice: strategic analysis. It is therefore centrally about the concerns of the Strategy as Practice perspective. It also examines practice in relation to different organizational contexts and seeks to understand the relationship between the two. Further, it raises important issues of research design and methodology in relation to our field. It also raises other issues for consideration in comparison to other papers included in the book: the extent and nature of theorizing and appropriateness of levels of analysis for example. And, as with the Barley paper (chapter 4), it is interesting to ask just how much the quantitative analysis adds to the qualitative analysis.

Paper summary

The departure point for this paper is to point out that surprisingly little is known about the use of formal strategic analysis in organizations: 'Is it in fact used at all? And, if so, when and why?' (598). The paper briefly identifies a number of motivators for the use of formal analysis, using appropriate citations. They include the use of formal analysis by specific staff: for control purposes; for the purpose of post-justifying decisions already made; for focusing attention, raising comfort levels and gaining commitment; as a tool in 'adversarial debate'; 'to deflect attention away from issues by giving the impression of action' (598); to convey rationality through symbolic and ritualistic uses of language. However Langley observes that there has actually 'been very little empirical research that has examined the purposes behind formal analysis in any systematic way' (598).

There is also an assumption that the use of analysis corresponds to particular organizational forms. It is machine bureaucracies that seem to rely most on analysis, adopting a 'rational / comprehensives mode of decision making with less of an emphasis on political influences'. However, 'in the study described here, it is noted that, far from being antithetical, formal analysis and social interaction are inextricably linked in organisational decision making' (599).

The overall research design of the research project is then summarized. It is a qualitative, grounded piece of research with multiple data sources. Langley acknowledges the small sample size and the concomitant problems of generalizability. She also acknowledges the problem of reliance on verbal data and the potential bias of interpretation of data by the researcher. However, Langley has sought to alleviate this problem by the use of extensive examples and quotes from the data and by means of second coding of data.

Research method

Bearing in mind that 'several authors have suggested that different organisation structures may produce different types of decision making processes' (599) the research design deliberately attempts to examine the role of analysis in the context of such differences. Specifically three organizational contexts were chosen: first, a machine bureaucracy, Servico, a public sector organization; second, a professional bureaucracy, St Gabriel's Hospital, reliant on highly trained professionals where the work is relatively routine and repetitive; and third, an adhocracy, again comprising highly trained professionals with less routine, more of an orientation towards innovation, more multidisciplinarity and 'one time outputs': The chosen organization, CAC, was involved in artistic production. In each of these organizations key strategic issues – twenty-seven in total – were studied, varying from diversification decisions through restructuring to closure of services.

Table 1. The Number and Frequency of Studies in Each Category of Analytical Sophistication by Organization

Studies	Servico		St. Gabriel's		CAC		Total	
	N	%	N	%	N	%	N	%
Armchair	2	4.3	4	10.0	30	31.3	36	19.7
Short	4	8.5	8	20.0	27	28.1	39	21.3
Medium	15	31.9	15	37.5	15	15.6	45	24.6
Major	16	34.0	11	27.5	14	14.6	41	22.4
Unclassified*	10	21.2	2	5.0	10	10.4	22	12.0
Total	47	100.0	40	100.0	96	100.0	183	100.0

* Insufficient information.

For every strategic issue in the sample, all documents related to this issue were collected. This set of documents formed the raw material for identifying individual formal analysis studies and classifying them according to a number of criteria. Documents that were merely descriptive reports of events (e.g., minutes of meetings) were rapidly excluded from consideration. The remainder were examined in more detail. Gradually, a set of conventions was developed by which individual formal analysis studies could be circumscribed and identified in a fairly consistent way across the three organizations. Eventually, a total of 183 individual incidences of formal analysis were identified for the 27 issues in the three organizations. Then, as some of these studies were clearly more analytically sophisticated than others, content analysis was used to place the studies in four different categories. The criteria for classification, described in Appendix A, were quantitative content, length of report, time input required, the number of alternatives considered, and the complexity of the methodology used. The four categories were labeled, in order of increasing analytical sophistication, armchair studies, short studies, medium-sized studies, and major studies. While the armchair studies were generally rather short and unstructured, involving the development of an argument based on relatively little data, the major studies usually required considerable quantitative data, multiple research methods, and a great deal of time. The distribution of the entire sample of studies between the four categories is illustrated in Table 1. This shows that very few lower-category studies were found for Servico, while a very large number were found for the CAC. St. Gabriel's Hospital falls somewhere in between. In fact, the absolute number of studies identified at the CAC was more than double that of each of the other organizations, although the number of issues examined was of the same order of magnitude. The difference is largely made up of reports of low sophistication.

The data sources used included documents, over eighty interviews and observation of twenty-six management meetings.

At the first stage of data analysis, I viewed the data as a large sample of 183 individual formal analysis studies, regardless of the issues to which they were related or the organizations in which they were carried out. Patterns were sought in the ways studies were used, and a typology of purposes behind formal analysis was derived. Later, comparisons were carried out to determine whether different patterns tended to be associated with different organizational contexts.

In order to understand the purposes behind these formal analyses Langley employed a grounded analysis approach. She is quite specific about how this was done.

In developing a typology of purposes, a number of a priori factors (e.g., my knowledge of previous literature and my previous work experience both as a consultant and as an internal analyst in two different organizations) suggested possible categories. I was also concerned to be as exhaustive as possible, while producing a parsimonious classification with a small number of components, each suggesting a distinct reality. The main objective, however, was to reflect the data accurately. To do this, in my first passes through the material, I generated a large number of purposes, sometimes using terms taken directly from interviewees: e.g., 'education,' 'assistance,' 'side-tracking,' etc. These were combined together into internally consistent groups. The typology that eventually emerged consisted of four broad categories of purposes: (1) information, (2) communication, (3) direction and control, and (4) symbolic purposes. Within each of these broad categories, the original, more specific categories survive as variants.

She notes that the broad categories correspond to previous research. She also notes that they are not mutually exclusive: whilst 55% were associated with one purpose, 39% were concerned with two, 5% with three and 1% with four.

The paper is also quite specific about the approach to data analysis:

A special 'purposes' data file was created for each study. This file included the following raw data items extracted from the complete data base: (1) extracts from all interview transcripts referring to reasons for initiating the study, (2) notes taken in meetings in which the reasons for doing a given study were discussed, and (3) all references to study objectives or purposes taken from the report itself or from other relevant documents (e.g., minutes of meetings, correspondence, etc.).

On average, each file coded contained information from 2.34 interviewees and from 1.34 documents. Twenty-one studies were excluded from the analysis because the information obtained was inadequate to make an assessment of the purposes behind the study. It is difficult to assess the effect of these exclusions on the overall results. However, the absence of adequate data on a given study is often symptomatic of the low importance accorded to it by people interviewed. Purposes were then assigned to individual studies by reading carefully through the special files to determine whether each of the types of purposes described in Appendix B was relevant to that study, based on the information contained in that file. The quotations from interviews given in the next section provide examples of the types of statements that were seen as indicating the presence of different kinds of purposes. Studies were classified solely on the basis of the information in the special files: the purpose had to be specifically indicated in documents or in the interview or meeting transcripts. Thus, the results on the relative frequencies of different purposes may be biased toward those purposes that were considered most presentable or legitimate in organizational terms and against those purposes that were less easily admitted.

Langley also used a second coder to examine the classification scheme developed, together with statistical tests on cross-coder reliability. Where there were disagreements, both coders had to justify their coding to each other in order to resolve the bases of such disagreements.

The paper then goes on to explain each of the categories in more detail, using quotations from interviews to exemplify what the categories mean.

The purposes behind formal analysis

Langley begins by explaining the typology of purposes behind formal analysis.

Information

This includes the conventional notion that the purpose of formal analysis is to obtain information to gain a better understanding of issues and Langley notes that in her interviews most 'people tend to be very willing to cite such reasons': indeed in 53% of the studies it was a stated purpose. Such information seeking may be undertaken open-mindedly but it may also be to confirm a tentative opinion. It may also be to verify other information sources, for example where top management require additional sources to verify information from specialists or technical experts. Langley also includes in this category what she calls 'pulse taking': where the emphasis is less on hard factual information and more on, for example, top management sensing the feelings of organizational members.

Communication

Formal analysis may also be used to communicate conviction and persuade; 57% of the analyses were at least in part to do with this. It could take different forms.

It might be 'bottom-up', where line managers use analysis to gain approval by senior management. It might be analysis done by a consultant or specialist thus helping the credibility of a case that is being made. It might be top-down, with top management employing analysed data as a basis for educating subordinates. Or it may be that top managers involve others in undertaking the analysis as a way of gaining their commitment. And again, analysis may be used for 'positioning purposes' even though there is little chance of influencing others views. Langley found this to be particularly common in CAC, characterizing the sort of 'armchair analysis' she found in that organization.

Direction and control

A third purpose was uncovered for the use of formal analysis in order to focus subordinates on particular issues for problems (found in 25% of the sample). Again this took different forms. It could be direct delegation of a formal study to specify in more detail what has to be done to implement a particular decision. But it also might involve senior management sending someone to 'help' with such detailed analysis.

Symbolic purposes for analysis

Here analysis is used not so much to serve an instrumental purpose as to legitimize activities, but also to symbolize rational decision making: a willingness to act with the participation of others in decision making and to be concerned with their views. None of this necessarily means that the information gained from the analysis will actually be used or have an influence. Indeed analysis may be used for the purposes of procrastination in order to divert attention until problems resolve themselves. However, whilst 19% of the sample were categorized as symbolic, Langley suggests that, since 'the best symbol is of course the real thing' (608) and that, therefore, empirical identification of symbolic uses is difficult, 19% could be an underestimate.

The purposes for analysis and its social interactive context

In this section of the paper Langley returns to the theme that there is a need to understand formal analysis in its social interactive context. In relation to this the paper identifies six interaction patterns. Moreover she suggests that an understanding of the hierarchical relationships between participants in the analysis process can help predict how analysis will be used. These hierarchical relationships were examined in relation to three roles:

I identified, for each incidence of analysis, the 'initiator' of the study (the person who first requested or suggested it), the 'executor' of the study (the individual or group responsible for carrying it out), and the main 'targets' (the individuals or groups to whom the study was principally addressed). By examining the hierarchical links between these three participants in the process, most incidences of analysis could be mapped onto one or more of six interaction patterns, built around the elemental interaction triad shown in Figure 1. This consists of a mini-organization chart connecting three types of people; a manager (M), a line person reporting to M (L), and a staff person (S). This staff person may be an internal analyst, reporting hierarchically to M, or an independent consultant. When the initiator, executor, and targets of any incidence of analysis are identified and linked on this skeleton organization chart, the interaction pattern for the analysis is obtained. Each interaction pattern is summarized by three letters

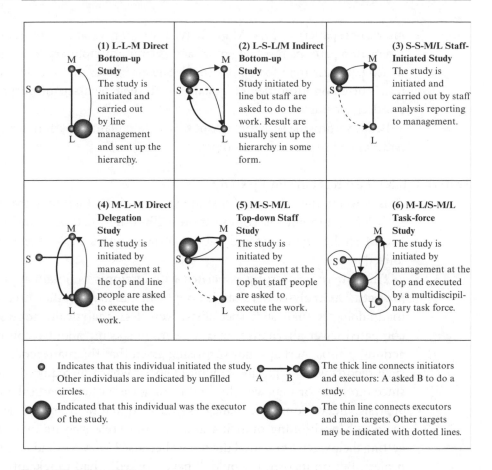

Fig. 2   The six interaction patterns.

identifying sequentially the relative hierarchical positions of the initiator, the executor and the main target(s) of the study. For example, interaction pattern 'L-L-M' indicates that a study is initiated by line management (L), executed by line management (L), and sent up the hierarchy to top management (the target – M).

Although there are in fact twenty-seven possible combinations resulting, 95% of the analyses studied conformed to one of the six patterns shown in figure 2.

Langley then turns to analysing the different interaction patterns. First, using both graphical displays and quantitative analysis, she shows the relationship between the interaction patterns and the different purposes of analysis. In these ways she demonstrates that: '1. Information motives are less frequent with direct bottom-up studies than with other pure interaction patterns . . . 2. Communication motives are more frequent for bottom-up interaction patterns . . . 3. Direction and control motives are more frequent for top-down interaction patterns . . . 4. Multiple types of motives are more frequent for interaction patterns involving more actors (multidisciplinary task forces and mixed patterns) than for others' (612). She also notes that the different patterns correspond to different 'gestalts', with their own sets of purposes and political dynamics.

Below we provide verbatim two of Langley's explanations of the interaction patterns and summarize the others.

Pattern L-L-M: the direct bottom-up study

This is where the content of a study is sent up the hierarchy from below. It is often present in combination with other patterns. Indeed pure L-L-M studies represent only about 30% of the sample, the rest being 'mixed'.

This pattern was largely associated with attempts to obtain approval for projects. The analyses were carried out by line managers; they used simpler methodologies than staff specialists, were less analytically sophisticated, compared fewer alternatives and were more specific about recommended actions. This is, perhaps, not surprising given that the managers preparing such reports were, typically, convinced about what was required. However, since more senior managers knew this, they were often sceptical about the analysis. Indeed some line managers indicated that their analysis was really to do with 'positioning' of their arguments and a relatively minor element in getting their way: 'I prepared the report because I knew we had to justify the project. But on its own it wouldn't have worked. I had to take other steps' (613).

Pattern L-S-L/M: the indirect bottom-up study

These studies were commissioned by line managers but executed by consultants. They represented about 10% of the sample. 'The line controls the mandate of the study but has less control over its content than with the direct bottom-up study.' These were studies for both information and communication purposes in which, typically, the initiator was looking for support for a preconceived idea, with the consultant providing, on the face of it, objective analysis to lend credibility. 'A trade-off has to be made between the risk that the analyst will not confirm one's ideas to the potential return if he/she does' (614). Such reports could be analytically sophisticated but might be unclear in their recommendations, not least, because of the potential discrepancies between the conclusions the analysts drew and what the line managers wanted the reports to show. In such circumstances the reports could go through a number of iterations as the line managers try to persuade the consultants to modify their reports.

Pattern S-S-M/L: the staff-initiated study

Langley found relatively few of these cases, in which studies were initiated by staff people then sent to line colleagues or management superiors. Generally they were unsuccessful in their outcomes. When they occurred they were for the purposes of information and communication but might well be 'done by analysts to symbolise activity and usefulness' (615). There could well be tensions between line managers and staff here too given that such reports might well be the product of staff specialists trying to pursue or advocate their own points of view or justify their existence. In so doing they might well gain senior management support without the senior managers being fully aware of their motivations. In such ways staff risked appearing to railroad senior executives and invade the territory of line managers.

Pattern M-L-M: The direct delegation study

Here, the study is initiated by a manager, and the work is delegated to a line subordinate. The manager at the top controls the definition of the mandate, while the line fully controls the response to it. Independent staff people are not involved, although the line may use subordinates to help respond to the request. About 19 percent of the sample used this pure interaction pattern, sometimes in combination with a bottom-up pattern.

As shown in Figure 3, direct delegation studies are associated with information and direction and control purposes. They represent the use of 'normal' formal organizational channels for carrying out analysis. This pattern expresses top-management confidence in the line's expertise and ability to implement decisions; 'The analyses were done by the different functional areas, . . . we said to ourselves. ' "We have to have confidence in each other – we receive the studies and they are accepted".' For these reasons, this pattern tends to be rather uncontroversial. It leaves full control of the content of the study to the line manager. However, if senior management is not satisfied with the information provided or with the actions taken, the situation could become more threatening. Persistent failure to satisfy management requirements would result in mandates being given to outside people – creating a much more tense situation: pattern M-S-M/L, the top-down staff study.

Pattern M-S-M/L: The top-down staff study

Here, management initiates a study and asks staff people to carry it out. Management therefore controls the mandate of the study, the staff control the content, and line people have virtually no control at all. This was a fairly common pattern, representing about 18 percent of the sample, sometimes in combination with other patterns.

As with direct delegation, two types of purposes tend to occur more frequently than average for top-down staff studies: the need for information from an expert source or the need for some kind of control with respect to line management . . . Staff people were sometimes asked to provide expert opinions, information, or suggestions to managers that involved no contact with or intrusion into the domain of line people lower in the hierarchy. Sometimes, however, the motivation had definite control elements. Staff analysts could be used because senior management had been unable to obtain what it required by direct delegation to line management, and sometimes, they were used to check out information provided by the line [reactive verification].

Certain staff analysts seemed to be particularly valued for their creativity and ability to challenge established ways of doing things, in spite of the fact that some or all of the time, their ideas were too 'way out' to be given serious consideration or too theoretical to be applied directly; 'His ideas can be a bit shocking – but they force you to think.' This idea of the top-down staff study as a 'challenge' appears particularly strongly when analysis was used for 'assistance' – to stimulate action and problem solving on the part of the line (a direction and control motive). As one analyst put it: 'I would say that 90 percent of consultant studies are not implemented. It has to be this way. If I was a manager, I wouldn't implement them either. The manager has to use his own judgment – he has to live with the thing – analyses only serve as a challenge.'

Sometimes this type of study could present a particularly strong 'challenge' to line managers. In at least one case, the line person involved was demoted as an indirect result of the study. Usually though, the line manager's job was not so seriously threatened and, in fact, staff people faced a difficult dilemma in handling the situation. To obtain the information they needed, they had to maintain good relations with the line, but they were often there to make recommendations that might reflect badly on the individuals concerned. Failure to maintain good relations would mean difficulty in obtaining information and a report that had little credibility. Excessive concern with good relations could, however, defeat the purpose of the exercise – to take an objective look at the situation.

The difficulties of maintaining objectivity also arose when top-down staff studies were used for 'reactive verification,' e.g., to evaluate a project proposed by somebody else. Sometimes, the line people proposing the projects were in fact more expert in the area than the analyst: 'When the administration realized the problem, they asked me to take a look at it. But it is difficult to get the credibility. I wasn't really an expert – I had just arrived. What was missing was a really objective analysis.' Moreover, over the long term, analysts would develop personal relationships with certain line managers, which made independent evaluation very difficult. In one of the three organizations, analysts were deliberately rotated round the organization in a conscious attempt to overcome the staff's tendency to develop loyalties that compromised their independence.

Pattern M-L/S-M/L: the multidisciplinary taskforce study

Here studies were initiated by managers but carried out by multidisciplinary taskforces or ad hoc working groups that could include both line and staff people, or perhaps line people from different functional areas. This represented 17% of the sample. Here the information, communication, direction and control, and symbolic purposes were all in evidence. These might be for several purposes. They might be a way of obtaining information from a wide variety of people in the organization. But they also might be ways of developing commitment to proposals or 'educating' those taking part. They might also be used to give the impression of participation in decision making. Or they might be used to help co-ordination between functional areas particularly in the implementation. Or there might be multiple purposes for such taskforces. In this context such taskforces could give rise to tensions, especially if the leadership or mandate of the study was unclear. As such they could be 'a secondary battleground' for career rivalries. Or they could result in the airing of many different points of view, without their resolution. Such taskforces needed clear leadership and/or a clear mandate or guidance from senior management.

Comparison of the three organizations

The paper then considers the differences and purposes behind analyses in their social context, i.e. in relation to the different structural configurations of the organizations studied. The expectation that the purposes will differ according to these contexts is shown in figure 4 (the paper shows that not all these differences are statistically significant, however).

Whilst accepting that the sample size does not allow firm conclusions about the causes of difference, there do seem to be systematic patterns that suggest a relationship between organizational context and the purposes of the analyses undertaken. In the paper Langley gives examples of such consistencies. One example is from CAC. Here there were a large number of 'minor analyses'. She argues that this is consistent with the situation at CAC. It was facing a major crisis at the time of the research and people wished to communicate their concerns with regard to the future of the organization. Moreover it was as an adhocracy in which there were relatively weak authority relationships and high participation in decision making.

The paper then moves on to describe further statistical analysis that was undertaken:

A final question concerns the degree to which the interaction patterns explored in the previous section can explain all the differences observed between the three organizations. The question is To what extent are these differences due to different relative frequencies of the interaction patterns, and to what extent are they due to other factors? To test this, linear models were fitted to the data . . . For example, to examine the importance of interaction pattern and organization in determining the frequency of communication purposes, the entire sample of studies was subdivided into six populations, classified by organization and by whether or not they involved bottom-up patterns (direct, indirect, staff-initiated, or mixed). The dependent variable was defined as the proportion of studies involving the communication motive, while the nominally

Statistically Significant Differences In Proportions (One-Tailed Tests)*

Purpose	Servico vs. St. Gabriel's			St. Gabriel's vs. CAC			Servico vs. CAC		
	C1	C2	A	C1	C2	A	C1	C2	A
Information	NS	*	*	**	***	NS	**	***	***
Communication	***	***	***	NS	NS	*	***	***	***
Direction & control	**	**	**	NS	NS	NS	**	NS	**
Symbolic purposes	Values too small			Values too small			Values too small		

* $p < .01$; ** $p < .05$; *** $p < .01$

* C1 = coder 1, C2 = coder 2, and A = agreed score. N = 41 for Servico.
N = 38 for St. Gabriel's and N = 83 for the CAC.

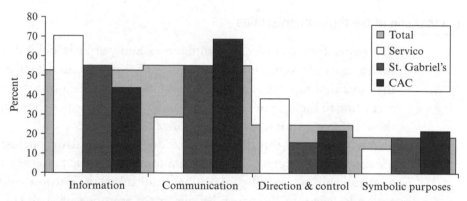

Fig. 4　Frequencies of different types of purposes by organization (% of studies associated with each type of purpose based on agreed classifications).

scaled independent variables were 'organization' (Servico, St. Gabriel's, or the CAC) and 'interaction pattern' (bottom-up or not). When a simple linear model was fitted using weighted least squares estimation (SAS Institute, 1985; 173), both interaction pattern and organization emerged as significant variables (with $p < .001$). In fact, it appeared that studies at Servico seemed to be consistently less communication oriented than elsewhere, even within the same interaction pattern group. For information and direction and control purposes, only the interaction pattern variable emerged as significant when similar linear models were tested. In the case of symbolic purposes, sample sizes were too small to draw useful conclusions. An inspection of the results for communication purposes suggests that the way in which the data were grouped in order to create sufficiently large sample sizes for statistical analysis partially influenced the results. Communication is logically much more consistently associated with direct bottom-up studies than with indirect or staff-initiated studies. However, the pure direct bottom-up pattern represents only 15 percent of the Servico bottom-up sample, while it is 60 percent of St. Gabriel's bottom-up sample and 66 percent of that for the CAC.

A more conceptually interesting element of explanation for the differences might be that the professional status of the people involved in analysis may change the dynamics and purposes behind it within the same interaction-pattern group. For example, it could be hypothesized that for top-down patterns (direct delegation, top-down staff studies, or task forces) in organizations involving professional operating staff (St. Gabriel's and the CAC), top-down communication (education) may replace direction and control as a purpose of analysis. But, given the small sample sizes and the small differences (not significant) observed for direction and control purposes, firm conclusions cannot be drawn.

The overall conclusion reached is that:

The study seems to indicate that different types of organizations may use formal analysis differently, in ways consistent with the nature of the structural configurations. Machine bureaucracies, with their top-down decision-making style, may use analysis most for information and direction and control purposes, to determine the substance of decisions, and to ensure that decisions made at top levels are detailed and implemented. Professional bureaucracies, in which strategic initiatives often come from the bottom up, may require analysis most for communication (direct persuasion) and information (reactive verification) as proposals move toward approval. Finally, in an adhocracy, the wide participation of individuals in decisions and the ambiguity surrounding formal authority may generate even greater uses of formal analysis for communication purposes (especially positioning and direct persuasion).

Discussion and conclusion

In the final section of the paper the discussion links the findings to different bodies of theory that inform the role of formal analysis and suggests implications for future research. The main bodies of theory considered are as follows.

Organizational decision making

Langley argues that despite the evidence of bounded, incremental decision making, at the time of the paper: 'Most treatments of organizational decision making still use variants of the stage based model . . . but these appear to have limited usefulness for describing the incremental contribution of analysis to decisions, because they de-emphasize the social interactive aspects of the process that are seen here to be critical to an understanding of its role' (623).

Information and principal-agent relationships in organizations

The results relate to explanations of organizational decision making that draw on agency theory. This in turn complements a political perspective on decision making and, for example, research that has shown that control over information is an important source of power. In this theoretical context, this research identifies interaction triads in relation to analytical studies and raises the question: 'Under what circumstances do such triads succeed in reducing information asymmetry and in aligning agents' goals with those principles, or vice versa?' (624).

Implementation and the role of staff analysts

The research is also of relevance to work concerned with the role of staff and specialists in analytic studies and the extent of implementation of staff's (or specialists') recommendations. Prior research has 'consistently identified two factors that enhance implementation prospects . . . top management support and, most importantly, participation of line managers' (624). However Langley also notes: 'The effectiveness of the staff–line dichotomy depends on the maintenance of a certain amount of tension between the two. When the tension disappears the staff may not be doing its job' (624). Moreover 'this study suggests that all staff recommendations do not have to be implemented for them to play a useful role in challenging line management' (624).

Institutional versus rational explanations for the use of formal analysis

Relating her findings to institutional theory, Langley asks what other reasons might exist for the undertaking of formal analysis. In particular: 'to what extent do these organizations adopt formal analysis because of institutional pressures – or because of pressures for effective decision making' (625). She briefly reviews the findings from the various research sites and concludes that 'neither purely rational nor purely institutional explanations seems sufficient to explain all uses of formal analysis in the organization studied' (626).

Editors' commentary

The paper makes the point that even those (process) papers that question the notion of rationality nonetheless fail to get to grips with just what goes on in analytical studies in organizations. And it moves us a good deal further forward in understanding the activities of strategic analysis. The paper is certainly to do with organizational processes but takes us 'beyond process' at least in comparison with the way in which most process research is undertaken. Whilst the concern is with organizational processes, these are not dealt with as generalized abstracted categories, but are examined in terms of the activities that go on within them. And as this summary has shown, those activities are related systematically to organizational context. Of course, it would have been possible to go further: arguably, for a paper that is concerned with why people undertake analytic studies, people and what they are actually doing are not central; they appear only in the quotes as illustrations of typologies. This in turn raises a question as to the value of such typologies. Are they useful or, as suggested by one academic in the Strategy as Practice field, 'premature abstractions in the absence of more doing'? Indeed it might have been possible to look in more detail at what went on within particular analytical studies. Such research would have provided greater insight within categories of analysis, but here the purpose was to compare across organizational contexts and it is difficult to see how this might be done without some form of categorization of activities.

A particular concern in the Strategy as Practice field is to examine links to strategic outcomes. There is evidence in this paper of such traceable links: for example the discussion in the paper about the role of staff/consultant led analytical studies and their failure to lead to outcomes. Indeed Langley considers the links between the activities of analysis and the consequences in terms of organizational context: she asks, in effect, how organizational contexts inform our understanding of the role of analyses and in turn how those analyses contribute to what sorts of outcome within those contexts. This is especially powerful since it is done on a comparative basis, but equally it could be done by tracing through such links within a given form of analysis. Again, then, in relation to the comment above, it might have been possible to trace through even finer-grained analysis of activities to outcomes in organizational context: but this would have been a different study and a different paper. It does however provide a potential research agenda for others.

In discussion with the author, it became clear that in the original PhD thesis on which the paper was based there was little in the way of theory. Theory was largely introduced into this paper as a result of the journal review process. Given that the thrust of the paper is essentially about the links between forms and purposes of analysis in context, it is certainly a good case for a need for theory upfront, as is now the case. Langley is, quite evidently, looking for links between organizational context and practice. That is a theoretically informed research issue and the research design and analysis certainly appear to be undertaken within that framing. It is explicit as the paper stands that theory was informing this research but may have been implicit in the original PhD work on which it is based. The question that then arises is the extent to which there is benefit in theory explicitly framing and explicitly driving a research project. Comparisons here might be made between this paper and the Barley paper (chapter 4). The impression is that in terms of research design and the operationalization of constructs, the research by Barley is more deeply informed by the theoretical position it takes than here, which would of course be consistent with the original absence of upfront theorizing.

The fact that the paper claimed to be grounded was a problem in the review process because reviewers said it was atheoretical: hence the introduction of a discussion of theory. Nonetheless the grounded element of the paper is spelled out in some detail and also qualified. In many other studies there is less explanation of the nature of the grounded analysis, and less qualification of it, than is provided in this paper. Here it is possible to see how Langley undertook that analysis in some detail. The broader question is the role of theory in relation to such grounded analysis. The question researchers need to ask is just how that theory informs their analysis. We would argue that those who are claiming to undertake grounded work would benefit from being explicit about the theories that inform their work and accept that this is a legitimate basis of guiding what they then may see as grounded, or perhaps more accurately inductive, analysis.

A further point of interest in this research design is the issue of organizational context, which plays an important part in this research. There are two points here. First, the design of the study is interesting in that there are three different organizations with different structural categories. The research design thus raises the question of the extent to which other researchers can 'control' for context in qualitative work as is the case here. A second point about the sample structure is that it is organized so that the researcher is *bound* to find something of interest; again a lesson worth noting for researchers.

The paper did not originally have the quantitative element. This was also added during the review process. Again the question of the extent to which the statistical analysis adds to the paper merits consideration. John Van Maanen's (1998) observations are interesting in this respect:

Her methods are mixed. They include some statistical hypothesis testing tucked inside a tightly packaged, taxonomically driven descriptive narrative. There is reflexive irony, for Langley's formal analysis suggests that, in the end, rationality – as displayed by the use of codified, numerical techniques – is largely and ordinarily a rhetorical category whose use and shape varies by circumstance and history.

Ann Langley's own view on the quantitative analysis in the paper is that it was needed to support the legitimacy of the argument in that particular journal at that particular point in history, and that this is indeed rather ironic given the message of the paper. On the other hand, this aspect of the paper is not incompatible with her own background and training (she has a bachelor's degree in mathematics). Twenty years later, she believes she might have presented the material differently – focusing in more depth on a smaller number of situations from the database to give a richer and less abstract portrait of how formal analysis contributes to strategic decisions. Indeed, there is no reason why this could not still be done. The issues addressed are to some extent timeless.

7

Sensemaking and sensegiving in strategic change initiation

(*Strategic Management Journal*, 12, 6 (1991): 433–48)

Dennis A. Gioia and Kumar Chittipeddi

Abstract

This paper reports an ethnographic study of the initiation of a strategic change effort in a large, public university. It develops a new framework for understanding the distinctive character of the beginning stages of strategic change by tracking the first year of the change through four phases (labeled as envisioning, signaling, re-visioning, and energizing). This interpretive approach suggests that the CEO's primary role in instigating the strategic change process might best be understood in terms of the emergent concepts of 'sensemaking' and 'sensegiving'. Relationships between these central concepts and other important theoretical domains are then drawn and implications for understanding strategic change initiation are discussed.

Editors' introduction

This illustrative paper on doing strategy in the university context combines a quite traditional top-management focus on strategizing with both innovative method and frame-breaking theorizing.

Most general texts on strategy describe the top manager as the major force in the process of strategy formation. Such a narrow view, where it is taken for granted that strategies get formulated at the top, is questioned in the Strategy as Practice perspective with its focus on activities and practices of strategizing. Strategies can emerge everywhere in the organization – anyone is a potential strategist – and different groups of people may also act as collective strategists. However, the top manager is certainly still a prime candidate for being an influential strategist, because of the power and strategic responsibility that resides with him/her as well as the overview and broad perspective on strategic issues that follow with the role (Mintzberg et al. 1998). But even when studying the top manager as an influential strategist we need to emphasize the unfolding of activities, the practices in use, and the social interaction between this strategist and other actors. Gioia and associates' seminal field work does exactly this through the in-depth study of the role, meaning and implications of a CEO's active participation in a major strategic change effort. The results from this study have been published in several articles (Gioia and Chittipeddi 1991; Gioa et al. 1994; Gioia and Thomas 1996). The first article, by Gioa and Chittipeddi (1991), is particularly interesting because of its well-performed ethnographic field work, with detailed real-time observations, and its convincing interpretive analysis resulting in trustworthy, expressive and attractive conceptualizations of the findings within the, at that time, emerging field of managerial and organizational cognition. We will elaborate on these and other strengths, as well as some limitations, in our commentary after the summary of this illustrative paper.

Paper summary

Introduction

What is the nature of strategic change and the CEO's role in instigating it? In general terms, change involves an attempt to alter the current way of thinking and acting by the organization's membership. More specifically, *strategic* change involves an attempt to change current modes of cognition and action to enable the organization to take advantage of important opportunities or to cope with consequential environmental threats. Organizational change has received significant study over the years; the distinctive character of strategic change, however, remains significantly under-studied (cf. Dutton and Duncan, 1987). In particular, the role of the CEO in the critical initial stages of the strategic change process have not been adequately described. Similarly, and in a directly related vein, the nature of processes used to launch a strategic change effort have not been well articulated.

In the very first paragraph, Gioia and Chittipeddi establish their view on strategic change, positioning themselves in an emerging stream of research on managerial and organizational cognition. The authors note that the CEO has the responsibility both for setting strategic directions and for ensuring their implementation. However, they note that the CEO's role may range from dominating these activities to a more intermediate and integrated role. They argue that terms such as formulation and implementation de-emphasize the symbolic elements of strategic leadership, and especially in the early stage 'when strategic change is just being instigated' (434).

In a theoretical overview, Gioia and Chittipeddi present the features of the literature dealing with the initial phases of a strategic change effort. It is stressed that any substantive change implies change of values and meaning systems, a view that becomes a major focus of this article. The CEO must make sense of the intended change in a way that eventually fits with a revised collective system of meanings. The communication of such *sensemaking* to other stakeholders is labelled *sensegiving* on the part of the CEO. It should be noted that although the concepts of sensemaking and sensegiving were in fact derived from the researchers' interpretive analysis of the data, they deliberately chose to introduce them at the beginning of their paper – an interesting rhetorical strategy. In the authors' interpretation, sensegiving is combined with symbolic actions to communicate that the existing interpretive scheme, or system of meanings, is not appropriate.

Such actions imply the creation of instability in members' ways of understanding the organization, and demand that they make some new sense of it (Poole, Gioia and Gray, 1989). Disconfirmation of an existing interpretive scheme, however, requires some revised scheme to take its place (Ransom, Hinings and Greenwood, 1980). Therefore, an opportunity is created for the CEO to articulate and advocate his or her vision or preferred interpretive scheme *for* the stakeholders (leading to another 'sensemaking' activity, this time by the stakeholders). Given that change efforts seldom happen by decree, but often hinge on consensus-building, a round of negotiated social construction is likely (Berger and Luckmann, 1966). Here the affected stakeholders try to negotiate revisions to the proposed vision (Strauss, 1978; Walsh and Fahey, 1986) . . .

Through these reciprocal activities of sensemaking and sensegiving the broad and abstract vision becomes more well defined.

In the light of this conceptual overview, the launching of a strategic change effort represents a critical time when several important processes that guide the entire change venture begin to coalesce. The initiation of strategic change can be viewed as a process whereby the CEO makes sense of an altered vision of the organization and engages in cycles of negotiated social construction activities to influence stakeholders and constituents to accept that vision.

The study also aimed to develop findings on how the vision became established as an interpretive framework in the face of possible resistance by some stakeholders.

Ground assumptions and methodology

Gioia and Chittipeddi searched for a method that could reveal both the nature and the sequence of the strategic change, including the assumed revision of interpretive schemes in the organization.

Such research needs to be 'interpretive' in nature (Rabinow and Sullivan, 1979), which implies an alternative paradigm applied to the study of strategic change (Burrell and Morgan, 1979; Kuhn, 1970).

Broadly stated, the interpretive approach turns on the assumption that human understanding and action are based on the *interpretation* of information and events by the people experiencing them (Rabinow and Sullivan, 1979). Understanding and action, therefore, depend upon the meaning assigned to any set of events (cf. Daft and Weick, 1984). Meaning, however, is a *socially-constructed phenomenon* (cf. Berger and Luckmann, 1966; Weick, 1979).

Gioia and Chittipeddi claim that the study of systems of meaning and how they are altered is crucial to the study of strategic change. The chosen perspective implies that in order to understand strategic leadership of deliberate change, the researcher needs to capture the meanings ascribed by the members of the organization. This takes the authors into the use of an ethnographic method of participant observation with the ambition to discover the conceptual lenses that actors use for their interpretations. This approach implies 'inductive reasoning' where the initial report from the ethnographic field study takes the form of a narrative mainly using the words of the organizational actors.

The reporting of the ethnographic account is framed around the dominant themes expressed by the participants and represents a *first-order analysis*. The researcher only later attempts to derive an explanatory framework to put the story into a more theoretical perspective by means of a *second-order analysis* (cf. Van Maanen, 1979). It is for this reason that ethnographic, interpretive research often appears 'inverted' when compared to the more traditional style of strategy research; rather than theory driving the data gathering, the theoretical perspective is grounded in, and emerges from the first-hand data (cf. Glaser and Strauss, 1967).

To avoid going totally 'native' in the field study, one member of the research team acted as an insider while the other acted as an outsider. The insider, doing the ethnography, was participating in the change process as a staff member within the Strategic Planning Office of the large public university that was the research site. The outside researcher 'conducted a more objective analysis of the data'. This combination was labelled a 'dual-researcher, grounded approach' (436).

According to Gioia and Chittipeddi, their research context, a university, is characterized by a multiplicity of goals and by diffused power. It is difficult to manage such an organization, as the professionals in it guard their autonomy.

The research project started with the arrival of a new President in the focal university (and continued with on-site research for two and a half years and another period of distant observations and a few follow-up interviews). He almost immediately launched a major strategic change effort with the goal of making the university into what he called a 'Top 10' public university. The President was the main architect of the strategic change but he also appointed a university-wide Strategic Planning Task Force (SPTF). Within the overall strategic change effort the President presented a short list of 'strategic initiatives in which he had a strong personal interest . . . most notably the creation of a new School of Communication' (436). These initiatives symbolized the determination and vision of the President to change the university.

The insider researcher was made a full-fledged member of the strategic taskforce, the SPTF, which gave him very good access to key informants, such as the President, the Provost and other senior executives, and with direct, often daily contact with many of them. This access involved multiple tape-recorded interviews with each of these informants. The interviews focused on their perceptions about the unfolding changes and the strategic leadership role of the President. Besides the interviews, the ethnographer wrote a diary with events and activities, and collected all relevant internal memos and (confidential) reports.

Finally, in addition to these data sources, a key member of the President's inner circle agreed to serve as a knowledgeable, independent reviewer of the data and their interpretation as findings and conclusions emerged. This individual was a trusted aide to the President who played a central role in the management of the strategic change process; in addition, however, he was also an active researcher who could analyze our emerging interpretations for their accuracy and credibility. He was not employed as a 'primary' informant, *per se*, but rather served as a 'hold-out' informant. In this role he could agree or disagree with the researchers' interpretations of events, thus either 'validating' research findings or suggesting avenues for further analysis.

First-order findings

Here the authors present a single narrative based on all accounts from the informants, the ethnographer's own experience, the archival sources and the 'hold-out' informant. The narrative is framed in four different phases that the ethnographer experienced as emerging during the first year, which is the period defined as the initiation stage of the entire strategic change effort.

Strategic change initiation phases

The initial stage of the change effort progressed from an 'Envisioning' to a 'Signaling' to a 'Re-Visioning' and eventually to an 'Energizing' phase. The labeling of the phases derives from the ethnographer's experience in interaction with the informants and other organization members.

The Envisioning Phase

This phase ran from approximately 3 months prior to the assumption of office by the new President until about 1 month after he became CEO. Thus, the strategic change process actually began *before* his formal term. Information-gathering visits to the university and many of his early job tenure activities were devoted to assessing potentials and possibilities. He quickly began to evolve an embryonic strategic vision for the university, which was based on a personal interpretive scheme derived from his prior institutional experience and applied to the university's current and historical context:

> *President (CEO):* When my appointment as President was announced I began to make trips to the university almost immediately. I met with all the Deans, got to know the place, read a great deal, talked to people here and elsewhere about this university. So, by the time I came on board I had a good idea of how the strategic planning process might be launched, and second I had an idea of how *I* thought it might come out.

The Signaling Phase

This phase overlapped the envisioning phase slightly and lasted approximately 3 months. It commenced with the arrival of the new President and was defined mainly by the public declaration of the strategic change effort. These virtually simultaneous events provided an ideal context for disrupting the status quo:

> *President:* It was important during my first year to indicate that the university was going to change, and to begin some of that change for a couple of reasons. First of all it was my mandate to lead this university. I was told in no uncertain terms by the people who hired me that they wanted strong leadership, and that they wanted the university to move to another plane. This meant that I couldn't wait for two or three years to demonstrate to the Board of Trustees that I had begun the next moves.

The announcement of the strategic change effort injected ambiguity into a heretofore stable, even complacent, university community. It infused the organization with some measure of anxiety, but also gave the CEO leverage in influencing desired changes. This leverage resulted not only from his position, but also from his ability to provide his own interpretation on the atmosphere of ambiguity that *he* had created by initiating the change effort.

The President used this 'ambiguity-by-design' to symbolize the reality of the change. But he and his top-management team were quite surprised by the positive effects that the ambiguity created in the change process. This was an important step in the President's introduction of a new framework for understanding the strategy and organization of the university that questioned some existing conceptions. At the same time, the President could reduce some of the ambiguity and anxiety by communicating to different stakeholders his inspiring vision of being a Top 10 public university.

The re-visioning phase

During this phase (from about the fourth to the tenth month) the President continued to be a 'vivid symbol' for the change effort. Members of the organization started to adjust to the new situation, accepting 'strategic planning' as the new watchword, even though no formal planning activities had yet begun.

Further, some opposition became visible from specific vested interests that questioned the need for any change at all.

As a consequence of this resistance, some tension developed within the top management team concerning differences in preferred approaches to managing the change process. The President favored a strong, somewhat directive leadership process, whereas the Executive Vice President (who was worried about the long-term costs of bypassing traditionally influential groups) argued for a more consultative process.

> *President:* Any time you change a massive institution, and do it within a reasonably short time span, people are going to be critical of [the leadership]. When a leader comes in with a bucket of goodwill, he spends it as he has to. If you do anything unilaterally, you lose some of that goodwill. I am perfectly prepared to see that happen.
>
> [The strategic change process] will create a sense of motion at the University, but it *can't* be a totally democratic process. You leave room for lots of participation, and you leave room for the constituency to change your mind – if it can. A CEO who leads a strategic change process has to have some idea of where it ought to go, or the process lacks motivation.

The Executive Vice-President thought that the President stressed 'action' at the expense of considering 'relationships', and the Dean of one college argued for a better balance between the need for both top-management activism and faculty involvement. The President continued to argue publicly for a fast pace of change but at the same time encouraged other members of his team to engage in more consultation.

The resistance that emerged during the re-visioning phase never coalesced into a united front, as different change initiatives affected various stakeholders within the university differently. Still, the effect of the resistance communicated in the feedback from different stakeholders was that the President modified some change initiatives.

The Energizing Phase

This phase overlapped the opposition period of the previous phase to some extent (because some resistance continued even after widespread commitment to the change effort became solidified), and extended up to and beyond the CEO's first anniversary. It was marked initially by the first substantive activities on the part of the formal Strategic Planning Task Force (SPTF)[3] and the widening circle of consultation and feedback from the various stakeholders affected by the proposed changes. The resulting consultation process began with the smallest and highest level groups and progressively expanded to include larger, more lower level audiences.

According to the authors' interpretation, the effect of this widening circle of sharing views on the change was a further reinterpretation by the President and his team of their change ideas and initiatives. All initiatives resulted in some change activity, but many initiatives were finetuned and revised. Many stakeholders could in this way influence different specifics of the overall change effort. A wider commitment emerged within the organization through this reciprocity between the top management and many stakeholders. This energizing phase became the end of the initiation stage of the President's change initiative, followed by a stage of implementation of more detailed plans.

Overall, then, the activities of the CEO and the top management team during the initiation stage of strategic change focused on figuring out new directions and communicating a renewed interpretive scheme and organizational resurgence to various stakeholders. Those activities, however, are not well captured in traditional conceptualizations of strategic management.

Second-order findings

As mentioned, the first-order analysis was conducted to discover themes and patterns through an ethnographic analysis of all informants' accounts, but with the main focus on interpretations by and about the President. The reporting of this first-order analysis was the narrative (summarized above) of the early stages of the strategic change. 'This narrative integrates the interpretations and experiences of the informants and the ethnographer' (437).

Analysis leading to second-order findings

The second-order analysis involves the examination of the ethnographic data from a more theoretical perspective by the research team. The objective was to discern deeper patterns seldom apparent to organizational members, and new dimensions of understanding that became important for subsequent conceptualizations. The research team reported the following five steps of the second-order analysis:

1. Examining each of the informants' accounts, via qualitative content analysis (cf. Miles and Huberman, 1994), to ascertain explanations for various events and activities that occurred
2. Determining whether the informants' accounts were internally consistent over time or were changing in some progressive fashion as the strategic change process evolved
3. Analyzing data *across* informants for significant patterns of convergence or divergence. The examined data were sampled based on their relevance to the research focus on the President's role in managing the strategic change process (a form of the 'theoretical sampling' method of Glaser and Strauss, 1967). This procedure was executed by repetitive or 'constant comparison' (Conrad, 1982; Glaser and Strauss, 1967), wherein the data from different sources and different times were repeatedly compared to discern the major themes or processes involved in the initiation of change

4. Extracting the theoretically explanatory dimensions from the emergent patterns in the data. In this step of the analysis, data related to emerging dimensions were constantly compared to other data until dimensional patterns became evident (Agar, 1980; Spradley, 1979: 1980)
5. Integrating these patterns into a theoretical or conceptual framework.

These steps lead to a new way of seeing the role of a CEO in the initiation stage of strategic change, building on the narratives that disclosed the informants' meaning systems. A theoretical view, grounded in the ethnographic observations, emerged and the second-order analysis resulted in an explanatory framework of sensemaking and sensegiving.

In the context of this study, 'sensemaking' has to do with meaning construction and reconstruction by the involved parties as they attempted to develop a meaningful framework for understanding the nature of the intended strategic change. 'Sensegiving' is concerned with the process of attempting to influence the sensemaking and meaning construction of others toward a preferred redefinition of organizational reality. We found that these processes took place in an iterative, sequential, and to some extent reciprocal fashion, and involved not only the President and his top-management team, but also the internal and external stakeholders and constituents of the university.

Sensemaking

Gioia and Chittipeddi then give meaning to these concepts by illustrating them with examples from the case narrative. According to them, a number of activities by the new President represent a 'sensemaking process in action' (442), such as his frequent visits to the university before he came into office in order to get impressions and make sense of the history and culture of the university. In the first stages of his tenure he also met with numerous people, from major stakeholders to lower-level members, with the same purpose. Quite early, his sensemaking process resulted in the formulation of the new vision. Members of the university organization and external stakeholders tried to figure out the meaning of the vision and the proposed strategic changes following from the vision, so that here again we have sensemaking processes in action.

Sensegiving

The formulated vision was communicated by the President in many ways and to different stakeholders. This sensegiving implies that he provided an interpretation of a new reality for the university, and he tried to influence stakeholders to adopt his vision, its underlying values and actual changes as their own interpretation. The term 'sensegiving' means that the President was

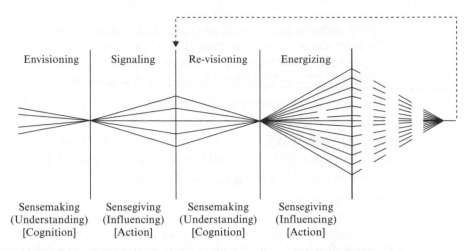

Fig. 3   Processes involved in the initiation of strategic change

making sense *for others*, supplying them with an acceptable interpretation. However, the target groups of the President's sensegiving first made their own sense of the vision and change actions and communicated back to the President their new interpretations. So the sensemaking/sensegiving process takes the form of reciprocal cycles between the President and a progressively expanding audience of stakeholders. Figure 3 illustrates the pattern found by the authors in their second-order analysis.

Stage 1 is a sensemaking effort by the CEO, wherein the President seeks to make sense of the new situation by creating some guiding vision for the university ('Envisioning'). Stage 2 is a sensegiving effort by the CEO, wherein he attempts to communicate this vision to the university's stakeholders and constituencies ('Signaling'). Stage 3 is a sensemaking effort by the stakeholders, wherein they try to figure out the meaning of the proposed vision to them and revise their understanding ('Re-Visioning'). Stage 4 is a sensegiving effort by these stakeholders, wherein they respond to the proposed vision and attempt to influence its realized form, but it also is a stage marked by the emergence and communication of an organization-wide commitment to action toward the vision ('Energizing'). (The feedback loop indicates that the sensegiving activities of the various stakeholders also leads to some modifications to the espoused vision [re-visioning] on the part of the CEO and top management team).

Furthermore, the authors identified a sequential pattern of understanding and influence related to periods of sensemaking and sensegiving, where sensemaking deals with understanding and sensigiving with influence. In a similar fashion they argue that each phase of sensemaking and understanding implies a cognitive process, while phases of sensegiving and influence incorporate action by the involved actors.

Discussion and implications

With its focus on the instigation of strategic change, this paper establishes a link between the early progress of change and a theoretical conceptualization related to the strategic cognition literature. The main finding is that the initiation process of strategic change can be described as reciprocal and iterating periods of sensemaking and sensegiving, where the CEO formulates and disseminates a vision that stakeholders make sense of and act upon as the first cycle of sensemaking–sensegiving–sensemaking.

The authors report interesting observations on the uncertainty, ambiguity and emotionality of organizational members, as many of them interpreted the initiated change as something ominous because of the implied changes in culture and practices. In other words, a cognitive reorientation of existing interpretive schemes was required for the President to achieve eventual acceptance of his initial change ideas. This acceptance emerged through the processes conceptualized as cycles of 'sensemaking-for-self' and 'sensegiving-for-others' (444). Furthermore, the four phases presented as first-order findings were found to fit with the progressive iterations of sensemaking and sensegiving. The envisioning and re-visioning phases can be understood as processes of sensemaking–understanding–cognition while the Signalling and energizing phases are dominated by processes of sensegiving–influencing–action.

Early literature on university organizations (e.g. Cohen and March 1974) noted the symbolic power of the presidency but questioned its potency for managing change. In contrast, this study shows that many presidential activities had a strong symbolic dimension that certainly helped to direct, motivate and facilitate the strategic change process. In particular, the vision, with its 'evocative imagery' (445), provided a guiding framework for the thinking and acting of different members of the organization. The case in this paper is also an early but strong account of changes in the sector of higher education implying that university presidents are increasingly acting strategically.

Furthermore, the authors note that strategic change does not need to be preceded by crisis. Given the lack of crisis 'the creation of "ambiguity-by-design" became a potent device for fostering an atmosphere of change' (445), leading to an opportunity for top managers to reframe the predominant interpretive schemes towards the direction of the vision. The findings show that the President's role in the initial stage of strategic change is about questioning obsolete interpretive schemes and framing a new collective interpretive scheme for the organization in order to provide guidance for actions toward the intended change.

This research also implies that a captivating vision is perhaps a key feature in the initiation of strategic change because it provides a symbolic foundation for stakeholders to develop an alternative interpretive scheme. On the basis of this study, it is clear that the symbolic role of the CEO during the initiation of strategic change can go beyond being merely 'expressive' of values, beliefs, actions, etc. as has traditionally been argued (cf. Edelman, 1964; Pfeffer, 1981). It also can be *instrumental* to the accomplishment of change. That is, the symbolic constructions used to create meaning for others (i.e. to give sense) are instrumental to the effectiveness of the critical stage of proposing and initiating an overall change effort.

Included in this view is the characterization of strategic change as a process of negotiations. The result of the initial stage of change was the 'negotiated reality' (446) that the President was able to reach with all important stakeholders. The authors note that a CEO can dominate the negotiated reality through the influence that his/her formulated vision may exert.

Conclusions

The conclusion of the sensemaking/sensegiving perspective on strategic change initiation is that the CEO and his/her top management team are architects, assimilators and facilitators of strategic change. Key processes are the acts of sensemaking and sensegiving in relation to a new vision. The authors argue that this perspective of the CEO as the prime 'sensemaker' *and* 'sensegiver' (446) captures the essence of the early stages of strategic change much better than the concepts of formulation and implementation.

Taken as a whole, then, the findings of our interpretive perspective and ethnographic approach to the study of strategic change imply that the initiation of the process involves a set of top management activities that are key to the effectiveness of the overall change process. These activities are simultaneously symbolic and substantive, involve reciprocal processes of cognition and action, and entail cycles of understanding and influence, all of which can be usefully captured under the concepts of sensemaking and sensegiving.

Editors' commentary

This paper is exemplary in several respects, offering both theoretical and methodological contributions to research on strategizing and Strategy as Practice. First it has a strong focus on doing strategy, in this case on what the CEO actually does in terms of some major strategic activities during his first year in office. Key activities are (1) gathering information, observing, and talking with stakeholders in order to interpret and understand the situation;

(2) translating his interpretations into an evocative vision; (3) communicating the vision and subsequent strategic initiatives to organizational members and external stakeholders; (4) meeting and talking with these people to get feedback on his strategic change efforts; (5) revising some strategic initiatives as an adjustment to the strategic resistance some stakeholders gave voice to; and finally (6) developing more detailed plans together with the strategic planning taskforce to implement the initiatives that would support the realization of the vision.

Second, the authors develop an explanatory framework using a new combination of theoretical concepts. The main contribution is the duality expressed by sensemaking, i.e. a cognitive process of interpretation to reach a new understanding of a complex strategic situation, and sensegiving, i.e. an action-orientated process with the purpose of influencing the sensemaking of others. The sensemaking–sensegiving cycles are defined as 'cycles of negotiated social construction', where the CEO tries to influence affected stakeholders to accept his socially constructed vision while these stakeholders in turn try to negotiate adjustments to the proposed vision. Together this conceptual framework gives a plausible explanation for the outcome of the initiating stage of strategic change in this case.

Third, the paper reports a quite unique methodological approach for field work and analysis that meets the demands of capturing the daily life of strategizing. This interpretive approach, using an ethnographic method, is not unique per se. Rather the uniqueness lies in its application to the field of strategic management at that time, and the empirical focus on a CEO doing strategy. It could also be added that the paper was published in a journal that traditionally has not published a great deal of qualitative research, which should be seen as frame-breaking. The interpretive approach is well conducted in the sense of remaining true to the underlying ideas of the approach. In this paper the interpretive approach implies both the practice of interpretation by the researchers of the observed 'reality', and also the efforts to observe and capture the interpretations made by the strategist(s) in this case.

Fourth, the design of the interpretive study implies a good balance between distance and closeness. Doing interpretive research using an ethnographic method means aiming for an authentic closeness to the studied actors. It is a situation of subject-to-subject relationships, where the ethnographer is accepted as a relevant participant in the daily life of an organization. At the same time, such closeness engenders an obvious risk of 'going native', with subsequent problems of distancing oneself as researcher for reflection and analysis. Such distance is necessary for a rigorous and theoretically fruitful analysis. This necessary, iterative balance between closeness and distance often emerges as a dilemma in interpretive research. However, in this paper the dilemma is addressed creatively (though not without problems) through the division of labour within the research team. One researcher reflects the closeness, being an 'insider' in the studied strategic change process, while the other researcher, the 'outsider', creates the distance necessary especially for the second-order analysis.

Fifth, the authors have explicitly described the steps and activities of their first-order and second-order analyses. These accounts of their methodology in action are valuable. Such details are quite often weakly reported in papers based on qualitative research approaches.

Moving to some limitations of the paper, first the paper conceptualizes sensemaking very much in line with later studies, meaning that sensemaking is a process through which people create and maintain an intersubjective world (cf. the paper by Balogun and Johnson also summarized here, chapter 10). However, although they may well have data relative to these, Gioia and Chittipeddi do not provide much concrete evidence of the social interaction between sensemaking people in this paper. The first-order narrative includes mainly self-reports from past-event interviews with the CEO and other key actors. Furthermore the narrative and analyses do not reveal in great depth the emotional and political dimensions almost certainly in play in the micro processes of sensemaking and sensegiving in this effort of a major strategic change.

Although the steps of the second-order analysis are presented, the interaction between the insider and the outsider in this stage of analysis could have been explained more clearly. It would have been interesting to know more about the interplay within the research team in the different stages of the research in order to evaluate better the pros and cons of the very promising insider–outsider combination in interpretive studies. Furthermore, there is a third member of the research team, a 'hold-out' informant who was validating the emerging research findings through agreements or disagreements with the researchers' interpretations. However, this informant was actually an important actor involved in the ongoing process of strategizing, with his own subjective view and vested interests, making the validation arguments around this 'independent' reviewer somewhat questionable. This discussion comes back to some of the dilemmas of in-depth ethnographic work discussed in chapter 3.

To conclude, this illustrative paper represents an interesting contribution to the understanding of Strategy as Practice. An important conclusion is that the duality of sensemaking and sensegiving includes negotiation processes. Future research could develop further this dimension by capturing in more depth the ongoing, daily social interaction of actors involved. Finally the processes of sensegiving are explained as activities of influencing others, something that future studies may deepen by focusing on the political and rhetorical sides of sensegiving.

8

Business planning as pedagogy: language and control in a changing institutional field

(*Administrative Science Quarterly*, 43 (1998): 257–92)

Leslie S. Oakes, Barbara Townley and David J. Cooper

Abstract

Language and power are central to an understanding of control. This paper uses the work of Pierre Bourdieu to argue that an enriched view of power, in the form of symbolic violence, is central. We examine the pedagogical function business plans played in the provincial museums and cultural heritage sites of Alberta, Canada. The struggle to name and legitimate practices occurs in the business planning process, excluding some knowledges and practices and teaching and utilizing other knowledges and ways of viewing the organization. We show that control involves both redirecting work and changing the identity of producers, in particular, how they understand their work through the construction of markets, consumers, and products. This process works by changing the capital, in its multiple forms – symbolic, cultural, political and economic – in an organizational and institutional field.

Editors' introduction

This paper is remarkable for several features. Above all, it surprises by revealing that the apparently mundane process of business planning in museums involves in fact a bitterly contested struggle for control, with considerable cultural significance. It makes a clear micro–macro link, connecting wider social processes of commercialization in the public sector to the detailed work of museum curators. The researchers demonstrate reflexivity about their role, almost to the point of self-consciousness. Finally, the paper introduces the social theory of Pierre Bourdieu to a new audience, in a manner that is clearly additive to other theoretical perspectives. On the other hand, as we discuss in the final commentary, opportunities for comparative analysis and close reporting of particular activities are not fully explored.

Paper summary

The introduction to the paper starts by setting out the traditional view of business planning as a technical, neutral instrument of explicit managerial control and change. It then quickly proposes that business planning may also involve less obvious issues of power, language and subjectivity, and have unequal effects on employees. This is the platform for introducing the sociology of Pierre Bourdieu. In this view, business planning may be a 'pedagogic practice' that invisibly exerts control and enforces change by altering organizational languages and identities. In Bourdieu's terms, this pedagogy is a form of 'symbolic violence', no less radical because scarcely acknowledged. The introduction concludes by laying out clearly the sequence of the paper, through theory, method, analysis, and final discussion and conclusions.

Bourdieu and institutional theory

In the first substantive section of the paper, Oakes, Townley and Cooper define two key terms in the analysis that follows.

Institutional field: this refers to all the organizations involved in an area of institutional life. It is thus a larger concept than just producers and consumers in a market and provides a bridge between the purely organizational and the societal.

Capital: fields have different kinds of capital at stake, social, symbolic and cultural as well as simply economic. The valuable kinds of capital in a field define actors' powers, and fields are often characterized by a contest between the holders of different kinds of capital.

Implications of capital and fields

Oakes et al. emphasize how Bourdieu's approach, unfamiliar then to many readers of the *Administrative Science Quarterly*, adds in three ways to the established institutional theory perspective, which is apparently closely related. First, it offers a less consensual notion of institutional field, emphasizing conflict and power. Second, the concept of capital offers a more political notion of legitimacy. Finally, the authors claim that the conflict and competition in Bourdieu's notion of field endows it with a dynamic character that institutional theory typically lacks.

The authors close this section with a clear statement of the paper's purpose: 'In this paper, we are interested in how the implementation of business planning affected the distribution of possible positions and the symbolic and cultural capital within the field' (264).

The methods section reproduced here in full is interesting particularly for the authors' display of reflexivity about their role as researchers; for the focus on discourse at many levels, inside the organizations and beyond them; and for its use of several methods: interviews, observation, feedback presentations and documentary analysis.

Methods

The research for this paper, which forms part of a longitudinal study on the introduction of business plans and performance measures into cultural and historical organizations, focuses on the period 1993, when the plans were introduced, to 1995. Our research resulted from our teaching a management course at the university for the provincial government and a request we made to participants to allow us to produce teaching cases for future courses. The assistant deputy minister (ADM) of the Department of Community Development initially provided access, and our plan to produce teaching cases soon shifted to a formal research agreement with the department. The means of access is always likely to affect research, and there is little doubt that senior managers liked the image of interacting with 'business types from the university' and hoped this would enhance their credibility in government. At the same time, it was apparent to the ADM that we were not managerialist enthusiasts. We emphasized the voluntary nature of our interactions with people in the organization and presented our research not as describing the development and implementation of business planning and performance measurement in the Albertan government. Our role was that of a 'peripheral member' (Adler and Adler, 1994), not only conducting formal interviews but also talking with insiders over coffee and beer, sharing the occasional meal, and attending workshops and meetings about planning and performance measurement, although not participating in the actual work of the participants. Yet we also saw ourselves as critical researchers, examining shifting forms of control and domination, recognizing that facts cannot be isolated from some form of ideological inscription and that our research work required self-conscious criticism (Kincheloe and McLaren, 1994: 139–140).

Our research draws on a number of sources from four levels of government (see figure 1): the provincial government, including the Treasury, the Department of Community Development, the Cultural Facilities and Historical Resources Division (CFHR), and the individual historical sites themselves. We analyzed policy documents, including memos, business plans, planning documents, and letters collected at all four levels of government. We studied discourses that museums and cultural facilities have traditionally drawn on, as well as the literature on performance measures and business planning that is frequently cited by the provincial government. We also conducted 56 semistructured interviews involving all four levels of government. Each interview lasted between one and a half and two and a half hours. With three exceptions, in which there was only one author present, two authors conducted each interview. The interviews were taped with the permission of the respondents and were transcribed. Although we constantly warned about how the people interviewed tried to present themselves to us (they were assured that no one else in the organization would have access to the tapes or the transcripts), we are somewhat reassured by our processes of cross checking with the data we obtained from other methods, particularly observation. These interviews involved the individuals responsible for developing, implementing, and monitoring business plans and managing each site. The discussion was loosely structured to cover the people's background and experience in the department, their involvement in business planning, their attitudes toward management and administration, and a description of their job, its challenges and rewards. In some cases, the interview focused on specific issues, such as planning and control of one site or the interaction between a site and the local community.

An important initial aim was to construct a history of the introduction of business planning and performance indicators within the CFHR, and we began to conduct interviews, attend meetings, and collect information at this level. Interviews, observation, and analysis of archival records allows for the interpretation of meaning as experienced by the subjects (Moch and Fields, 1985). To understand changes at this level, however, we also needed to extend our observations to higher levels in government (e.g., the Department of Community Development and Treasury) and at the actual museums and historical sites. The sites vary considerably in the number of people employed, from one to three full-time employees at the smaller sites and museums to almost 100 at the larger sites. At each site, we interviewed the director, or manager (who frequently had been trained in a related profession – curator, historian, etc.) and those involved in business planning. Many of the people at the site and division level had worked either in CFHR or in similar cultural facilities for most of their working lives. We also collected archival data and developed a historical perspective on the division and the sites (Moch and Fields, 1985).

The three researchers worked to practice epistemic reflexivity (Bourdieu and Wacquant, 1992: 36–47), that is, acknowledging and acting on a view of themselves as researchers who help to produce culture and theory as well as being a product of their own sociohistorical conditions (Pels, 1995). Being a member of a culturally and theoretically diverse team that included both genders facilitated self-analysis of the objects of the research and ourselves as objects. Bourdieu, however, insisted that researchers go beyond narcissistic reflexivity by requiring the analyst to recognize her or his own position in the intellectual field, to subject 'the *position* of the observer to the same critical analysis as that of the constructed object at hand' (Barnard, 1990: 75). We actively discussed the parallels between our own experiences as workers in a publicly funded and increasingly manageralist university with those of the managers in the department and division. We cannot pretend to have fully examined our own position in the intellectual field, but we have begun the attempt (Townley, 1995, 1996; Cooper and Neu, 1996).

All three researchers worked iteratively through the collected material and reviewed transcribed interviews for common themes. Frequently, however, an interview or document would raise questions or appear to contradict material collected earlier or contradict the authors' preliminary understanding of the material being collected. These points of difficulty were important aspects of the research process for two reasons. First, they encouraged us to conduct further interviews and attend additional meetings and to use the techniques of 'snowball sampling' (Goodman, 1961; Dawes, 1987), in which an original group of respondents suggests additional lines of inquiry, leading to additional respondents. Acceptance of this method reflects our understanding that neither the processes we were studying nor our study itself was linear but, rather, reflected the twists and turns that are normal in this type of research (Silverman, 1985). Second, we recognized the importance of coming to grips with these difficult points of contradiction (Calhoun, 1995). Bourdieu's work, in particular, his description of fields of restricted and large-scale production and the capital involved, proved useful in explaining the changes that we were identifying. For example, Bourdieu's work is useful in understanding why actors might appear contradictory, because they are often operating within or moving between several fields in which differential capital and positions are available.[2]

Finally, as part of our research agreement, the authors presented their research to several seminars in the department. These presentations generated considerable debate and were, on several occasions, followed up in more private meetings. The department has reviewed several versions of this paper, suggested amendments, and finally agreed to the publication of the paper, without endorsing its arguments.

Cultural and historical sites as a field of restricted production

In this section Oakes, Townley and Cooper establish the traditional practices of the Albertan museum sector, emphasizing the scholarly, non-commercial values of its staff. The museum sector is portrayed as a field with some degree of autonomy from both government (its funders) and the public, with cultural capital accruing to those with strong educational credentials, such as PhDs. This autonomy and set of values are to be challenged by the introduction of business planning.

Subtle control through business planning and pedagogy

This section introduces the challenge represented by the 1993 election in Alberta of a cost-cutting new government committed to a new, more commercial form of public management. It also extends the theoretical discussion of Bourdieu and states clearly the authors' view of business planning in this light:

We consider business planning as pedagogic action, in which the format of the plans simultaneously excludes and inculcates. Business planning excludes certain ideas as unthinkable, such as not being businesslike, efficient, customer-oriented, and revenue-seeking, while also promoting a vision of the organization as a business, subject to instrumental reasoning. The process of business planning also acts as a form of learning by doing. Business planning has significant implications for the capital of a field and, with this, positional and organizational identity. What is valued in the field shifts, in our case from representing a historian's view of authentic culture and artifacts to a concern with what will generate revenues and visitors. Economic capital becomes more important, and cultural capital remains valued to the extent that it can be transformed into economic capital. Further, business plans not only announce that change is coming, but it is through the activity of business planning itself – the introduction of new vocabularies such as revenue generation, products, and customers – that change occurs.

From here, the paper proceeds to the substantive empirical analysis. We reproduce verbatim the first empirical section because it represents well the paper's strength in artfully weaving theory, interviews, documents and observation together into a convincing and coherent account. The section spells out very precisely three ways in which the authors view business planning as pedagogical. The second empirical section explains how the micro practices of business planning – writing plans, carrying out workshops, hiring consultants – transformed the whole field, from one in which the dominant form of capital was cultural to one where economic capital dominates. We use the authors' own highly systematic table to summarize this. We shall present only a brief summary of the final empirical section on the roles of managerial action and control, as it uses a similar mix of theory, interviews, documents and observation.

Business Planning as Pedagogy in Action

In its first budget, the provincial treasurer discussed the creation of a new 'management control structure for all departments' (Dinning, 1993: 118). 'This fall, . . . each department, agency and organization receiving government funds will be called upon to develop a three year business plan by January 1994. . . . These plans will include measures of outcome and performance and strategies to reduce costs. Future funding will be tied to the achievement of those results' (Dinning, 1993: 14–15). Alberta's 'New Approach to Government' was not just about planning and performance measurement. It was about *business* planning, and it is in this undefined term that we see pedagogic processes at work. Business planning, designed to incorporate alleged business values (such as economy, efficiency, output orientation, and entrepreneurialism) in a system of accountable planning, is central to this new approach, as is the changing discourse. Thus, the first business plan of the CFHR division stated: '[The division] will focus on the economic contribution of its facilities, programs and services by emphasizing quality, aggressive regional marketing and sound reinvestment in infrastructure. One of the primary goals is to develop regional anchors for national and international tourism, thereby helping to sustain community vitality and prosperity' (Alberta Community Development, 1994: 5). Further, services came to be described as 'products,' and the aim of the government emphasized 'results, results, results.' As an Albertan commentator noted, 'People all over were reading . . . economic and management theories from the likes of Peter Drucker, Tom Peters, Kenichi Ohmae, Ted Gaebler, and David Osborne, and others' (Lisac, 1995: 43).

The CFHR division, although at the time a field of restricted production, also exists within the larger political and economic field, one that gave rise to the Klein government. Senior division managers described the changes in philosophy and practices emanating from the Klein government as fundamental changes – changes in fact, not in rhetoric. At times they even anticipated (and helped constitute) the changes. And, as Meyer and Rowan (1991: 53) noted, in 'institutionally elaborated environments, sagacious conformity is required: Leadership (in a university, hospital, business) requires an understanding of changing fashions and governmental programs.' We observed this throughout 1994 as all levels of government struggled to come to terms with the changes that were occurring. During this period, divisional representatives met frequently to attempt to learn how the department was interpreting the actions of the provincial treasurer and to attempt to determine what constituted a successful business plan. Pedagogy worked here as a form of learning through discovery and self-reflection. The CFHR believed that it would have to change the way the managers and people working in these sites viewed themselves, their activities, and the management of the sites to survive this government retrenchment. As one senior divisional manager observed: 'We know what we are trying to do. We know what we are trying to accomplish as an organization. We think we know what the government wants us to do. And that is what drives us. We think we know what the government wants us to do. As civil servants . . . we see that as our job. How we get there varies enormously.'

The division thus began its own, somewhat independent business planning process for the historical sites and, in late 1993, hired consultants from Alberta's Department of Economic Development and Tourism to conduct a series of five day-long workshops on business plans and to visit the sites to provide specific advice. Business planning in the CFHR division followed the SWOT design school model, in which organizations conceptualize their environment in terms of opportunities and threats and their own capabilities in terms of strengths and weaknesses (Mintzberg, 1994). Business plans in Bourdieu's terms, are 'culturally arbitrary.' There is no reason why a business plan should contain certain things and not others. The SWOT model, however, was presented as a legitimated vocabulary, a technical procedure, the way things should be done if business planning was to be done properly. Fiol and Huff (1992: 282) emphasized that 'the categories "threat" and "opportunity" are important mapping devices influencing the way managers act on issues.' For example, other historic sites were now labeled as competitors and threats. Charging entrance fees was seen as an opportunity to create discretionary funds. Symbolic power operates through a process of naming and categorization.

As Mintzberg (1994) suggested, the goals implicit in the use of business planning are forced on an organization that relies on the process. In the CFHR division, business planning has been premised on cultural and historical sites being, if not businesses, organizations that may be likened to businesses. Thus, isomorphism is implicit in this initial step. Described as competitors for a fixed amount of tax payers' leisure, time, and money, cultural and historical sites were asked to identify other organizations in Alberta that attract visitors and encourage spending. West Edmonton Mall, Canada's largest shopping mall, became a point of comparison. Thus, planning in the CFHR followed the pattern described by DiMaggio's (1991: 287) history of art museums in which 'unreflective allusions to organizational models from other fields . . . was the object of fateful debate.'

Business plans were presented as an integrated hierarchy of ordered and organized actions, a cascade through goals, outcomes, strategies, and performance measures. Emphasis was on content, principally increased gate visitation and revenue generation activities, and strategies for implementation. Planning thus controlled the premises that underlay the decisions, if not the actual decisions themselves (Mintzberg, 1994: 198). Most sites were obliged to engage in this process; those that were not obliged worried about the implications of their exclusion. Although sites are front-line organizations with high performance ambiguity (Smith, 1965) and may be assumed to have a decentralized power structure (Jermier and Berkes, 1979), our view is that the opportunities for loose coupling between actions and talk were minimized, and change was real.

The pedagogic effect of planning was that it was appropriate to expand revenue, increase admissions, introduce new products, or improve the coffee shop. Sites were not encouraged to include plans for collections, research, or restoration. Such plans, where produced, were rejected as irrelevant. Plans that were long and individualized were rejected in favor of simple and abbreviated plans. Thus, mechanisms of transcription (like business plans) were never neutral but involved strict, although unstated rules about what was appropriate. A second reason why these sites, even though they are front line organizations, had limited opportunition not to conform to divisional and government pressures was that their plans and performance measures were reported through standardized annual accountability reports.

The business planning process was pedagogical in three ways. First, it required a receptivity to change. By receptivity, Bourdieu (1991) did not mean a welcoming or acceptance, but simply a preparation for change. In this situation, receptivity was invoked by a changing discourse at the provincial level as well as through budget cuts and the rapid pace and unpredictability of change. In a period of destabilization, the very indeterminacy of the business planning exercise was also acutely disorienting. Second, business planning actively involves organizational actors who appear to be creating the process as they go along. The business planning process was very unstructured, although it is unclear whether the lack of instruction at the governmental level was intentional. Some of those interviewed felt it epitomized the new approach – that the process of developing plans could be quite varied and that all that mattered was results. For others, there was a great deal of tension surrounding getting the business plan and the performance measures 'right.' Frequently, managers remarked on the lack of a blueprint for change and spoke about 'feeling their way,' an expression that symbolizes managers' attempts to 'read' the government's actions specifically and the wider Albertan power structure more generally. In this sense, business planning encouraged managers to try to learn a feel for the new situation and to try to absorb some of the cultural capital to be gained by appearing entrepreneurial. For example, a divisional manager stated: 'We wanted to be entrepreneurial and if we wanted to be players in the private sector we were going to have business plans. We were going to operate our facilities like small businesses. So we got small business planners in and we went through that educational process.' Managers generally began to use the business planning process to gain legitimacy in the larger environment by using 'the language of business.' Business plans were also used to signal to lower-level managers and employees that their organizations were changing.

Third, the planning process involved the pedagogy of learning the new official language, and, as Meyer and Rowan (1991) argued, the evolution of organizational language is the most important aspect of isomorphism. As one site manager noted. 'It is very important to us to have these business plans be credible with business people . . . it has recently become a good public relations tool with us. It has also allowed us to, you know how your Mama always told you, speak to people in a language that they understand? It is wise to have a common language with people in business. It has also taught some of our people to get out of their own professional jargon and into somebody else's.' The meaning of everyday words like 'goals' and 'objectives' became precarious. The difficulty in remembering a new language and all its categories – goals, objectives, measures, etc. – was expressed several times. As one site manager lamented, 'Well, as you are aware, there is a whole field of planning, with all the charts and all the steps. I have tried, I can't even remember them, I can't even classify them and by background I am a classifier. That is what we do. We are interested in taxonomy and I can't lump these buggers together.' It was a language that was alien to most personnel: 'Out of [planning] comes the goals, strategies, actions – sorry, goals, objectives, strategies, and actions. And to those we attach measures' (division manager). Some departments presented their completed business plans to the legislature only to be told that what they described as objectives were really goals and that what they defined as outcomes were really processes or outputs.

A significant part of Bourdieu's general argument is that the dualism between the content (e.g., Porter, 1980) and process of business plans (e.g., Pettigrew, 1985; Hart and Barbury, 1994) is often unhelpful in understanding the production and reproduction of social life. In our study, managers were learning and producing strategy in the process of forming strategies. The content of the strategies not only came out of the process, it informed the continuing process. Pedagogy helps us understand how organizational actors make sense of and construct change through both participation and resistance. Meaningful pedagogical exercises cause the capital and positions within a field to shift. These shifts create points of examination at which members of a field are encouraged to examine their existing activities and identities. At such a point, people name and categorize themselves (Bourdieu, 1991). This leads some people to try to remake themselves, while others may stop contributing or withdraw completely. Some, particularly those with curatorial backgrounds, felt uncomfortable and tended to become less involved as they no longer understood the rules of the game; others not only embraced the new field but helped give it shape. These processes are both conscious and preconscious in that they occur as participants recognize in their own language and dispositions that either they fit or do not fit in a field (Bourdieu, 1977).

Business planning was an act of symbolic violence. Through a process of naming, categorizing, and regularizing, business planning replaced one set of meanings, defined by the producers within the field, with another set that was defined in reference to the external market. By doing so, this change threatened the relative autonomy of the field and its cultural and symbolic capital. In concrete terms, it reduced the control that people in the field had over their own work lives. The appearance of business plans as mere acts of technical transcription concealed the force this process involved. In particular, it directed attention away from the shifting of cultural capital toward economic capital and the diminution of existing identities.

Table 1. Comparison of Fields of Restricted and Large-scale Cultural Production

	Field of Restricted Production	Field of Large-scale Production
Orientation between capital and field		
Dominant capital	Cultural	Economic
Orientation of field	Definition of capital and distribution of positions is based on rules internal to the field.	Definition of capital and distribution of positions more dependent on rules external to the field.
Function of management	Focused on preservation of cultural capital. Accomplished through facility and exhibition planning based on professional interpretation of the necessities of history and culture.	Focused on ease and speed of convertibility of cultural to economic capital. Accomplished through business planning and performance monitoring.
Organizational identity	Cultural/historical site capable of preserving and generating cultural capital.	Small business capable of generating economic capital.
Product	Collection, preservation, study, interpretation, and exhibition of artifact.	Products for revenue generation.
Positions within the field		
Professional identity	Curator, researcher, interpreter, educator, historian accountable to artifact and profession.	Entrepreneur, accountable to the bottom line.
Orientation	Internal: Based on professional standards. Able to define and educate appropriate consumers.	External: Dependent on finding and attracting consumers who are willing to pay.
Criteria for evaluation	Aesthetic, historical and representational faithfulness.	Visitor counts and admission fees; entertainment value.

Fields of large-scale production

The second empirical section explores how the introduction of business planning transforms the museums from a field of 'restricted cultural production'
to one of 'large-scale cultural production'. Under the traditional field of
restricted production, cultural capital was dominant; in the new field of large-
scale production, economic capital dominates. Oakes et al. systematically
explore the different implications of this transformation, not only for the
dominant forms of capital but also for issues such as the function of management, products and professional identity. Using brief quotations and illustrative examples, the authors show how business planning has achieved a radical
transformation in every dimension. The contrasts are summarized clearly in
the authors' own Table 1.

Capital and fields of cultural production: the role of strategic action and control

The third substantive empirical section introduces a sense of human agency, which, the authors suggest, is lacking in conventional accounts from institutional theory. Museum managers are portrayed as being sometimes active exploiters of the potential in business planning for realizing their own objectives and values. Some curators take delight in discovering the ability of their newly commercial operations to attract new audiences. Others use business planning as a smokescreen to protect core elements of what they have traditionally valued. Again, the authors use a mix of quotation and anecdote.

Discussion and conclusion

Oakes, Townley and Cooper summarize key elements of their argument. In particular, they write: 'In Bourdieu's terms, the planning process was pedagogical in that it fundamentally changed the allocation of capital to positions within the field and thus changed the valued positions within the [museum] field. The attrition of the field's traditional cultural capital leaves the division and its members increasingly vulnerable to further external challenges in the name of economic capital' (284).

The authors then go on to state explicitly how Bourdieu's concepts enrich institutional theory. Here they stress change, multilevel notions of institutional fields, and the political notion of capital. They continue by reflecting on the ease of operationalization of Bourdieu's concepts, considering their potential for future research. They acknowledge certain criticisms, but also offer other examples of research using these concepts. Finally, the authors link this micro case of business planning in the Alberta museum sector to global processes of commercialization in the public sector, underlining their study's wider significance.

Editors' commentary[1]

There are many things to admire about this paper. It was of course one of the first papers to apply practice theory to strategy and the first to use Bourdieu. Particularly noteworthy here is the clarity with which the paper establishes

[1] The authors would like to acknowledge the helpful remarks of Satirios Paroutis and other participants in the Strategy as Practice workshop at Nottingham Trent University, October 2005.

Bourdieu's distinctive contribution in relation to conventional institutional theory, to which his perspective could easily be reduced. Second, the paper is explicitly multilevel, connecting the macro level of field change with the micro level of actors' experience and activity. The minutiae of planning and broad trends in government are part of the same story. Third, there is a strong critical component, revealing a neglected aspect of business planning as involving shifts in organizational power. This critical component is extended to the authors themselves, who are determinedly reflexive in their exposition and, through their feedback seminars in the department, show themselves to be open to the criticism of their research subjects. Finally, the empirical data are wide ranging and clearly presented. There are both quotations and accounts of particular incidents, and tables are used effectively to structure and summarize material.

There is, then, a lot already in this paper, but we highlight here two dimensions that future researchers might want to explore further in similar projects. The first dimension is the actual practical activity of business planning. This paper relies heavily on interview quotations that have a somewhat general and retrospective character. The authors do not take the opportunity to examine in detail how the new techniques and language were successfully deployed in particular planning episodes in order to overcome traditional approaches to museum management. Although there is a section entitled 'Business planning as pedagogy in action', there is not in fact much *action* – people working, calculating, presenting, meeting and arguing together, more or less successfully. Besides knowing the general effect that business planning had, we need to see more of what people actually did in particular episodes in order to understand what difference business planning really made in practice. Here the ideal data would be reports from direct, real-time observation of particular episodes or sequences of episodes. If observation is infeasible, then interviews should be tightly focused, undertaken soon after the event, involve several participants, and preferably be supported by documentary and other kinds of data. Isolated interview quotations tend to be too general to capture detailed activity.

The second dimension that future researchers might want to develop further in this kind of study is a more systematic comparative analysis. The key contribution of this paper is to establish the general pedagogic effects of business planning. However, while the authors do suggest that some museum managers were more enthusiastic and proactive with regard to the new techniques than others, they do not take the next step of exploring systematically what influenced the responses of different managers and museums. Comparison of organizational units and managers that were either particularly proactive or particularly resistant would help tease out the conditions and activities required to implement business planning effectively. Thus within the larger single case of Alberta museums, there is the potential to take a finer lens to explore variability of outcomes. Comparisons of units achieving different outcomes within the same field help reveal key differentiating factors. Strategy as Practice researchers will get more explanatory leverage the more they take opportunities for such systematic comparison.

9

Strategizing as lived experience and strategists' everyday efforts to shape strategic direction

(*Journal of Management Studies*, 40, 1 (2003): 141–74)

Dalvir Samra-Fredericks

Abstract

This paper draws together the ethnographic and ethnomethodological/conversation analytic traditions to outline an innovative and multidisciplinary approach for researching strategists-at-work. Ethnography is premised upon close-up observation of naturally occuring routines over time/space dimensions and ethnomethodology/conversation analysis, upon a study of people's practices and inherent tacit 'methods' for doing social and political life, much of which is accomplished through talk. Through the observation and recording of strategists talk-based interactive routines and from drawing upon seminal studies within the social sciences, the paper aims to map out a number of analytical routes for a fine-grained analysis of strategists' linguistic skills and forms of knowledge for strategizing. This includes their speaking of morals and the assembly of emotion as they construct a shared definition of the future. To illustrate the approach and its scope, the paper draws upon one ethnomethodologically informed ethnography. It will specifically focus upon aspects of the relational-rhetorical basis of strategic effectiveness as constituted by one strategist who was judged, from amongst a group of six, to have influenced strategic processes.

Editors' introduction

More than any other paper presented in this book, this article gets down to the micro level of *doing strategy*. It first appeared in the 2003 special issue of *Journal of Management Studies* on micro strategy and strategizing, and it was chosen for this book both because of its clear contribution to research on the practice of strategy and because of its innovative methodological approach (i.e. conversation analysis, see chapter 3).

In substantive terms, the paper shows how strategists can shape strategic direction in interaction with their colleagues. It is theoretically grounded in an ethnomethodological tradition that views meaning as constructed in interaction and that set outs to reveal, through fine-grained analysis of those interactions, exactly how this happens. While situated squarely under the social practice theoretical umbrella, this paper thus adds to the theoretical resources for studies of strategy practice identified in chapter 2.

The summary provided here aims primarily to illustrate the richness of this form of analysis. The interesting way in which Samra-Fredericks explicitly relates micro practices to more macro outcomes (an issue raised in chapter 1) is also noteworthy, as well as the way she addresses certain methodological issues raised in chapter 3.

Paper summary

The introduction of the paper draws the reader directly into context for the study:

Introduction

. . . if you have a policy if you have a strategy (.) then anything else becomes irrelevant . . .

[and, shortly after, the same strategist says . . .]

. . . but the danger of not having a policy [strategy] is like a ship that doesn't have a rudder you don't know where the hell you're going to end up (. . .)

The significance of strategizing is concisely voiced here by one strategist during the ebb-and-flow of human exchange between a group of six strategists. Here, he metaphorically expresses one dominant and orthodox belief – a strategy tells you where 'you're going to end up' and like a ship's rudder, steers the organization to some future destination. Barry and Elmes (1997, p. 430) have more formally asserted that 'strategy must rank as one of the most prominent, influential and costly stories told in organizations'. They add that what is needed is a study of how language is used by strategists to establish meanings and create a 'discourse of direction' (see also Smircich, 1983). This paper makes a distinctive contribution through outlining an innovative approach for the study of how strategizing is accomplished during 'real-time' talk-based *interaction*. From observing and recording such interaction over time/space dimensions, it draws upon a specific intellectual infrastructure, ethnomethodology (Garfinkel, 1967) and conversation analysis (Sacks, 1992; Sacks et al., 1974) to undertake a systematic and fine-grained analysis which provides for scrutiny of strategists' linguistic skills and forms of knowledge for accomplishing strategic direction. Furthermore, in researching strategizing as a *lived* experience as opposed to a 'reported' experience in interviews, theorizing the ever-present and intricate nature of the emotional and moral domains of human interaction is also made available for close analysis.

After this introductory paragraph, Samra-Fredericks places her contribution within the emerging stream of work on Strategy as Practice and argues for the particular importance of looking in some detail at talk among strategists, noting that it is through talk that strategy is negotiated and in talk that knowledge relevant to strategy is articulated and embedded.

Samra-Fredericks goes on to describe the context for her study: a manufacturing firm in which the speaker in the initial quotation (subsequently labelled SA in the paper) succeeded in significantly influencing the firm's strategic direction. She describes the two main objectives of her study as outlining an innovative approach to investigating strategizing and, second, to present a fine-grained analysis of how SA achieved this influence during interaction among six strategists. In particular, she notes that the paper will focus on how SA 'subtly raised and constituted two fundamental organizational weaknesses' (144):

One weakness was in IT capability and the other in strategic thinking, leading to decisions to invest in IT and to terminate the employment of others (in particular, one executive director who will be referred to as strategist B in the transcripts and SB in the text). It was during the ebb-and-flow of everyday human exchange that SA shaped the attention of others and began to lay the building blocks for shaping future possibilities. How he did so will be concisely illustrated alongside the selection and discussion of six features here. They are the ability to: speak forms of knowledge; mitigate and observe the protocols of human interaction (the moral order); question and query; display appropriate emotion; deploy metaphors and finally; put history 'to work'. Knowing *when* to do this (the 'right time') is, of course, a tacit form of *knowing* which will also be discussed here.

In the above paragraph, Samra-Fredericks introduces the six features that will be the focus of the paper. Four strips of interaction are reproduced in her paper and are used to illustrate these six features. Although the six features of interaction were successful for the strategist in question, Samra-Fredericks stops short of drawing simplistic normative conclusions from this observation but expresses her broader objective more modestly as follows:

An overall goal is to begin a conversation with others (researchers and practitioners) in order to develop wisdom concerning everyday strategizing. The conversation started here is also one where simple prescription regarding strategic (or managerial) competence remains an elusive ideal since there can be no simple claims such as: being metaphorically articulate provides for interpersonal leverage. It is rather more complex, fragile and dynamic as this paper reveals and as practitioners know too well.

A turn to strategists' talk-in-interaction

In the following section of the paper, Samra-Fredericks relates her methodological approach to the broader literature on linguistic approaches. After introducing the basic principles of ethnomethodology and conversation analysis, she then describes her method in more detail. She notes that an emphasis on talk-in-interaction requires capturing 'strategizing as lived' rather than drawing inferences from interviews, and that such an approach requires careful recording, including details of hesitations and overlaps in speech considered significant in conversation analysis.

Such an approach clearly poses practical problems of access (cf. chapter 3). Samra-Fredericks notes these difficulties, but indicates that after 'protracted negotiations' she obtained access to private sector firms who allowed her not only to observe but also to make electronic recordings of conversations in both formal and informal settings. (The reader cannot help being curious as to the content of these negotiations.)

Samra-Fredericks goes on to note another methodological challenge – that associated with reporting rich ethnographic material within the constraints of an academic article. Her approach to this involves first providing a descriptive ethnographic account of the context for the study, and then following this with the detailed analysis of four strips of interaction using conversation analysis techniques. These steps are summarized below.

Ethnographic account: what was happening?

In this section, we learn that the manufacturing firm observed over a period of a year (in visits varying from a half-day to two or three days) is a subsidiary of a French firm and is in the process of building a new manufacturing facility. They are also attempting to develop a five-year strategy to build on this initiative. Strategist SA (not the managing director) is seen to be having a particularly strong influence on the development of this strategy. As indicated earlier, the focus of the paper is on SA's ability to persuade other strategists subtly of the importance of two weaknesses, one concerning IT competencies and the other concerning weaknesses in strategic thinking that led to the departure of SB.

Samra-Fredericks looks in this section at the particular knowledge and experience assets of SA and SB to see whether these might explain the findings and concludes that each had different strengths that would not allow an *a priori* prediction of the outcome. She concludes that it is not in these assets in themselves but in the ability to express them at appropriate times and to use associated linguistic skills in interaction that differences become evident.

In an important subsection, she then presents the reasoning that enables her to link the particular rhetorical strategies used with the outcomes described. This recalls the issues raised around figure 1.1 in chapter 1 and to some extent the discussion of micro and macro perspectives in chapter 2.

Linking outcomes (macro) to everyday talk (micro)

To account for the linkages between strategists' talk and the outcomes in the form of the two weaknesses is challenging primarily because human activity across time and space is so rich, dynamic and complex. Boden's (1994) work which draws upon the conversation analytic tradition offers us two key concepts for doing so. They are the notion of 'minor moves' and 'laminate'. In the new *Shorter Oxford Dictionary* (1993, p. 1524) *laminate* is defined as a manufacturing process where layers of materials such as metal are 'bonded' together. It is a process characterized by 'placing layer upon layer', a 'succession of layers' to produce something more durable and yet, still flexible. What this term 'laminate' also encapsulates is the important concepts of process, time, interaction and outcome. The former two have been recognized as key issues for empirical research within strategic management (Pettigrew, 1985, 1992b). Generally speaking, outcomes are what everyone is interested in and are available for easy expression after the 'event' as evidenced in the ethnographic account. Actual interaction, through which something more durable is fashioned, seems to be routinely ignored but only through placing interaction centre-stage, can the '*how*' surrounding the accomplishment of outcomes be answered. In this light then, each strip of interaction reproduced here is conceptualized as *one* layer or 'minor move' *in a succession* shaping or 'producing' beliefs, opinions, values, assumptions, feelings, perceptions, meanings and so on. Each minor move laminated to produce a plausible and subsequently, collectively agreed sense of 'organizational weaknesses' *and* (at various points) 'decisions' were taken to rectify them.

It is with this understanding that efforts to trace the empirically 'lived' linkages between talk and such outcomes are 'unpicked' theoretically and analytically and clearly, the ethnographic component is crucial. The four extracts will illustrate the everyday 'lived' linkages and have been selected on the basis of two criteria. The first criterion is that these moments were brief but important turning points or 'minor moves' in terms of the two weaknesses outlined above (both at that time given the increase in interpersonal energy and confirmed with hindsight given what was eventually accomplished). They arose during a day long 'meeting'/event regularly convened to discuss what was happening in terms of the strategic investment/changes and what else they needed to do. The second criterion is that the extracts concisely illustrate *how*, in terms of the six features, SA persuaded his fellow strategists and thus effectively laid the building blocks for shaping strategic direction within this company.

Lived experience – strategists' at-work/talk and how it was all made to happen

In this section, the author presents her key findings, drawing on four strips of interaction. To illustrate her approach, we will focus on two strips of interaction – extracts 1 and 3. In a first section, extract 1 is used to sketch the six relational-rhetorical features of strategist A's talk (emphasized in bold and italics). The subsequent discussion elaborates on these findings, drawing on this and the three other extracts.

Extract 1

Strategist A	= can I [come back to *simple* manufacturing man's
MD	[yeah
Strategist A	language and and (.) and leave the intelligent stuff so we'll
	keep it at manufacturing level urm (.) I would query why
5	we need another (.) analyst for two reasons number one it
	is one of the other stated policies that you told me about
	(.) that the stated policy is that the *manager* and the user
	department will develop the expertise and systems under-
	standing necessary to identify their requirements and to
10	be able to spell out what they need =
Strategist B	= um um
Strategist A	given that why the *hell do you need an analyst* number two (.)
	our bottleneck is obviously right now and it looks as
	though [glances at collection of papers] it has been for
15	some time and our our skill shortage and our bottleneck
	is programming (.) so if you get another analyst all you do
	is increase the work on the bottleneck =
MD	= um =
Strategist A	= which can't process it anyway =
20 **MD**	= yeah um =
Strategist B	yeah but I think
MD	I think thats a [fair
Strategist A	[now you've got two analysts =
MD	= thats a fair point =

(SA is represented here as strategist A. The MD is noted as such as opposed to
being labelled as another strategist since he formally chaired the range of meet-
ings/encounters)

Whilst the talk here was about a seemingly trivial matter regarding what IT analysts and programmers actually do, it was transformed into an opportunity by SA to draw others' attention
to his perception of more significant problems (the weaknesses). This extract will also allow a
concise illustration of all six features (italicized below). First, in describing himself as a 'simple
manufacturing man', he swiftly displaced the prior technically informed monologue by
Strategist C (SC). Overall, a logic and sense of reasonableness pervades SA's utterances alongside the articulation of frustration and exasperation at the lack of logical thinking surrounding
the apparent move to appoint analysts as opposed to programmers. Reasonableness is initially
linguistically conveyed through **mitigation** ('can I'). Then, through what may seem like a self-
depreciating comment ('simple manufacturing man's'), he **queries** (L4) what he has been told
and thus the **past** is mundanely invoked. On this simple basis he warrants his switch to a more
assertive style and conveys both frustration and worry leading to his more overt expression of
anger (L12). This emotional display is legitimated through the rational component where what
he was told was not happening and secondly, through articulating the belief that analysts add

to the bottleneck. This contested the typified *knowledge* held by SB regarding what analysts and programmers do.

In describing a situation where analysts 'increase the work on bottlenecks' (*metaphorical* expression) and where inefficiencies had apparently been tolerated for some time (L13–15, the past again), a *moral* responsibility is also being evoked. In terms of this moral component, what is witnessed here is the subtle everyday and usually elusive speaking of what is right (e.g., 'manufacturing man's language') and wrong ('intelligent stuff') or good (solving problems) and bad (tolerating inefficiencies) management. The latter two aspects are not easily displaced since they comprise a form of 'wisdom' and provide one small example of the everyday speaking of an economic sensibility informing management practice. Indeed, we can even conceptualise this as a one grounded example of what Foucauldians would term a 'Discourse of efficiency' which is deemed to pervade strategic/management practice and has 'effects', for example, for constituting subjectivity (see Knights and Morgan, 1991). On an everyday level, such Discourses, as 'ways of reasoning/constituting the social world' (Alvesson and Karreman, 2000a, p.1125) are linguistically invoked and 'put to work' (as glimpsed here) by individuals during their efforts to make meaning with others.

Samra-Fredericks then describes in detail the six features she develops on the basis of the four strips of interaction. We will abridge her analysis to focus on how the six features are manifested in extracts 1 and 3. We will also provide greater depth on one of the features of the talk ('Questions for courtroom performance') while briefly sketching the others. The code (. . .) indicates places where the original text has been shortened.

Speaking knowledge 'of' and knowledge 'how to'

In this section, Samra-Fredericks describes two forms of knowledge that are mobilized by the six strategists in interaction. Knowledge of 'how to' concerns the ways in which people reveal their tacit understanding of how to go on appropriately within conversations (respecting rules of turn-taking, etc.). Knowledge 'of' is more concerned with content and category-based knowledge. Samra-Fredericks draws attention to SA's use of this second form of knowledge in extract 1:

In terms of extract 1 and this second form of knowledge, there is the simple and routine expression of knowledge of 'typified' organizational 'categories' (Berger and Luckmann, 1967; see also Boden, 1994, p. 134; Garfinkel, 1967). They are expressed through the selection and combination of lexemes or words such as 'manufacturing', 'policies', 'manager', 'user department' and 'bottlenecks'. In selecting and combining them, SA inserts forms of everyday know-how and expertise which 'constituted the context' out of which he then developed next possibilities. In ethnomethodological terms, these typified categories (and others across all the extracts) allowed these strategists to sense-make, to reason and ultimately, to deploy a rhetoric to 'do' organization (Bittner, 1973; Garfinkel, 1967). Furthermore, a Schutzian (1932/1972) principle which interested Garfinkel was where we are deemed to 'hold' knowledge in 'typified forms' but that it is incomplete and progressively clarified and expanded during interaction (Samra-Fredericks, 1996, p. 232).

In this case (extract 1), what IT analysts and programmers were deemed to do was progressively clarified through speaking and contesting typified knowledge surrounding these human resources as seen here. In doing so, SA constituted a 'reality' where particular human resources were to be valued 'more than' another group. This evaluation was based upon their apparent contribution to organizational effectiveness and efficiencies, again, spoken in ways glimpsed here. In other words, SA did legitimate his beliefs that 'analysts' would add to the 'bottlenecks'. He also begins to surface the possibility that SB was failing in his strategic role, here, because SB was implicated in this situation of tolerating 'inefficiencies' and supporting the recruitment of 'analysts'. (. . .)

The basic requirement to mitigate and 'speak' the moral order

In this section, Samra-Fredericks draws attention to two further important aspects of the talk observed. The first concerns the ways in which the strategists 'mitigate' their utterances to avoid overt conflict and conserve face even when the content of their remarks suggests criticism or discord. As described by Samra-Fredericks, it is this that enables them to voice such views without seeming to violate social norms.

The second aspect concerns the way in which different strategists and in particular SA manage to establish the moral order ('right' and 'wrong') through their talk. As Samra-Fredericks notes (156) referring to extract 1, '*SA speaks a set of beliefs where it is "right" to speak manufacturing language and "wrong" to deviate from stated policies and not resolve bottlenecks (which, by implication, must impact upon organizational effectiveness and efficiencies).*' SA's particular skill at establishing moral norms (often at the expense of SB) is revealed in other extracts. For example, in extract 2 (not reproduced here), SA is shown establishing the primacy of 'strategic thinking' over cost concerns – another moral issue that places SB at a disadvantage. As Samra-Fredericks notes, the cumulative effect of a series of such 'minor moves' is very powerful, contributing gradually but forcefully to the constitution of a weakness in strategic thinking and associating that weakness with SB.

The next feature examined by Samra-Fredericks further reveals SA's relational-rhetorical skills in constituting these weaknesses. This section is reproduced in its entirety. It provides a compelling illustration of the way in which Samra-Fredericks effectively builds up her arguments by relating her micro analysis of two empirical extracts to the findings from previous ethnomethodology and conversation analysis work.

Questions for a Courtroom Performance

The ability to lodge questions and queries (see also extract 1, L4) not only inserts the speaker into the split-second ebb-and-flow of interaction, it can also curb or constrain the action possibilities of another. This was found to be something SA consistently did and clearly was allied with his use of 'ethnomethods' (Garfinkel, 1967) such as *knowing* when and *how to* 'let pass, gloss and question' (Turner, 1988). Again, through doing so, SA shaped the attention of others and from this basis, influenced process. Empirical studies within the field of conversation analysis and pragmatics have shown that the use of such a basic linguistic resource is a powerful mode of interpersonal control (Harris, 1995; see also Boden, 1994; Dillon, 1990; Molotch and Boden, 1985). Such studies have shown how through posing questions in institutional settings, the membership role/identity of magistrate, teacher and doctor, as well as, settings (courtrooms, classrooms and doctors surgeries) are socially constructed. It is where institutional representatives are seen to deprive others of this most fundamental architecture of social structure and thus, reflexively constitute that institutionality. Such studies also empirically reveal what is meant by the 'constraining and enabling' features that 'social structure' affords members (Giddens, 1976, 1984).

Much of this work though has been undertaken in courtrooms, classrooms and doctors surgeries, primarily because the right to question and the obligation to supply an answer is reasonably clear-cut (although it is always based upon members' observance of contextual norms). On occasions though there was a striking similarity between strategists' talk and courtroom questioning where the construction of 'reasonableness' was simultaneously performed whilst curbing anothers' possibilities for a counter move. What transpired was intriguing, not least, because those subjected to such a process also appeared to be left wondering 'what happened' and 'how did I end up in this position?' Being able to 'backtrack' and explore 'how' it all happened, the analysis highlighted that on these occasions the question was skilfully utilized by SA to deprive another individual of the means to configure a social reality, even when the contextual norms were not tightly prescribed as in courtroom interaction. Extract 3 is one concise illustration of this. Alongside simple question-and-answer format (adjacency pairs, see Samra-Fredericks, 1998), queries, as seen here and evident in courtroom contexts (Dillon, 1990) tend to be 'chained together' to follow a line of reasoning or lead to a particular position' (Boden, 1994, p. 124). It is where information is pieced together to mean something in particular. Again, as one crucial resource providing rhetorical leverage, it also simultaneously realises social and political relations as glimpsed here.

Extract 3

```
                      [[interrupts]
      MD              [but thats not policy =
      Strategist A    = what I was trying to get at =
      Strategist B    = well of course it isn't but =
  5   Strategist A    = but what I was trying to drive is but what is [the policy?
      MD                                                              [hang on
                                                                      [name of
             strategist C] just let me go in a second =
```

	Strategist A	= and thats the question that I asked of yourself and [name of strategist C] what is the company policy?
10	**Strategist B**	yes
	Strategist A	now you defined it for me as (.) company wide activity should utilise the mainframe
	Strategist B	yes =
	Strategist A	= specific internal department's special needs can utilise
15		PCs
	Strategist B	yes
	Strategist A	having *accepted* that as the policy (.) I'm saying we ain't working to the policy
	Strategist C	[hes right
20	**Strategist B**	[interrupts

At L11–12 and L14–15, points arising from prior talk (the past being invoked and 'put to work') are *queried* again by SA. He begins though with re-stating the question (twice, L5 and 9) he asked during this prior talk. The subsequent queries, though, curbed the possibilities for an answer very much like courtroom interaction where, for example, prosecutors attempt to have their account confirmed. To do so, they present questions, queries and statements in such a way that a minimal response is deemed necessary (Dillon, 1990). Here, a simple 'yes' (L10, L13 and L16) elicited from SB demonstrates a form of interpersonal control where SB was positioned to supply an answer in a way which deprived him of this basic resource – to ask a corresponding question or to elaborate. However, unlike courtroom interaction, SB may of course have done this. The interpretation made here regarding why he did not was because SA explicitly reported past conversations which could not be easily disputed without implying that SA had either failed to understand, was misrepresenting him or, was even lying. Furthermore, SA's assertive style (constituted from posing the questions and queries) would have necessitated immense interpersonal effort on SB's part to undertake any of these talk-based counter-*actions.*

This exchange also provides us with a stark contrast between what characterises a 'winning' form of talk from that which correspondingly failed. SB failed to secure the floor primarily because SA combined his store of linguistic skills (ability to query) and forms of knowledge (surrounding for example, the 'rights and obligations' that surround even artifacts such as policies), allied with *knowing* when and how to deploy the 'past' and chain such queries. Furthermore, to accomplish a negative evaluation or positioning of SB (and by association, SC, the collective 'you') there was the initial indexing of political and social relations through personal pronouns. Here, there is the use of 'I', 'I was' 'I'm saying' and 'we' by SA. Significantly, it illustrates the mundane toing-and-froing of the active and arguably responsible individual who also takes on the institutional role through 'we' (Drew and Sorjonen, 1997; further detailed in Samra-Fredericks, 2000b). In doing so, its rhetorical possibilities are also realised. This is set against the outsiders, 'yourself' (L8) and 'you' (L11) and thus, the relational domain is reconfigured. 'You defined it for me' (L11) does hold SB accountable and is skilfully contrasted with 'I'm saying we . . .' (L17). Interpersonal boundaries, with associated possibilities for future action are linguistically or symbolically 'drawn' through such basic resources. There is perhaps some realisation of the significance of what *could* (and did) transpire here given the serial employment of the mitigating discourse marker, 'but', at L2, L4 and L5, signalling 'speaker return to pointmake' (Schiffrin, 1987).

A simple 'fact' that was established was that policy was not being implemented. What was also simultaneously and interpersonally accomplished in the space of seconds, was a political and morally laden appraisal of another's competence since SB was positioned to be a part of this problem. Yet, SA preserved a sense of reasonableness as he utilised the context (including others in the sense that he reported earlier conversations). Without doubt, through chaining queries, timed to perfection following the re-statement of the question 'what is the policy?', SA *did* 'gain far more "readability" than a memo or report' and thus, he acquired a 'great deal of interactional "value" . . . packed into a fleeting moment of talk' (Boden, 1994, p. 113). As another 'minor move', it shaped a sense of what had happened and continued to happen. It was through such efforts, that SA influenced process and ultimately, shaped strategic direction. What such an analysis also demonstrates in all its complexity is Mangham and Pye's (1991) assertion that *effective performance is relational*. 'Check-lists' of skills determining or accounting for an *individual's* performance miss the crux of what constitutes effectiveness. The fourth extract further substantiates this stance and illustrates two more features consistently deployed by SA. They were his ability to assemble and express the emotional domain alongside use of metaphors.

The two remaining features presented by Samra-Fredericks rely on the same kind of detailed analysis as that seen above. We briefly summarize these two remaining features.

The emotional realm and metaphor use

Here, Samra-Fredericks elaborates on the ways in which the strategists used emotions and metaphors to make their points more powerfully. She observes that SA expressed emotions such as anger and despair more often than his colleagues, but that he also systematically tied these expressions of emotion to rational components of strategizing that he had previously established as important for the firm. In addition, SA was more skilful in metaphor use than his colleagues (see, for example, the introductory extract).

Putting history 'to work'

Finally, in this section, Samra-Fredericks describes how the strategists referred selectively to the past in their interactions and used these references to further their aims in the present. SA in particular is seen to 'put history to work' more actively and effectively than the other strategists. In each of the extracts presented, he refers back to previous events or conversations, drawing attention to decisions that had not been implemented or considerations that had been raised but not followed through, essentially choosing from the multiple available interpretations of the past to create a consistent storyline. As Samra Fredericks puts it: '*What was "meaningfully" made to be "consistent" by SA was taken as "what actually occurred" with profound consequences for others. Ultimately, a specific social and political reality was accomplished by SA*' (166).

At the end of this section, Samra-Fredericks summarizes the cumulative understanding of what was happening in this firm based on her analysis of the full range of relational-rhetorical features. To reinforce understanding of this process, the reader may wish to refer back to the earlier section in which extract 1 was initially introduced.

As 'minor moves' laminated onto next 'move' 'facts' surrounding the two weaknesses were fashioned by SA and decisions were made. Those incapable of 'biting bullets' and thinking strategically were removed (employment terminated) and financial and human resources for developing IT competence was allocated.

Without taking these actions, it was felt that their strategy of 'targeted growth' would remain 'just talk'. Yet, paradoxically, it was through skilled talk that SA translated his perceptions and beliefs to constitute the weaknesses and decisions. He also articulated and thus constituted strategic thinking or competence to *mean*: being able to rise above a functional role; to think long-term; to take tough action and avoid being 'frozen in time'; to remove inefficiencies; to ensure implementation of policies and so forth. The strategic decision to invest and develop a core competence in IT is simple enough to understand given the logic condensed earlier. The need for strategic thinking as a crucial organizational competence has also been specifically recognised by Grant (1995, p. 125) who argued that the 'knowledge, skills, reasoning and decision-making' capabilities of the senior management team are a crucial 'intangible resource'. SA's set of intangible resources, uniquely combined and through *knowing* 'when and how' to express or deploy them, did influence 'what the organization will look like' next year and the years after that.

Conclusions

In her conclusion, the author returns first to the objectives of the paper. She then considers the limitations of her methodological approach, but notes its relative superiority to interview-based studies as well as its potential for informing strategy practice. She ends by calling for a continuation of the conversation among researchers on a view of strategizing as lived experience.

Editors' commentary

This innovative paper provides a truly micro-level perspective on doing strategy. Within the four strips of conversation, two of which are illustrated above, we see the way in which strategic weaknesses are constituted in everyday interactions. The author provides an insightful account of the relational-rhetorical strategies associated with effective persuasion in episodes of inter-action between management colleagues concerning organizational strategy.

The research is exemplary in many ways. The quality of access obtained by the researcher is exceptional, and encouraging for those who wish to capture the detail of doing strategy in vivo. The conversation analysis approach is very impressive, although one senses that this approach is not necessarily easily accessible to all. Samra-Fredericks builds on an extensive knowledge-base in linguistic studies and ethnomethodology that enables her to apply this approach with confidence. In her fine-grained analyses of particular conversations, the author illustrates how much can be revealed in even the smallest of interactions. At the same time, she takes care to embed these small interactions in the organizational context. The analyses she presents would not have been possible without this surrounding ethnographic material. The accu-mulation of similar observations across different extracts that combine to produce a coherent overall gestalt is also very powerful. One may hope with the author that others will take up the challenge of this kind of fine-grained work.

Nevertheless, it is important to note that the particular interactions described in Samra-Fredericks' paper essentially turn around how one manager succeeds in putting down and undermining the credibility of another manager to the point where the latter was eventually fired. There is something rather disturbing about using this illustration as exemplary of effective strategizing. Is learning how to put down colleagues really some-thing that should be developed as a key skill for an effective strategist? It would be interesting to see how the same or different relational-rhetorical moves might be implicated in a more constructive, integrative and transfor-mational form of intervention than this one. The development of support and enthusiasm around a new strategic orientation in a more inclusive way might well unfold somewhat differently and would be very interesting to observe.

With its focus on the small strips of conversation, the paper also raises another question: can research on the activities of strategists become so micro as to lose its connection with strategy or its relevance and usefulness for strategists? The author clearly maintains the connection systematically in her paper. Nevertheless, not every sneeze or hiccough in a meeting has strat-egic significance. Distinguishing between that which is worth observing and recording and that which is not relevant to the matter at hand is clearly an ongoing challenge.

Overall, however, this paper illustrates the potential of the ethnomethod-ological/conversation analysis perspective for improving understanding of Strategy as Practice, adding to the theoretical and methodological resources available to researchers involved in this endeavour.

10 Organizational restructuring and middle manager sensemaking

(*Academy of Management Journal*, 47, 4 (2004): 523–40)

Julia Balogun and Gerry Johnson

Abstract

This longitudinal, qualitative study examined 'sensemaking' during an imposed shift from hierarchical to decentralized organization. We identified a 'replacement' pattern of schema development in which middle managers moved from shared through clustered sensemaking, to shared but differentiated sensemaking. Our findings provide evidence that different change processes lead to different patterns of schema development. Further, they highlight the socially negotiated nature of schema change and the significance of middle managers' lateral social interactions in shaping change in the absence of senior management.

Editors' introduction

This paper was selected for several reasons. First, it is a very interesting exploration of the role of middle managers in 'doing strategy'. It responds to the calls in chapter 1 for plurality in levels of analysis and in actors and it also takes a dynamic perspective, tracing strategy activities over time. Secondly, it is an illustration of the mobilization of the sensemaking perspective – one of the possible theoretical resources for studies of Strategy as Practice introduced in chapter 2. Finally, as mentioned in chapter 3, the paper uses an innovative set of methods, including diaries and focus groups.

The introduction to the paper describes the context and objectives for the research.

In this research, we examined the middle manager role in processes of change, as opposed to the more commonly researched senior manager role in change. We studied the 'sensemaking' (Gephart, 1993, 1997; Weick, 1995) of middle managers during a top-down change initiative in which senior managers outlined a new structure that replaced a traditional integrated hierarchy with a more modular and decentralized organization of semiautonomous business units. The seniors then left it to middle managers who were primarily individuals based outside the head office, to develop the operational details of this structure. The middle managers were thus recipients of change as much as its implementers. They had to make the new structure work but had little involvement in the up-front change design or decision making.

Conceptual background

The theoretical roots of this work are already announced in the previous para-graph. The authors are particularly concerned to understand the processes of 'sensemaking' (Weick, 1995) among middle managers faced with the change. They define sensemaking as 'a conversational and narrative process through which people create and maintain an intersubjective world' (524). Thus, sensemaking is seen not as a passive process but as a process that involves social interaction, communication and mutual observation. In order to study sensemaking during the change process, the authors draw strongly on the concept of 'schemata', seen as cognitive structures or 'data reduction devices' that summarize the meanings developed by organization members as they try to make sense of the world.

The focus of the research then becomes how participants' schemata (or syn-onymously 'interpretive schemes') change over time as they deal with organ-izational restructuring. Balogun and Johnson refer to previous studies of schema change that have suggested a variety of different models by which this may occur. For example, Bartunek (1984) proposes a *conflict model* in which schemata are gradually replaced through the dialectical interaction of old and new understandings; Labianca et al. (2000) describe a *conversion model* in which schemata change suddenly and dramatically in the face of new stimuli; Weber and Crocker (1983) identify the *book-keeping* model in which schemata are incrementally adapted over time and the *subtyping model* where 'subcate-gories develop within higher order schemata' (525).

After reviewing the literature on schema change, the authors restate their research questions in more theoretical terms as follows.

Our concern here is with organizations' structural change from integrated hierarchy to a more decentralized form and how middle managers make sense of such change. Our guiding premise is that such change will challenge existing middle manager interpretive schemes, leading to cognitive disorder (McKinley & Scherer, 2000). The middle managers will engage in active sensemaking (Gephart, 1993, 1997; Weick, 1995) as they try to resolve the ambiguity and uncertainty that result from the tension created by the need to be differentiated from other middle managers by work goals, yet achieve coordination (Lawrence & Lorsch, 1967). Both ver-tical and horizontal communications will be important, but hierarchical barriers will tend to make lateral communication the more significant mechanism for middle managers trying to make sense of restructuring, and key interpretations will be generated through these lateral processes. To address these issues, we examined the process of schema development and the schemata used by middle managers before and during change. We sought to answer three related questions: What are the patterns of schema change? How does middle manager sense-making inform the schema development process? What is the relationship between schema change and restructuring?

Method

The methods used for this research project are particularly interesting and some extended extracts will therefore be provided here. Essentially, the research takes the form of a longitudinal case study of a single organization implementing a significant structural and strategic change. The organization studied is a recently privatized utility company in the UK. A decision had been taken to subdivide an integrated business into three separate components: a 'Core Division' with strategic responsibilities and two support divisions, and 'Engineering' and 'Services' which became suppliers to the Core Division creating an 'internal market'. The relationships between the divisions were thus transformed from a hierarchical one to a contractual one, with the Core Division being ultimately empowered to purchase services elsewhere if it was dissatisfied with the performance of its internal suppliers. The objectives of this change included cost reduction, quality improvement and the move from a 'risk-averse culture' to an 'empowered, customer-focused organization' (526).

Data collection for the research project occurred over approximately one year between August 1993 and July 1994. The project began as soon as the management teams in each of the three new divisions had been appointed. The focus of the research was on a set of middle managers operating below divisional management level, who had mostly been reassigned from positions within the integrated structure. In return for research access, the first author provided feedback to divisional managers on the progress of the change (526).

Data sources

As described in the next extract, a particularly innovative aspect of this study is the use of diaries as a primary data collection device (see also chapter 3).

Diaries, a form of personal document (Denzin, 1989; Taylor & Bogdan, 1984), were the primary data collection mechanism. Although data collection through diaries has a variety of strengths and weaknesses (Balogun, Huff & Johnson, 2003), a key strength is that they provide an insider's account of a situation (Burgess, 1984) and can be used to track what participants do in the absence of a researcher (Perlow, 1997, 1999).

Twenty-six middle managers from a group of about 90 managers at the level of interest across the three divisions acted as diarists. The first author requested identification of potential diarists from the new organization charts with a view toward having most departments and interfaces represented. At an initial briefing, the diarists received individual diaries, which initially they completed fortnightly, but they moved to monthly reporting as the pace of change slackened. The diaries contained separate entries for each time period with five questions:

What is going well and why? What is going badly and why? What problems do you foresee? What have been the significant events? What rumours and stories are circulating? The diaries were solicited logs (Burgess, 1984) rather than intimate journals. In line with our focus on sensemaking, the questions were designed to elicit the thought processes of the diarists, giving insight into how they were interpreting the changes and why, and the impact of this interpretation on them and on the change process. Within each division, a change manager worked alongside the divisional director to help implement the changes. These managers also acted as diarists.

Frequent contact was maintained with the diarists by telephone to follow up on queries raised by the diary entries. Review meetings were held with the change managers and diarists every six to eight weeks on a divisional basis to feed back initial interpretations from the diaries and get feedback on the accuracy of these. Beginning in April 1993, which was prior to the start of the tracking, and continuing throughout the change process, the first author spent time individually (and occasionally collectively) with the three divisional change managers to discuss their views on how change was progressing. These meetings also provided information on the senior manager perspective on change. The regular visits to the site for meetings and interviews provided observation and background data on the nature of the organization.

In addition to the diary data, the authors conducted individual interviews with diarists at the beginning and the end of the research process. The first interviews enabled the researcher to present the diary process and obtain initial impressions. The second interviews were useful for allowing diarists to reflect back on the process. In addition, during the last few months of the research process after the second interviews, diaries were replaced by focus groups, another innovative approach to obtaining data on strategy practice. Three focus groups were held in the Core Division and two each in the other two divisions. The focus groups, the interviews and the diaries all emphasized similar questions: 'What is going well and why, and what is going less well and why' (527). All the interview and focus group data were fully transcribed for analysis. Documentary sources concerning the change were also collected for background purposes.

Data analysis: patterns of schema change

The data analysis involved the search for patterns of schema change among the middle managers as the change rolled out. The authors describe their analysis as composed of three steps, contributing cumulatively to the overall findings.

First, a detailed narrative of the change process and managers' interpretations of it was developed for each of the three divisions by drawing together the diarists' accounts. This enabled the identification of two types of schemata: those associated with the content of change (organization) and those associated with the change process. In a second stage, the data were examined more finely using the NUD.IST software to derive detailed descriptions of the schemata and sub-schemata that composed them. The authors' unusually explicit presentation of the way in which these descriptions were developed using the software is worth reproducing.

We then examined the data, by division, for more detailed emergent classifications and patterns (Taylor & Bogdan, 1984) that connected to form the tentative schemata identified from the stories. Initially our categories were very detailed, and based on the terminology of the diarists to create 'in vivo' codes (Strauss & Corbin, 1990; Van Maanen, 1979). This stage was equivalent to 'open coding' as performed in grounded theory (Strauss & Corbin, 1990: 61). As our coding progressed, we were able to create broader categories of related data items. In keeping with our definition of schemata as thematically related knowledge with embedded subschemata, separated by perceived similarities and differences, we first clustered thematically related categories to create subschemata and then grouped thematically related subschemata into higher-level schemata. We used NUD.IST, a text analysis program (Wolfe, Gephart & Johnson, 1993), to code and search our data and to enable reorganization of data into emerging themes (Gephart, 1997) or subschemata. As our coding progressed, we were able to use the tree-based search facilities of NUD.IST to reorganize the detailed codings into related categories, and then into emergent lower-level schemata, which we could then group into our higher-level schemata relating to either the organization (change content), or the change process. We included only subschemata identified for more than one diarist to omit idiosyncratic data. While we recognize that particular individuals may have particular ways of seeing things, we were looking for shared themes.

Finally, drawing on the narratives, the authors associated different organizational and change process schemata with different time periods: the initial situation (time 0); early days when people were still being appointed to new positions (time 1); as change progressed (time 2); and finally, as contracts came into place (time 3).

Results

The presentation of the findings in the paper takes several forms. First, the organizational and change process schemata (and subschemata) for each time period and each of the three divisions are presented in the form of four tables. Each table describes the content of the schemata and indicates how they evolve over time. We reproduce two of these tables here. The first (Table 1) shows the schema shared by all organizational members at time 0. Here the organization is seen as a hierarchy with a common purpose. No schema elements relative

Table 1. Shared Organizational Schema prior to Change

Schema and Subschema	Time 0
Organization as hierarchy	
Common purpose	Keeping the lights on.
	Work done on basis of goodwill and cooperation.
	We work for one company as equals.
	We run cost centers.
	Technical excellence
Control	Senior managers controlling.
	Blamed for making mistakes.

to change are indicated since the change has not begun. The second table shows schema development in the Engineering Division over the three time periods (Table 3).

Table 3 is particularly interesting because it shows how schemata evolved over time in the division where there was perhaps the greatest degree of upheaval and change. Similar tables with similar subcategories are presented in the paper for the Core Division and for the Services Division, but these are somewhat less complex. In fact, the Engineering Division not only became a supplier to the Core Division, but was also itself divided into three business units (repairs, construction and maintenance) that contracted independently with the Core Division. When one of these sub-businesses needed resources from a sister business, it further had to contract with that business for those resources through what was called the IBT or interbusiness trading system. For this reason, inter-business relationships are a key component of the Engineering Division's schemata, not present in the schemata for the Core and Service divisions.

In the remainder of the results section, the authors explore stage by stage the evolution of schemata shown in Tables 1 to 4. For each stage, two types of analysis are presented: a 'first order analysis' and a 'second-order analysis'. The first-order analysis tells the story of the change from the perspectives of the diarists and provides evidence for the categories described in the tables using extensive quotations. For example, the following extract illustrates clearly the shared schema described in Table 1.

Time 1 First-Order Analysis: August–September 1993

From common purpose to interdivisional and interbusiness tensions. Prior to the imposed structural change, a shared schema of *common purpose* captured how the middle managers worked together (see Table 1). Their work involved 'keeping the lights on' (delivering the service

Table 3. Engineering Division Schema Development

Schema and Subschema	Time 1 August–September 1993	Time 2 October 1993–March 1994	Time 3 April–July 1994
Change process	This is not like any change we have done before, Workload.	Workload. 'Business as usual' needs to cease. We need contracts asap to tell us who does what. 'Business as usual' used as an excuse. Review group output not detailed enough/black holes. No interdivisional problem resolution.	Workload. 'Business as usual' needs to cease. 'Business as usual' used as an excuse. Review group output not detailed enough/black holes. No interdivisional problem resolution. 'Business as usual' necessary initially. Contracts starting to end 'business as usual.'
Organization as multidivisional Interdivisional relationship	We run profit centers.	Contracts will make things worse.	Contracts resolving who does what. We can work together contractually. We can cooperate.
	Interdivisional tensions. Attitudes of them and us. Defense of turf. We are now contractors/ no longer own assets. Core behaving like prima donnas. We are doing Core's work/ 'business as usual.'	Interdivisional tensions. Attitudes of them and us. We are doing Core's work/ 'business as usual.'	Interdivisional tensions. Attitudes of them and us. Defense of turf. We are doing Core's work/ 'business as usual.'
	Who does what.	Who does what. Pressure greater in Engineering.	Who does what. Pressure greater in Engineering.

Table 3. (continued)

Schema and Subschema	Time 1 August–September 1993	Time 2 October 1993–March 1994	Time 3 April–July 1994

Interbusiness relationship	IBT means we can build real businesses.
	
	Them and us.
	  Walls between businesses.
	  Different workloads/perks.
	  Defense of turf (e.g., sharing of tools, ring fencing own business).
	
	Who does what/who pays for what.
		IBT means we can build real businesses.
		We cooperate.
		Them and us.
		  Walls between businesses.
		  Different workloads/perks.
		  Defense of turf (e.g., sharing of tools, ring fencing own business).
		
		Who does what/who pays for what.
			IBT means we can build real businesses.
			We are cooperating.
			Them and us.
			  Walls between businesses.
			  Different workloads/perks.
			  Defense of turf (e.g., sharing of tools, ring fencing own business).
			
			Who does what/who pays for what.

Control	Senior managers controlling.	Senior managers controlling. Blamed for making mistakes.	Senior managers controlling. Blamed for making mistakes.

[a] IBT is the utility's interbusiness trading system.

to people's houses) and technical excellence. They worked together cooperatively on the basis of goodwill, and as equals, within cost centers, to achieve this

> I think people still remember the days when they were all together with the same terms of conditions, and if something applied to one of them it applied to all of them, and now it doesn't. (Engineering, interview)

> We over the years have just accepted that the cost of the job is the cost after all the oncosts have been added on, which is totally unrealistic, because these are group average oncosts to pay for everything . . . head office, group finance . . . (Engineering, interview)

> The engineer was king at one time. With the accountant beginning to come in, the engineer is now the end product of the job. . . . Technical quality not cost and profit was what mattered. (Engineering, interview)

> If you ask one of the engineers to design and make you a penknife, it will take 6 months and cost £150K, but it will last forever. (Core, preliminary meeting)

The first-order analysis of time 1 moves on to describe how these schemata changed as the change process began:

By the end of September, all staff members had been appointed to their new positions in the new structure. This imposed change from hierarchy to decentralization involved a significant shift in working patterns and challenged the old assumptions of common purpose since there were now three divisions with different, although linked, priorities. The future introduction of contracts pointed to the need for all three divisions to operate as stand-alone (profitable) businesses, with Engineering and Services only doing work required by the Core Division. Diarists in Engineering and Services saw the introduction of contracts as a shift to profit center management.

> If you're going to be a profit center manager you've got to be able to identify all your costs, and this (IBT) is a way of doing it. To me it's the first time we've ever really looked at costs, and it's really focusing everybody's attention. (Engineering, interview).

The changes also affected the degree of collaboration perceived among division members. The first-order analysis details how Core Division managers perceived these emerging tensions and then goes on to describe how these issues were viewed in the Engineering Division (cf. Table 3):

Engineering Division members (see Table 3, time 1) were also commenting on a 'them and us' attitude, defense of turf in the Core Division, and issues of 'who does what.' In addition, the Engineering managers were starting to think of themselves as *contractors* instead of as equals working cooperatively. The Core Division people were 'prima donnas' who were 'giving orders.' 'Business as usual' (carrying out both old and new duties until the old were assumed by someone else) was unpopular since it meant Engineering continued to do Core's work.

> Core staff are reluctant to take on responsibility but quick to give orders with a 'make them have it attitude.' We all need to work together. (Engineering, diary)

> Engineering staff have had a pride in the ownership of the network but now are made to feel like contractors. We must be careful not to destroy this pride. (Engineering, diary)

> I was the policy maker . . . I no longer have that power. Operational issues are a Core thing. (Engineering, diary)

> People in Engineering feel that the Core . . . (are) . . . prima donnas . . . in what they are and what they aren't going to dictate to Engineering who up until 5 or 6 months ago were their colleagues . . . Core seem to think that it is their system and they are going to run it and from day one they will dictate all the rules and everything else. Basically they will try and tread on you, give you as hard a time as possible. (Engineering, interview)

> My problem is that in Engineering we are under a lot of pressure with less staff and Core have taken the staff . . . . If there is an interdivisional problem, you get a glib answer. 'Oh it is business as usual, we've not taken that duty on yet.' (Engineering, interview)

Managers in the Services Division are shown to share similar preoccupations. However, the Engineering Division's particular situation engenders other concerns (see Table 3):

The problems between the divisions were reflected on a smaller scale within Engineering, now split into three new businesses (see Table 3, time 1). This split created another divide in what had been a united workforce working cooperatively to 'keep the lights on.' There were noticeable differences between the three businesses, although it was argued that these were due to the different goals of each business unit:

> The workloads between the three businesses seem imbalanced. Construction numbers have been reduced, yet Repairs seem overstaffed for the amount of work. Low fault incidence means that staff are underutilized. (Engineering, diary)

Just as contracts had been introduced between the divisions, signaling a move to a more commercial environment, the IBT system had been introduced into Engineering as a device to enable each business to be managed as a profit center. On the one hand, the introduction of IBT was welcomed as it enabled the diarists to 'build real businesses' by highlighting who used what services and how much these services cost. On the other hand, walls between businesses were developing, with defense of turf. There were also 'who does what' conflicts, particularly between repairs and maintenance.

> The teams in repairs, construction and maintenance all seem to be working against each other, building barriers. (Engineering, diary)

> Plant and equipment is being locked away or chained up. Staff are reluctant to help each other – even to the point of not answering somebody else's phone. (Engineering, diary)

> In my region I am fighting a losing battle every day. I seem to be at the losing end with Repairs every day (about what's what). (Engineering, diary)

At this stage, few schemata elements concerning the change process are present (see Table 3). However, there is considerable uncertainty as to what will happen next:

Similarly, the Engineering diarists recognized that this change was different from any other change they had been through. In an interview, one said, 'I think it's just a totally different way of doing the job than we have ever done.'

We have presented these extended extracts from the authors' first-order analysis of time 1 to illustrate how they draw on extensive data quotations to illustrate convincingly the schemata categories summarized in Tables 1 to 4. The material presented here supports the data in Table 3 related to middle managers in the Engineering Division. However a similar degree of support is offered in the paper for the evolving schemata exhibited in the other divisions.

Having presented the first-order analysis of time 1, the authors then move on to a 'second-order analysis' that provides a conceptual interpretation of the processes described. The second-order analysis for time 1 is presented below in its entirety, accompanied by Figure 2 that illustrates the evolution of schemata through all time periods as well as the patterns of overlap in schemata between the different divisions. (Figure 1 referenced in the text is not essential to understanding as its elements are equally well illustrated within figure 2.)

Second-Order Analysis, Time 1: Middle Manager Sensemaking and Schema Change

The 'big bang' imposition of a decentralized organizational form destroyed shared middle manager sensemaking around old norms of common purpose. Figure 1, which outlines the pattern of schema development among the utility's middle managers throughout the period studied, highlights this change. (See the headings 'Time 0' and 'Time 1'). Instead, patterns of clustered sensemaking developed around new divisional goals and identities. The new contractual structure replaced the old 'organization as hierarchy' schema with an 'organization as multidivisional' schema at time 1 in all three new divisions. Yet the subthemes that surfaced within these divisional schemata were very different, revealing little commonality in the newly formed middle manager groups' interpretations of the new structure and its impact. Interdivisional tensions developed as a result, as well as interbusiness tensions between the three new businesses in Engineering, as individual middle managers sought to build

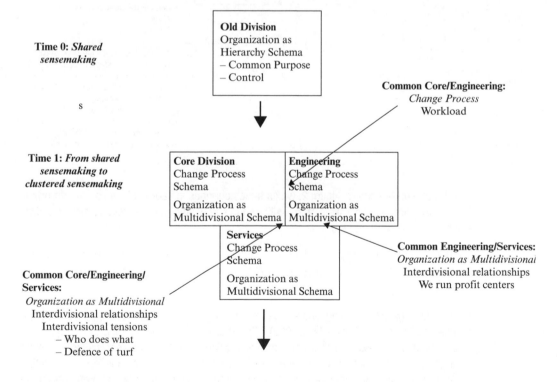

Fig. 2   Increasing Overlap in Understanding between Divisions

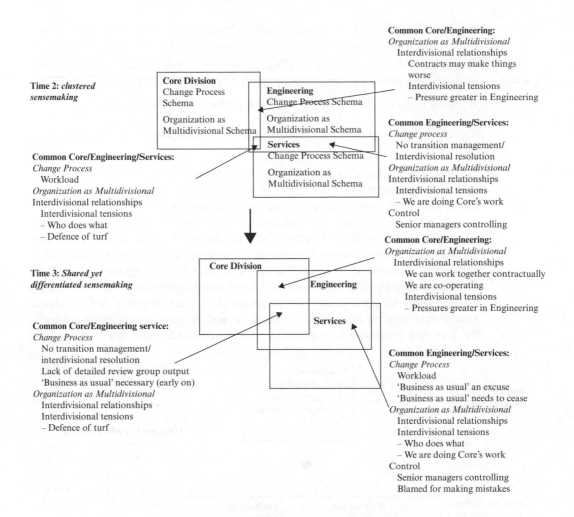

stand-alone profit centers. Figure 2, which traces changes in degree of overlap of interpretations in the three new divisions of the utility, shows how little the members of the three divisions had in common at time 1.

In the above paragraph and in the figure, the authors thus summarize the changes in schema development across the divisions observed between time 0 and time 1.

Work settings have four components – organizing arrangements, social factors, physical setting, and technology (Porras & Robertson, 1992) – that shape the behavior of organization members. In the change process observed here, changes in organizing arrangements were imposed through the new structure, goals, and contractual relationships, and the new accounting systems under development to allow for more precise allocation of costs and profit. Structural change also led to some imposition in technology with the specification of new responsibilities and workflows between divisions (and between businesses in Engineering). In addition, there was imposed change in the middle managers' physical setting, with staff increasingly located together in offices within their new divisions, businesses, and teams. However, although the divisional directors had espoused changes in social factors, such as a shift from control to empowerment, nothing was formally done to shape either the company's management style (the schema of *control*, Table 1) or other aspects of its operation, such as interaction processes (the schema of *common purpose*, Table 1), or, more generally, its culture. Since changes in one component require accompanying changes in others, the imposition of changes to organizing arrangements, technology, and physical setting forced evolution of old schemata – particularly the common purpose schema.

The new schemata developed and were sustained by horizontal processes of social interaction between middle managers. The new modular structure created sensemaking fault lines by fragmenting one group into three new communities, which then had to establish new patterns of interaction and coordination consistent with their new (individual) goals through negotiation with each other. The new structure forced a process of 'deidentification' (Fiol, 2002) through destruction of the old and replacement with something new. Through the diarists' reflections on the way things were, the first-order analysis revealed that the old schema concerning equality, cooperation, service (keeping the lights on), and technical excellence before cost was challenged by the restructuring into internal customer supplier divisions. Deidentification led to a loss of meaning and to ambiguity and uncertainty – a situation that leads to active sensemaking. Deidentification also disrupted the focus on a common goal, here represented by the common purpose schema. It was no longer possible for the middle managers to develop the future through recourse to past experience; current experience and experimentation were the only available means. Poole and his colleagues argued that 'by accepting institutionalized schemas, an organization member acquires trustworthy formulas for obtaining desirable consequences when handling situations and interpreting the organizational world' (1989: 272). The new structure rendered existing trustworthy middle manager formulas for coordination of their work obsolete. The first-order analysis shows how, instead, the middle managers developed their new interpretations through, for example, their direct experiences of the behavior of others, gossip and rumor about senior management behavior, and shared stories of their experiences with and interpretations of the new structure. Reciprocal behavior and symbolic reinforcement (Johnson, Smith & Codling, 2000) are important influences on developing interpretations. The behavioral responses the diarists encountered in others, such as defense of turf, prima donna behaviors, and lack of cooperation, provided feedback for their developing schemata about how the new structure was to work. Cooperation was blocked by differences in meaning and, during time 1, a lack of shared communication behaviors (Donnellon et al., 1986). Similarly, visible and symbolic indicators affected interpretations. The new structure itself, with its maintenance and development of company assets through contractual relationships, was highly symbolic, and it contributed to early interpretations by members of Engineering that their new status was that of contractors. Physical indicators were also present, such as the centralization of Core Division at a site away from Engineering and Services, the colocation of staff within businesses within Engineering, and perceived differences in working patterns, hours, and potential job security.

In this concluding section of the second-order analysis for time 1, the authors thus theorize about the process of movement in schemata that they have presented in the figure. They note the deidentification produced by the structural change, and they argue that ongoing interactions and mutual observations of behaviour among members of different divisions and businesses reinforced a feeling of separation, lack of cooperation and uncertainty in this initial period.

The analyses for times 2 and 3 follow the same pattern as for time 1. The authors first present a first-order analysis supporting the schema changes described in Tables 1 to 4, and then theorize about these changes in their second-order analysis. Because of space limitations, we will not present these analyses in depth. However, the main components of the analysis and interpretation are summarized below.

The analysis for time 2 essentially reveals increasing frustration with the change process itself, and these frustrations are shared by middle managers from different divisions (as illustrated in the descriptions of overlap in figure 2). The heart of tensions among divisions lies in the practice of 'business as usual' in which the Engineering and Services divisions continue to work as before while waiting for formal contracting procedures to be properly implemented. This is seen as increasing the workload unfairly on some divisions as opposed to others. Despite attempts by Core Division managers to develop linkages to the other divisions, there are increasing complaints about the absence of senior management interventions to resolve the tensions among the divisions. In theorizing about the sensemaking processes during this period, the authors note two parallel types of negotiation and communication processes going on. On the one hand, there is an increase in horizontal communication and negotiations among divisions. These are leading to certain shared perceptions (including those about the inadequacy of the change processes). However, they are accompanied by vertical negotiations in which the engrained hierarchical mode of functioning is seen by middle managers to be dominant and is said to be hampering the creation of local initiatives that would allow the organization to develop towards the espoused more decentralized mode of functioning.

By time 3, although differences remain, there is increasing overlap among schemata for the different divisions (see figure 2). Interpreting the schema changes observed, the authors suggest that middle managers were going through a 'reidentification' period 'as they come to terms with the new goals of their different divisions/businesses' (543). They conclude that the increasing commonality among schemata is the result of 'ongoing horizontal processes of social interaction of middle managers around the contracts leading to patterns of shared yet differentiated sensemaking' (543). They note the remaining differences among schemata between the divisions and discuss whether or not higher degrees of commonality are always necessary to achieve coordination. They argue in fact that the communication processes associated with contracting may sometimes be sufficient in themselves.

Discussion

The discussion section of the paper first summarizes the changes in schemata observed across the three time periods (1–3), noting the initial fragmentation of the divisions into clustered schemata and the eventual development of shared but differentiated schemata across divisional lines in time 3. They argue that this development was largely a result of the patterns of interdivisional communication observed. They note that the Core Division's liaison initiatives in time 2 and the implementation of contracting in time 3 were instrumental in allowing the emergence of these new schemata.

Balogun and Johnson then return to the literature on schema change mentioned in the conceptual background in order to compare and contrast their findings with those of previous studies, most notably the work of Labianca et al. (2000) and Bartunek (1984). Their observations confirm some of their findings about schema change but contradict others. Balogun and Johnson conclude by suggesting that a contingency framework may be needed and they suggest some contextual factors that may explain why different types of schema change occur.

One of the most interesting aspects of the discussion is centred on the importance of horizontal processes of sensemaking among middle managers in making sense of change in this particular case.

In addition to identifying patterns of schema change, we also need to understand what informs the schema development process. How is middle manager cognitive disorder resolved, and what is the relationship between managers' sensemaking and the way restructuring develops? Clearly, middle managers do a lot of experimentation in the absence of a clear and shared view of how a new structure is to be made operational. They use both vertical and horizontal social processes of interaction, but, as expected, given vertical structural barriers, most interaction occurs horizontally, between middle managers. The nature of the relationships that develop, and the way the new structure operates, are thus determined by these middle manager processes of interaction. Change outcomes – here, interdivisional and interbusiness tensions leading to poor customer response times – may not be the ones intended by senior managers. Middle manager sensemaking occurs primarily outside of senior management control. This may be because, as here, middle managers are largely remote from their seniors. Yet the delayering that often accompanies decentralization removes hierarchical layers between senior and middle managers, simultaneously reducing opportunities for interaction up the management chain. The middle manager lateral processes occurring in change contexts, which have so far received less attention than vertical processes, are therefore critically important.

It is not only the formal lateral processes that play a significant role in schema change, but also the multiple (and largely informal) conversational vehicles: stories, gossip, and rumour; behaviours and actions; discussions and negotiations; and sharing of personal experience and interpretations of change interventions. Our findings regarding what gets shared through such conversations support other research on the importance of senior management's symbolic influence on the change recipient sensemaking process (Donnellon et al., 1986; Gioia & Chittipeddi, 1991; Gioia et al., 1994; Isabella, 1990; Morgan et al., 1983; Pettigrew, 1985; Pondy, 1978, 1983; Poole et al., 1989). However, our findings also suggest that the actions, behaviours, gestures, and language of peers and their shared personal experiences and interpretations have a more direct impact on change outcomes, and therefore on the way a structural blueprint designed by seniors works in practice.

Implications for practice and research

The above discussion leads the authors directly towards a review of the implications of their work. First, they consider the advantages and different modes of schema change from the viewpoint of top managers. Second, and perhaps most interestingly from a Strategy as Practice perspective, they draw attention to the important role of middle managers in strategy development. Middle managers are usually viewed as change recipients, and prescriptive recommendations about change generally focus on ways to improve vertical communications with them. However, this perspective ignores the degree to which middle managers will make sense of change (and therefore influence its success) through conversations and interactions that may be largely outside direct management control. The paper ends with a discussion of future research avenues, emphasizing the importance of a focus on sensemaking and on the role of middle managers.

Editors' commentary

From the viewpoint of a focus on 'doing strategy,' the strengths of this paper lie in at least two areas.

First, the paper describes in considerable detail how middle managers become involved in the definition of strategy. We see through the analysis and the empirical data how important middle managers are in determining how a strategy is enacted and what its consequences may be. Indeed, it is clear that the strategy is 'done' in large part by this level of management. While top management may have had a vision, the data presented here show that they seem largely absent from how it comes to be operationalized. Indeed, there are suggestions that senior management is perhaps somewhat problematic in this process, remaining attached to old ways of behaving even longer than middle managers, who are seen to be struggling to understand the meaning of changes and who work across new organizational boundaries to make the new structure work.

Second, the paper uses an innovative set of methods. The use of diaries and focus groups is particularly interesting. Diaries are temporally embedded and allow the tracing of understandings about the change process over time among a fairly broad sample. This is particularly important in a study that aims to capture schemata as they evolve. Focus groups are another useful way to capture views from a large number of people quite economically. The analysis presented in the paper is interesting for the way in which temporally embedded details are carefully traced among the three business units. The multiple quotations from the various data sources render the description of the evolving schemata particularly credible. The presentation of first-order descriptions followed by second-order interpretations is also well done.

A third aspect of the paper that is of considerable interest is the type of relationships developed between the researchers and the researched during this study. This is not explicitly examined in much detail in the paper. However, it is clear that the interactive focus groups probably constituted not only a way of collecting data but also a way for the researchers to provide forums for interaction among organization members that contributed to their own learning. More generally, one may ask the question as to how the fact of being obliged to write a diary every two weeks or every month might lead a person to make sense differently of what was going on in his or her organization. Clearly, these issues suggest that the research approach adopted may itself have contributed to the nature of sensemaking among organizational participants. If, as the authors claim, sensemaking occurs through interaction, this surely includes interactions with the researchers. There would be room for more analysis of how the research process itself (not only in this study but in other studies of strategy practice) may affect the phenomenon being studied, and the advantages and disadvantages of these effects.

In terms of its contribution to knowledge about strategizing, this paper positions itself with respect to other articles on sensemaking and schema change over time (see chapter 2). To judge from discussions with one of the authors, it seems that reviewers pushed the authors in this direction. The similarities and differences the paper identifies with respect to previous literature are undoubtedly interesting, and a series of contingency hypotheses emerge from this analysis about effective modes of schema change in different contexts. Yet the data collected could have been presented differently and a different presentation might have told us a little more than the current paper about the 'doing' of strategy. We find out a lot about how people felt about the imposed change. Yet, we believe that the everyday doings of people within the middle management group as they coped with the changes could have been the focus of more concerted attention. We hope that these issues will be addressed in future research.

11

From metaphor to practice in the crafting of strategy

Journal of Management Inquiry, 14, 1 (2005): 78–94

P. T. Bürgi, C. D. Jacobs and J. Roos

Abstract

This article explores how the link between the hand and the mind might be exploited in the making of strategy. Using Mintzberg's image of a potter undergoing iterative and recursive learning and knowledge-building processes as a point of departure, the authors develop a three-level theoretical schema, progressing from the physiological to the psychological to the social to trace the consequences of the hand–mind link. To illustrate their theoretical schema, the authors present an illustration case of managers from a large telecommunications firm experimenting with a process for strategy making in which they actively use their hands to construct representations of their organization and its environment. The authors conclude that new and potent forms of strategy making might be attained if the fundamental human experience of using one's hands is put in the service of all kinds of organizational learning.

Editors' introduction

This paper is an unusual action research study of a semi-consultancy intervention in the strategy making of a large mobile phone company, Orange. The authors are themselves the leaders of the intervention, though they do not describe themselves as consultants. The paper is noteworthy both for the intimacy of the empirical insight into strategy making in practice and for its sophisticated theorization of a strategy tool, the Lego Serious Play technique. The paper also provides an opportunity to reflect on the opportunities and constraints of action research.

The authors' starting point is Henry Mintzberg's (1987) famous metaphor of the potter at the wheel to characterize the hands-on crafting process of strategy making. While Mintzberg used the crafting metaphor to marginalize formal strategy, the authors carry forward its implications into the reality of deliberate strategizing. The paper's core is a case of senior managers using Lego bricks to model a company's strategy, using the same kind of hands-on, iterative interaction with physical materials as a potter uses in moulding clay. As the authors summarize, the paper 'takes what appears to be an evocative turn of phrase (crafting strategy) and grounds it in practice' (91). By introducing the crafting of physical models of strategy, the paper cleverly takes Mintzberg literally in order to return formal strategizing to the foreground. This returning of strategy making activity to the foreground is at the heart of the Strategy as Practice endeavour.

Paper summary

The article opens with a paragraph directly quoted from Henry Mintzberg (1987), with the final line being: 'Managers are craftsmen and strategy is their clay' (66). With this quotation the authors simultaneously establish their concern for the hands-on, signal their location in the strategy process tradition broadly conceived, and claim the legitimacy of a well-respected theorist. This choice of opening quotation is in itself a clever piece of craftsmanship on the part of the authors.

The article continues by introducing three streams of theoretical literature making the case for the role of literal hands-on crafting in strategy. The first draws from research in physiology and communications on the importance of the hand in developing understanding: in English, French, German and Spanish, the words meaning hand and understanding are closely linked (consider 'to grasp'). The second stream of literature draws from the Piagetian tradition in psychology, in which effective learning is closely connected with hands-on recursive cycles of activity. The third stream is social constructionism, in which knowledge is seen as emerging from intense social interaction. The authors do not use these streams of literature to develop precise propositions, but they do knit them together convincingly into a coherent justification for their empirical focus on hands-on strategizing. They summarize the argument so far thus:

We began with a discussion of three areas of theory related to the strategy-as-crafting metaphor, all of them linked thematically and substantively by the ideas of recursivity and enactment. The physiological one focuses on the hand as the primary tool for manipulating the world and also as an often-overlooked means of stimulating cognition. The psychological one deals with the role of practical activity as a means of shaping understanding. The third uses social constructionism, which emphasizes that what we know of reality is constructed through discursive interactions of meaning making. Together, three bodies of literature help us extend Mintzberg's (1987) metaphor of crafting strategy as embodied recursive enactment, involving the psychological, social, and physiological domain of the hand-mind connection.

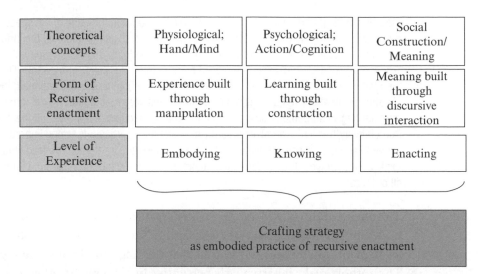

Theoretical concepts	Physiological; Hand/Mind	Psychological; Action/Cognition	Social Construction/ Meaning
Form of Recursive enactment	Experience built through manipulation	Learning built through construction	Meaning built through discursive interaction
Level of Experience	Embodying	Knowing	Enacting

Crafting strategy
as embodied practice of recursive enactment

Fig. 1   The Concept of Crafting as Strategic Practice

Their theoretical position is also neatly encapsulated in Figure 1.

What this exploration of quite recondite theory has also established is that the authors are by no means simple consultants: this is a serious study. This provides them with a secure platform to introduce their 'illustrative case study', a two-day Lego Serious Play workshop in the phone company Orange.

The case study begins by introducing the company's three strategic issues of identity, branding and increased competition, established by interviews with senior managers before the workshop. The workshop itself is then described, using the authors' own observation, quotations from participants' remarks during the workshop, and post-workshop interviews and email correspondence.

The workshop involved the participants working together around a table to build a Lego brick model of their company's strategy. A flavour of the workshop can be got from the following extract, describing an incident on the second day when they had already constructed a so-called flotilla model of their strategic position:

In the next phase of the workshop, participants began to populate the area around their flotilla model, with different constructions representing aspects of their social, economic, and competitive context. One participant, for example, sought to illustrate how a very large competitor with its power base in another part of the world was likely to enter into direct competition with Orange, and she placed the large, blocky figure representing this competitor on a bookshelf on the wall behind the table. The competitor was, as she put it, 'coming in from left field,' an assertion made patent in the physical location of the figure at the edge of the space where the group was working. Two of the other participants eagerly began to question the individual who had arrived at this particular contribution: Did she really think this competitor was interested? Yes, she responded, that's why I've placed them coming right over at the table. Do they have the resources to really come in and shake things up? Absolutely, she continued, look at how big and threatening I've built this model of them. This very resourceful way of introducing and representing a competitor, said a participant in the subsequent interviews, 'hit them in the gut.' Cumulatively, this and several other surprises made for a particularly strong impression on participants about their competitive position. One participant commented the following: 'I used to think we had maybe three or four competitors. But now the table just isn't big enough to hold all of them!'

This incident directly relates to the key strategic issue of increasing competition. But it is particularly well chosen for how it conveys the imagination, excitement, interaction and impact that the Lego modelling could generate. The authors make it particularly persuasive by weaving together a vivid sense of the experience at the time with punchy commentary from a participant in subsequent interview.

In another particularly striking episode, the authors describe how one of the participants moves the icon representing the Orange brand from the front of the company's flotilla to behind:

Up to the morning of the second day, the group had placed an icon of its brand in the front of the flotilla, as if that was what drew them further. In a moment of experimentation, one participant placed the icon of the brand at the rear of the flotilla. After a moment's hesitation, participants nodded in acceptance of this radical statement of the importance of the brand to their present situation, even though the notion that the brand was somehow behind them clearly struck several people as an almost taboo thought.

If attempted in words, this challenge to the value of the famous Orange brand might have been hard to articulate or liable to provoke furious intervention before completion. The simplicity of the physical move, however, made possible a reversal of given understandings of the place of the brand in the company's strategy.

The final part of the paper is made up of five sections: Discussion; Contributions to theory and practice from our theoretical framework; Implications; Caveats; and Conclusion. The Discussion integrates the empirical material in a second figure, with one axis based on the three earlier dimensions of physiology, psychology and social construction and the other axis based on the company's three strategic issues of identity, competition and brand. The consistency of theoretical dimensions and the visual echo of the first figure together provide a persuasive sense of completion and coherence.

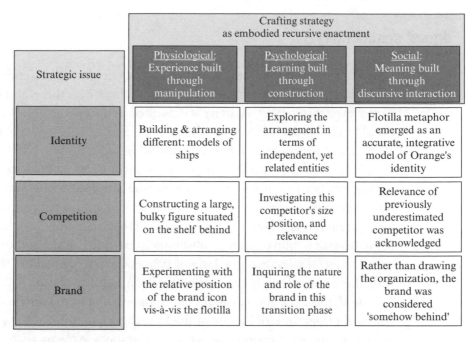

	Crafting strategy as embodied recursive enactment		
Strategic issue	_Physiological:_ Experience built through manipulation	_Psychological:_ Learning built through construction	_Social:_ Meaning built through discursive interaction
Identity	Building & arranging different: models of ships	Exploring the arrangement in terms of independent, yet related entities	Flotilla metaphor emerged as an accurate, integrative model of Orange's identity
Competition	Constructing a large, bulky figure situated on the shelf behind	Investigating this competitor's size position, and relevance	Relevance of previously underestimated competitor was acknowledged
Brand	Experimenting with the relative position of the brand icon vis-à-vis the flotilla	Inquiring the nature and role of the brand in this transition phase	Rather than drawing the organization, the brand was considered 'somehow behind'

Fig. 2   Crafting Strategy at Orange: Synopsis of Case Episodes

The Contributions section develops the theoretical discussion, underlining the paper's distinctiveness in demonstrating the importance of the physiological. The Implications section then widens out the discussion to argue for the potential value generally of the kind of visualization and dramatization approaches exemplified here. Readers are thus invited to see the particular Lego phenomenon as something much more than an idiosyncratic consulting tool. The Caveats section does, however, concede that this is a single case and underlines its status as 'a provisional and largely suggestive illustration' (91).

The Conclusion section is brief, and in a final paragraph returns to Mintzberg's opening metaphor in order to summarize the argument in broad and quite inspiring terms:

This article develops and illustrates an integrative framework to move Mintzberg's idea from metaphor to practice; crafting strategy is a process of embodied, recursive enactment. The implication of our thesis is that crafting strategy could one day no longer be simply a compelling image of an organization uncovering new opportunities through trial and error but a technique through which individuals collectively use their hands to develop a different type of strategy content. Instead of a detached, analytical, and cerebral activity inside organizations, the process of developing strategy can offer passion, involvement, and discovery in employees' work.

Editors' commentary

This article is unusual both in method and in subject. The action research method achieves remarkable intimacy. The authors were there, and that sense is conveyed throughout. Activity is described in a vivid detail not easily captured by retrospective interviews. The significance of putting the block on the shelf, or the icon behind the flotilla, would have been very hard to grasp by people outside the process. Readers learn something about both strategy consulting practice in general – for example, the routines of pre-workshop and post-workshop interviews – and a particular and innovative consulting tool, Lego Serious Play. But all this is also related carefully to theory. The Mintzbergian notion of craft is substantially extended, as the authors demonstrate its literal relevance to a kind of deliberate strategy making that Henry Mintzberg himself might originally have been sceptical about.

Indeed, there is a good deal of craft in the writing of the article itself. This runs right from the striking use of the Mintzberg quotation at the start to the closure of the final paragraph, where the authors leave us with an almost ironic extension to Mintzberg and a rhetorical appeal to 'passion, involvement and discovery'. The authors' early emphasis on theory carefully marks them as more than consultants. The authors are aware of the rhetorical power of three: there are three theoretical themes and three strategic issues, producing two nine-cell figures, neatly echoing each other. The various incidents during the workshop are narrated with a good deal of vigour. Scepticism is disarmed by an explicit Caveats section, as well as a light smattering of references to participants' occasional 'frustration' or 'critical comments'. Credibility is reinforced by the fact that the naming of the company itself, and the provision of several of the participants' job titles, leaves readers with the sense that they could check this account for themselves.

This is an impressive paper that researchers can learn a good deal from. There are, though, three things which researchers following this path might consider adding. First, this kind of action research provides rich opportunities for the analysis of photographic records of activity. Elsewhere these authors have made some use of photographs, largely for illustration (Burgi and Roos 2003; Roos, Victor and Statler 2004), and researchers in the practice tradition more widely (e.g. Latour 1999; Molloy and Whittington 2005) have shown that photographs can uncover details of activity that are not easily captured in textual narrative. Given the emphasis on visualization and the physiological in this article especially, it would have been good to see more of the participants' social interaction and hands-on activity. Here of course one may simply run into the limitations of journal editors' policies on the reproduction of photographic materials. However, photographic evidence is an under-exploited resource generally and in this kind of research has a good deal of potential (see chapter 3).

A second point is the desirability of providing more details of the relationship between the action researchers and research subjects. This article avoids the term 'consulting', although the episode has many of the features of such an engagement. The authors simply identify themselves as members of the Imagination Lab Foundation, which their website (www.imagilab.org) describes as an independent non-profit research institute. The exact relationship in terms of funding and pre-publication reviewing rights between the authors and Orange is left unclear. For good reason, the terms of funding relationships are now typically made explicit in scientific and medical research. Even if independence was retained in this particular case, it seems a good general rule to be equally explicit about the terms of the relationship in this kind of Strategy as Practice research where the mutual involvement of researchers and subjects is necessarily so intimate.

Finally there is the question of authorship: this is particularly sensitive for action research. In this paper, the authors are all from one side of the relationship. Their credibility is reinforced by the naming of the company, but nonetheless the company's perspective is not represented directly. Other researchers, for example Gioia et al. (1991) and Vaara et al. (2005), have used mixed teams of authors, incorporating both independent researchers and participating managers. While this may well not have been feasible (or desired) in this particular case, a more complete authorial team does add confidence in the rounded nature of the account provided. The subjects in many Strategy as Practice research projects are highly educated, and well capable of contributing directly to the writing of research. Mixed authorial teams, with both practitioners and researchers, promise both greater insight and greater authority.

Part III

Our enthusiasm for Strategy as Practice should be evident in the chapters and commentaries that have preceded this one. This enthusiasm is similarly to be found in the community of academics that has grown up around it, as we indicate above. A good deal of this arises because Strategy as Practice provides a real opportunity to place an emphasis on people and what people do in relation to strategy – something which, as chapter 1 suggested, has been somewhat absent in much of what is now researched in the strategy field. We should however remember that this interest and enthusiasm is part of a long legacy. It builds on the legacy of the subject of strategic management back into the 1950s and 60s and it has been the continuing central concern of academics such as Henry Mintzberg, Robert Burgelman and Andrew Pettigrew. So this is not an entirely new perspective: it builds on and extends a tradition.

Our objectives in this final part are twofold. First, we reflect collectively on the journey followed in this book, summarizing the central substantive, empirical and methodological themes developed in Parts I and II, and broadening the field of vision to draw in some of the most promising recent initiatives in this area. Second, each of the authors provides individual reflections on the contributions and future opportunities of Strategy as Practice, emphasizing those areas that are of greatest interest and concern to him or her personally. All of us have been independently involved in empirical work relevant to Strategy as Practice and were drawn to this area with slightly different motivations and interests. We give space here to these personal reflections in the belief that they may find a kind of resonance with readers that more traditional and more detached academic discourse cannot achieve. We also believe that the recognition of individuality and diversity within an academic community is a healthy thing to be celebrated.

12

Reflections

Ann Langley, Gerry Johnson, Leif Melin and Richard Whittington

Collective reflections: looking back and looking forward

We began this book by inviting readers to consider strategy in a different way – as a practice – something *people do*, rather than something *organizations have*. Building on this foundation, we mapped in some detail the domain of the Strategy as Practice perspective, arguing that strategic activities carried out by organization members (i.e. the doing of strategy) both influence and are influenced by organizational-level actions and institutional-level practices, and that the greatest potential for developing new and valuable knowledge for the strategic management field lies in exploring and understanding these relationships (shown schematically in figure 1.1). We provided many examples of research questions that address the various linkages and drew attention to previous research that has begun to explore these issues.

The particular interest of the Strategy as Practice perspective lies, however, not only in its empirical relevance as described in chapter 1, but also in its theoretical richness. Thus, chapter 2 examined some of the most promising theoretical resources available for its development. We first located the perspective with respect to the 'practice turn' in philosophy and the social sciences generally. Then four broad theoretical traditions were identified as holding particular potential: the Situated Learning perspective; sensemaking and routine related views; institutional theory; and actor-network theory.

Chapter 3 then explored some of the methodological tools available for connecting empirical research questions with relevant theoretical frameworks. We discussed the particular challenges of approaching, bounding, capturing and understanding Strategy as Practice in empirical research. This chapter drew extensively on a series of illustrative papers that exemplify these research challenges and their potential solutions. The chapter provides a bridge to Part II of the book in which several illustrative research papers are presented in depth.

The content and form of Part II is rather unusual. We chose in this section to present extended annotated extracts from published research studies that are relevant to the Strategy as Practice perspective and that illustrate substantively, theoretically or methodologically types of work that we believe can contribute to developing knowledge in the area. The choice of the eight papers to be included in this volume was not an easy one and required much discussion among the authors. Several of the papers are quite well known. Five of them (Barley, Eisenhardt, Gioia and Chittipeddi, Langley, Oakes et al.) can be described as precursors: they were written and published at a time when 'Strategy as Practice' had not been pinpointed as a distinct domain within the strategy field. However, all are – in different ways – relevant to understanding the doing of strategy. The three more recently published papers (Balogun and Johnson, Bürgi et al., Samra-Fredericks) have more explicit and self-identified affinities with the perspective. The commentaries we provide on each of the individual papers are intended to draw readers' attention to the particular strengths of each piece of work and to relate these strengths to the practice agenda. We briefly summarize in the next few paragraphs some of the themes emerging from a horizontal look at this set of papers.

At the substantive level, the eight chosen contributions in Part II address a variety of research questions. The Langley and Eisenhardt papers look at patterns in top managers' strategic decision making activities, including formal decision tools, and examine either how these are affected by organizational context (Langley) or how they affect decision speed and outcomes (Eisenhardt). These two contributions are relatively traditional in style. Nevertheless, they focus on key dimensions of strategy related activities and relate these to other phenomena.

Another set of papers examines activities related to sensemaking among strategists. The paper by Gioia and Chittipeddi is a classic contribution showing the importance of both sensemaking and sensegiving to the initiation of strategic change, while the paper by Balogun and Johnson explores the sensemaking activities of middle managers and their role in implementing strategic restructuring. The paper by Oakes et al. links managerial sensemaking to the institutional environment, showing how the meaning of 'business planning' comes to be shared at operational levels based on the specific language that is used to refer to it.

Finally, the papers by Bürgi et al., by Samra-Fredericks and by Barley are those that are most strongly focused on the micro level of analysis. Burgi et al. show how the physical manipulation of objects in a social context contributes to collective strategic sensemaking. In different ways, both Samra-Fredericks and Barley show us the importance of 'small' interactions for cumulatively generating potentially large 'strategic' effects. While Barley's study is not directly related to what we normally think of as strategy, his insights about how disturbances of routine (caused in this case by technology) generate new micro-interactions that cumulatively lead to new structures could be immensely relevant to the development of a deeper understanding of the relationships between strategy and structure. Samra-Fredericks' study similarly shows how apparently small conversations among strategists can cumulatively lead to major strategic change. There is clearly room for more work that relates micro-level interactions to organizational and more macro-level results.

The eight illustrative papers are also diverse in terms of the theoretical resources mobilized. Theorizations more obviously associated with the 'practice turn' such as structuration theory (Barley), ethnomethodology and conversation analysis (Samra-Fredericks), sensemaking theory (Balogun and Johnson; Gioia and Chittipeddi) and Bourdieu's theory of fields of production (Oakes et al.) join more classical middle-range approaches reflected in the work of Eisenhardt and Langley. However, as we noted in chapter 2, there are many theoretical opportunities that remain to be fully tapped. Even the most well-studied phenomena such as strategic planning or decision making may take on new richness when examined by drawing on some of the resources we described in that chapter.

Finally, the eight papers provide a rich panorama of the types of methods that may be successfully used to study Strategy as Practice. We have commented extensively on these methodological issues both in chapter 3 and in our editorials. As mentioned in chapter 3, the challenges of empirical research in strategy practice are considerable. However, the eight illustrative papers show that they can be met.

It is clearly impossible to do justice to the full potential of Strategy as Practice as a research area purely on the basis of the work featured in this book. We therefore urge interested readers to widen their field of vision to recently published and ongoing work that has identified itself with Strategy as Practice, or that otherwise contributes to it. There is a dynamic community of scholars who have taken up the ball and are running with it. A special issue of *Journal of Management Studies* (2003) featured a series of ground-breaking papers, many of which have already been cited in this book (Jarzabkowski 2003; Johnson et al. 2003; Maitlis and Lawrence 2003; Regnér 2003; Salvato 2003; Samra-Fredericks 2003). Further papers will be published in special issues of Human Relations and Long Range Planning in 2007. Tracks, symposia and workshops at the Strategic Management Society, the European Group for Organization Studies, the Academy of Management, the European

Academy of Management and other meetings have been created and are enthusiastically attended.

Significant publications outside these specialized fora which identify themselves with the perspective are emerging (e.g. Balogun and Johnson 2004, 2005; Jarzabkoswki 2005; Mantere 2005; Rouleau 2005; Whittington 2006). There are also substantial numbers of doctoral theses being completed or underway (e.g. see Nordqvist 2005). A website www.strategy as practice.org/ and listserv sap@domeus.co.uk have also been created to allow intellectual exchange around these issues.

A look at recent sets of papers presented at the European Group for Organization Studies (2005 and 2006) under the Strategy as Practice banner suggests that a considerable body of work is now emerging that focuses on long-neglected aspects of strategic activity, including strategy workshops, strategy consulting, the use of strategy tools, strategy project organization, and communication practices. At the same time both these and other more traditional topics such as strategic decision making, strategic planning and the dynamics of top management teams appear using theoretical frameworks associated with the practice turn in social theory. In addition, there is an increasing tendency for authors working in this area to draw on each other's work. The Strategy as Practice 'conversation' (Huff 1999) is in full swing and open for participation!

Personal reflections: looking around and looking forward

In this section, each of the authors of this book provides a personal perspective on how they see the Strategy as Practice perspective and where it might lead. Each of these reflections is very individual in style. We have worked well together as an authorial team despite our diversity. However, we all welcome the chance to be freed, if only for a moment, from the bonds of collective authorship so that our individual voices can be heard. We hope that these final thoughts – like good music that is largely harmonious but that incorporates occasional and rather satisfying discords – will provide an interesting counterpoint to the more detached discussion we have provided so far.

Ann Langley: Strategy as Practice – opening up a new identity within a closed field

For me 'Strategy as Practice' is a bit like prose. Apparently, I have been doing it without knowing it for a long time. When I first heard about a group of people who were developing this perspective, I was very interested in the work itself but I did not really buy into the idea of developing this as a specific perspective or as a school of thought in strategy. I am not by nature a joiner or a creator of schools of thought. I do the research that I do; what it is called and what school of thought or perspective it belongs to have never really preoccupied me very much. Ever since my doctoral thesis days when no one was quite sure what discipline I should be classified under (Strategy? Organization theory? Public administration?), labelling and boundary-drawing have always seemed to me to be a bit of a distraction. The labels and boundaries of academic disciplines appeared to be 'mere' social constructions that really didn't seem to be worth fighting over – what seemed important was to do interesting and relevant work, not to put it into an established category (let alone to establish a new category that would include it).

Yet here I am, co-signing a book that is introducing a new label for the type of work that I and many others do or have done and that is in fact defining and delineating a subfield of strategy research. How did this happen? How did I get co-opted into this enterprise?

I have to say that I have been fascinated by the energy and purposefulness that intellectual leaders Gerry Johnson, Leif Melin and Richard Whittington (joined by Paula Jarzabkowski, David Seidl, Julia Balogun, Linda Rouleau, Patrick Regnér and many others) have put into creating and developing the Strategy as Practice perspective. When I went to the EGOS conference in 2003 (the second of a series dealing with micro-strategy as it was then labelled), I actually presented a paper that dealt with the use of actor-network theory in strategy. As I listened to the papers, the discussion and the developing discourse about an emerging perspective that was then being defined by the participants, I could not help thinking that Latour's work was a perfect description of what the convenors were up to. Here I was in the presence of an archetypal and highly organized 'translation' process. The Strategy as Practice perspective was being socially constructed before my very eyes.

In fact, through a series of formal and informal meetings, through a *Journal of Management Studies* special issue, through interest groups in the major European and North American conferences, through the development of a website, and in a variety of other fora, the network of participants has been extended and the perspective has indeed come to be – and of course, this book also contributes to its existence. Moreover, as a co-author of it, I find myself irrevocably 'enrolled' (Latour 1987). I am both flattered and a little bewildered that this has happened to me – could it be that an unclassifiable non-joiner has at last found a home?!

Of course, I would not be here if I did not find the home comfortable. Quite naturally, the Strategy as Practice perspective appeals to me first and foremost because it reflects my own research interests. I have been fascinated by how strategy is actually made, lived and 'done' by people in organizations. I am an inveterate sceptic as far as normative recipes are concerned, while having enormous respect for those who attempt to apply the recipes or who find other ways to do strategy. Some of these people are successful at doing strategy at least some of the time. Understanding their successes and setbacks is surely a worthwhile enterprise.

The Strategy as Practice perspective as presented in this book also appeals to me because it puts some theoretical flesh onto these highly empiricist bones. Indeed, the label 'Strategy as Practice' is richer in its implications than other possible labels that have been experimented with (activity-based view, micro-strategy) because of its reference to the practice turn in social theory. This implicitly draws in a whole range of theoretical resources that deepen its possibilities and potential, as we saw in chapter 2. The idea of 'practice' also implicitly links to application: strategy is not just an abstract concept. It is a practice and it has practitioners who apply practical knowledge. The Strategy as Practice approach aims in some sense both to capture that knowledge and, if possible, to enrich it.

Finally, the Strategy as Practice perspective offers space for creativity and dialogue in a broad academic field (strategy) that has sometimes seemed rather closed in recent years. It is a 'perspective', not a tightly knit theoretical frame whose concepts are well defined. A wide variety of contributions are possible. In my opinion, that must remain so. Dogmatism about what is and is not a valuable contribution to Strategy as Practice will kill it – at least for me. As things stand, there are great opportunities for theoretical and methodological innovation under a broad umbrella that provides a community of congenial and like-minded colleagues, opportunities for rich conversations (Huff 1997), and – yes – a source of legitimacy and support for ideas that might otherwise remain marginal and isolated voices in the wilderness.

For as Pfeffer (1993) noted in his controversial statement about the state of organization studies, shared ideas or paradigms provide a source of power, influence and legitimacy. I would never suggest (as Pfeffer might) that the whole world should accept my preferred paradigm. However, having an intellectual home is a source of strength. Labels and boundaries in academic fields are indeed social constructions. However, there is nothing 'mere' about them. They can be powerful.

So if the research objects, ideas and methods presented in this book appeal to you, my message would be: 'Come join us.' The Strategy as Practice perspective has potential to inject fresh air and fresh ideas into the strategy field. Research in this area is not without its particular challenges but those challenges can be met, as we show in this book. There is a clear need for creative, theoretically grounded and rigorous research on strategy practice, and there is an emerging community of scholars who are open, interested and eager to participate in this effort.

Gerry Johnson: benefits, boundaries and pragmatics

In these concluding comments I would like to highlight some benefits I see in the pursuit of the Strategy as Practice agenda; but also to highlight some potential risks that we need to be aware of and avoid.

Many benefits have been highlighted throughout the book. I would emphasize two in particular. As I write this, I have just returned from the 2006 EURAM conference in Oslo. Jay Barney made a keynote speech there in which he suggested that, although he believed his research had relevance for managers, that was not its motivation. The research was purely for academic purposes; relevance was an incidental benefit. Whilst I understand the arguments for this distinction, I cannot make it myself. To me strategy – indeed management – is an applied subject and I feel the need to understand the relevance and implications of research in the field. For this reason I am frustrated by much of the research in strategy as currently represented in mainstream academic literature; in particular by the reliance on an abstraction of explanation. This was discussed in chapter 1 with regard to the Resource Based View of the firm, but also to empirical fields of enquiry such as diversification and even much of the current 'strategy process'. The problem with such abstraction is twofold. First, as Priem and Butler (2001) have pointed out about the Resource Based View of the firm, unless such abstractions are brought down to the more specific explanation, they do not have a lot of meaning. They need substance to gain that meaning. Second, it is very difficult for practitioners to understand or benefit from such concepts unless that meaning is made real. So to me one of the big benefits of the Strategy as Practice perspective is that it can bring the specifics of action and doing to the strategy field.

A second benefit is that, in so doing, it can help to integrate that field. People's activities underpin most of the questions raised over the years in research on strategy. As the discussion about figure 1.1 in chapter 1 made clear, by the time we get to investigate activities and praxis, divisions such as strategy content and process become redundant. Bringing the two benefits together, I see the further benefit that Strategy as Practice is, then, not an alternative to mainstream strategy research but complementary to it.

I do, however, have concerns for the future as the Strategy as Practice perspective develops. One arises from what I have highlighted already, in particular in relation to the emphasis on the 'doing of strategy' that I see as fundamental. Whilst I am happy that Strategy as Practice should be broad in terms of research questions, methods and theory, there is a risk that it will drift away from this emphasis on 'doing' and thus lose its distinctive focus and interest. In particular there is a tendency to equate 'doing' with 'strategy processes' and that tends to take research claiming to be Strategy as Practice towards a concern for 'processes' at the organizational level of analysis rather than a concern with what people actually do. There are reasons for this of course. There is already a tradition of 'process research' that examines organizational processes and therefore a temptation to relabel such work. There is, moreover, an undeniable overlap between such research and the Strategy as Practice agenda. In practical terms it may also be difficult to do research on the doing of strategy if it means gaining access to strategizing events and episodes. It is also challenging to relate an attention to detailed activities to the development of generalized theory. However, to me, by definition Strategy as Practice research needs to involve an attention to activities; to the bottom-most level of figure 1.1 in chapter 1. That is where both the originality and the potential of this perspective lie.

This in turn raises two other concerns, however. Research on 'doing' can sometimes lead to rich case studies that may be interesting in themselves but that do not get us very far in terms of a contribution to a wider understanding of strategic issues. One pragmatic consequence is that they are unlikely to get published. A second is that it is difficult to build more general bodies of explanation upon them. Readers need go no further than the papers in this book to realize that the influence and impact of many of them is precisely because they have lifted their contribution beyond case study narrative. The study of activities – the study of the micro – is the more powerful when it is related to other levels, be they organizational or institutional, and to the theoretical debates associated with those levels.

There is a related concern. Like others interested in Strategy as Practice, I believe that, if we are to understand the doing of strategy, we have to be prepared to engage with levels of analysis that take us into the micro aspects of strategizing; with the discourse and activities of strategizing. Pragmatically, however, we have to ask if we are interested in seriously influencing and having an impact in the strategy field. If we do, we need to realize that such a level of analysis is foreign territory for most scholars of strategy, indeed of management. Their question will be, 'So what?' What does such a level of analysis tell us about strategy, strategy development or strategic management? Unless such studies build explanatory linkages to outcomes at other levels, most obviously in terms of effects on strategy or strategy processes at the organizational level, they will be of limited influence.

All of this raises a final issue. Returning to my opening comment: it is a significant benefit that the Strategy as Practice perspective can embrace, even help integrate, a broad community of interest. However it must not become so all-embracing that it is meaningless. Without boundaries, Strategy as Practice risks losing its identity, indeed its existence. To me the boundary is clear. Strategy as Practice provides an opportunity to research a wide variety of strategic issues – the sort of issues identified in chapter 1 and summarized in figure 1.1 – provided that research focuses on people's activities; on 'doing'.

I believe all these concerns can be turned into opportunities. If Strategy as Practice can take the 'doing of strategy' seriously, build empirical findings and theoretical insights that link that doing to outcomes, or understand that doing in terms of context, then there is a very significant opportunity to influence the current debate on strategy for the better: not least to help move away from vague abstraction so as to offer real insight to fellow academics but also to practitioners.

Leif Melin: a perspective with potential to renew the field of strategy

Having spent over thirty years of doing research, mainly process orientated, in the field of strategy, I am absolutely convinced that Strategy as Practice is a perspective capable of influencing the whole field. This new perspective has the potential of resulting in a necessary renewal of the strategy field, overcoming the taken for grantedness of the *who* and *where* of strategizing (directors and executive officers in the top of the organization), and the ignorance of *how* strategizing actually takes place. Such a renewal will mean adding new research topics, new theoretical lenses and new methods, eventually contributing new understanding and more relevance to the strategy field, especially regarding the role and meaning of different strategists in doing strategy, i.e. in creating strategic outcomes. It is also my belief that Strategy as Practice implies an integrative force, meaning a useful integration of the strategy field with related management fields, such as leadership and organizing.

Furthermore, the Strategy as Practice perspective is an inclusive approach, with potential to embrace different kinds of scholars. We have already seen an interest from many strategy researchers who wish to apply different aspects of the perspective to different parts of the broad and complex phenomenon of strategizing, emphasizing micro-processes, daily activities, institutionalized practices and/or discourses. It is important that the future development of the Strategy as Practice perspective continues to be characterized by inclusiveness rather than exclusiveness. The inclusiveness also means active bridging to other perspectives, for example inviting and welcoming both process people and resource-based people who want to be more practice and/or micro orientated to understand what would conventionally be seen as 'content' issues of strategy.

In the remainder of this personal reflection I want to emphasize three issues that we should carefully consider in the future development of the Strategy as Practice perspective. The first issue is a reminder that we should not forget about the practitioner. So far this perspective, with its strong arguments for understanding the practice of the actors who actually strategize – i.e. the practitioners that are doing strategy – has shown less interest in talking to practitioners in the dissemination of findings. It is important to neutralize this paradox and for it to become the predominant pattern. We discuss a good deal about how to get close to practitioners in field work when gathering data, for example in the methods chapter of this book, but we should also both discuss more and experiment on how to disseminate our results in ways that directly talk to and with practitioners. If the Strategy as Practice perspective delivers on its promise to produce new knowledge on the 'secrets' of doing strategy, we need to develop new channels, arenas and methods that may stimulate practitioners to active reflections about the doing of strategy. For example, methodologically we might consider co-production as a means to develop more accurate empirical accounts of practices of strategy. However we should also think more about the potential co-learning side of such an approach. Furthermore, we focus on publishing in high-ranked academic journals, which is both legitimate and important. But we should also think about communication channels, maybe new types of media (in the internet age) and arenas (beyond the MBA context) that could support dialogues with practitioners of strategy, with the aim to influence and stimulate them to reflective learning based on the growing knowledge about practices of strategy.

My second issue is about the practice of thinking as an inherent part of strategizing. The strong focus on activities, practices and routines in the Strategy as Practice perspective is certainly relevant to both the thinking and the acting side of strategizing. However, there may be a tendency for the latter to be overemphasized (even if there are recent examples focusing on the thinking side, including the Balogun and Johnson paper presented in this book). I have three reasons to emphasize the thinking dimension of strategizing in the Strategy as Practice perspective. First, how strategists think is a crucial part of a micro perspective on strategizing. Second, to regard thinking as a practice makes sense, as modes of thinking tend to become routinized and institutionalized (e.g. as industry recipes) as, indeed, most practices are. Third, strategy as a mental construct naturally bridges the micro and organizational side of strategizing, i.e. the micro process of individual thinking activities and the organizational process of intended, or emergent, strategy outcome.

Maybe the most critical type of strategizing includes activities and practices that eventually lead to a major strategic renewal. In this context, and on the level of individual or small groups of strategists, what does successful strategizing actually mean when it implies major rethinking of predominant beliefs and wisdom about the rules of the strategic game? And, related to this question, what type of strategists' behaviour may lead to new and innovative strategies; that is, what type of thinking practices support the creation of new and the renewal of predominant strategies. Established views on strategy making most often emphasize analytical practices and tools, while practices of intuition and creativity are still largely unexplored.

The third and final issue that I want to raise relates to paradigmatic standpoints in social sciences. My view is that Strategy as Practice implies a freshness, not only in terms of research topics and theories but also in terms of epistemology. For the Strategy as Practice perspective to realize its potential, there is a need to overcome the obvious risk of converging on the mainstream epistemology of puzzle solving that dominates the field of strategy. There are strong pressures to conform to the predominant logic of building explanatory theory based on the magic of generalizable empirical evidence. But such an approach requires data, most often taken from existing databases and characterized by distance and cross-sectionality, that are far from the daily practices of strategists doing strategy. In this book we have noted this trade-off or dilemma. On the one hand we argue for micro, depth, and closeness with the aim to develop trustworthy empirical accounts (stories, narratives, etc.) on the doing of strategy, the activities of strategizing, and the daily interaction between strategists. On the other hand we comment on the generalization problem such an approach implies. My personal view is that our plea for the micro perspective and the closeness to the actual practitioners doing strategy may imply an alternative epistemological stand compared to the predominant neopositivism, with its aim to generalize empirical evidence to more or less universal truths. Based on close access to micro activities and actual interaction between strategizing actors, the Strategy as Practice perspective will rather result in the type of theorizing that builds on iterative interpretations between well-grounded observations and relevant theory, in line with the interpretative approach of first- and second-order analysis illustrated by several papers in Part II of this book.

Richard Whittington: research that makes a difference, one way or another

The Strategy as Practice research community is a new one. We have proposed here a shared central interest for this community – curiosity about what people actually do in strategy. We have also suggested some directions and models for future research. What we cannot do is predict exactly how the community will take things forward. We can help and, perhaps, nudge. But we should also expect some surprises.

That said, I will make two pleas in this final part of the book. First, I shall argue that, in keeping with the emergent nature of our community, we should be pluralistic. Here I shall underline both pluralism of concerns and pluralism of methods. Second, I shall urge that, for all kinds of reasons, our research should be, in some sense, practical. In short, I hope that our research will make a difference, one way or another.

The first kind of pluralism I want to assert regards the underlying concerns that drive Strategy as Practice research, whether these concerns are thought of as 'dependent variables' or simple sparks of interest. There have been many attempts to define strategy as essentially concerned with the performance of organizations, somehow measured (by profitability, survival or similar). Of course, organizational performance matters intensely, whether it is that of the world's great corporations, of entrepreneurial start-ups, or of organizations in the public and third sectors. But there is plenty else at stake in the practice of strategy that conventional definitions too casually exclude. I shall highlight two.

Conventional strategy is too indifferent to the performance of strategy's practitioners. These are the people who sit in our executive education classes and whom our MBA and other students seek to join. It is they who are our direct responsibility; the organizations that employ them stand second in line. To be sure, general guidelines about which organizational strategies pay, and in what circumstances, will be useful to these practitioners, actual and would-be. But also useful will be knowledge of how to get along in strategy work, how to perform the strategist role, how to be a player. For this we shall need to understand a good deal more about strategy work and then to communicate the practical wisdom involved. Strategy work includes such apparently mundane but actually artful activity as participating in strategy workshops, managing strategy project teams and building strategy story-boards. If strategy is something people do, we should be concerned to give the people in our classes more insight into how to get the strategy job done – all of it.

The other exclusion from the concerns of conventional strategy is the tools of this strategy job. These include the tools and techniques of the standard strategy course, for example Porter's Five Forces or the Boston Consulting Group matrix. But, if we recall Andrew-the-Strategist from chapter 2, they also include the taken-for-granted information technologies and supporting infrastructure which makes strategy work possible. I think there is a two-sided agenda here. First, and oddly, the standard strategy course tools (Porter's Five Forces and so on) are hardly ever researched any more: from a Strategy as Practice perspective, we clearly need to understand more about what people do with them. Understanding tools-in-use can inform strategy tool design, dissemination and critique. It can also make practitioners more skilful users. Second, we need to investigate more of the taken-for-granted technologies of strategy work, the video-conferencing, the Blackberries, the flip-charts, the PowerPoints. The skilled strategist probably needs to be able to drive a flip-chart as much as draw a Five Forces. An interesting question here will be how such technologies shape the nature of strategy work. Does the standard PowerPoint slide-pack lead to strategic glibness and simplification; can new intranet and electronic voting technologies facilitate greater inclusion and participation in strategy? In short, we should be concerned too for the impact of strategy's tools – all of them.

The second kind of pluralism to plead for is a pluralism of method. The papers by Barley and Langley in this book use both qualitative and quantitative methods. That is something to applaud, though they are tough acts to follow. But even if we cannot always combine methods in a single study, we should recognize the potential complementary of different methods across studies. Ethnography will play a central role in future Strategy as Practice research. As in chapter 3, new technologies such as email records, the track-changes on evolving strategy documents, digital photography and video filming all promise exciting opportunities to deepen the ethnographic interrogation.

But Strategy as Practice has other methods available beyond the ethnographic. Surveys have an important place, at the least to establish the prevalence and influence of the particular kinds of strategy practice requiring ethnographic study. The historical method may be useful too: for example,

archival research would illuminate the difference that new information technologies have made to strategy work and its outputs. Interviews need not be
scorned – consider the vivid insights of Studs Terkel's (1972) *Working*. The
boardroom and the bedroom have similar privacy constraints, yet Alfred
Kinsey's (1948) mass interviews in *Sexual Behavior in the Human Male*
revealed a great deal about what turned out to be ordinary activity. The same
can be true of Strategy as Practice. Nor should we rule out the methods of economics. After all, Alfred Marshall's *Principles of Economics* originally defined
the discipline as about 'the study of mankind in the ordinary business of life'
in a way that finds a surprising echo in the Strategy as Practice community's
concern for the everyday practice of strategizing (Knight 1941).

These pluralisms of concern and of method also point to a diversity of practical impacts. We can make a difference to people's performance as strategists.
We can help in the design of more effective strategy tools. We can promote
new technologies that facilitate inclusion and participation. We can critique
concepts and practices that race through business with faddish enthusiasm
but that may have unintended and dangerous consequences. The study of
Strategy as Practice is a platform for intervening in many practical ways.

And Strategy as Practice scholars should try to make a difference, in one way
or another. There are at least three good reasons to search for practical impact.
The first is to recall some of Strategy as Practice's roots, in the philosophical
pragmatist tradition introduced in chapter 2. The pragmatists sought to help
people in their ordinary lives, particularly through education. If we are
inspired by the pragmatists' philosophy, then we should be true too to their
commitment to practical assistance. We should respect the practical in our
community's title.

The second reason to make a difference is less idealistic, but recognizes the
realities of academic competition. Conventional strategy academics promise
the philosopher's stone of superior organizational performance, and have made
some progress at least in defining what is likely to deliver inferior performance.
Their promise is a seductive one – for research grants, consulting interest and
ambitious new PhD students. If Strategy as Practice is to compete for resources,
interest and minds, it will need to demonstrate its utility. It is hard to believe
that rigorous research on what people really do in strategy does not have the
potential for considerable practical value. Now we have to deliver it.

Finally, we should make a difference simply because we owe it to our students. Student fees typically pay a large part of our salaries; we take a good deal
of their time at critical stages in their lives. Yet much of what is taught in strategy is at a level of abstraction that is both remote from the likely immediate

responsibilities of most of them and alienating to practically minded people. We can do better. By taking strategy as a practical activity that will be part of their job either to undertake or to influence, we can offer students a more immediate and tangible set of skills than the abstract principles that are typically the stuff of strategy courses. They need these principles, but they also need to know how to do a strategy workshop, to manage a strategy project, to build a strategy story-board, and lots more besides. At the moment, a good deal of strategy is taught like a dead language, Latin or Ancient Greek, best appreciated on the written page. We need to teach it more as a living language, one which is evolving and which can be given greater power through the skill with which it is spoken.

Like my fellow authors, I hope that readers will have found some useful things in this book. I hope too that it will encourage readers to do substantive and impactful research in this exciting new domain. So the task now for readers is to get on and do something new. Surprise us.

References

Abrahamson, E. 1996 Management fashion, *Academy of Management Review*, 21: 254–85

Abrahamson, E. and Fairchild, G. 1999 Management fashion: lifecycles, triggers and collective learning processes, *Administrative Science Quarterly*, 44, 4: 708–41

Adler, P. A. and Adler, P. 1994 Observational techniques. In N. K. Denzin and Y. S. Lincoln (eds.), *Handbook of qualitative research*, 377–92, Thousand Oaks, CA: Sage

Ager, M. H. 1980 *The professional stranger: and informal introduction to ethnography*, New York: Academic Press

Akrich, M., Callon, M. and Latour, B. 2002 The key to success in innovation part 1: the art of interessement, *International Journal of Innovation Management*, 6, 2: 87–206

Alberta Community Development 1994 *Business plan: 1994/5 to 1996/7*, Edmonton: Alberta Community Development, February

Allison, G. 1971 *Essence of decision*, Boston, MA: Little Brown

Alvesson, M. and Karreman, D. 2000 Varieties of discourse: on the study of organizations through discourse analysis, *Human Relations*, 53, 9: 1125–49

Alvesson, M. and Sveningsson, S. 2003 Beyond neo-positivists, romantics and localists: a reflexive approach to interviews in organizational research, *Academy of Management Review*, 28, 1: 13–33

Ambrosini, V. 2003 *Tacit and ambiguous resources as sources of competitive Advantage*, New York: Palgrave Macmillan

Ambrosini, V. and Bowman, C. 2001 Tacit knowledge: some suggestions for operationalisation, *Journal of Management Studies*, 38, 6: 811–29

Argote, L. McEvily, B. and Reagans, R. 2003 Introduction to the special issue on managing knowledge in organizations, *Management Science*, 49, 4: v–ix

Argyris, C. 1990 The dilemma of implementing controls: the case of managerial accounting, *Accounting, Organizations and Society*, 15, 6: 503–11

Argyris, C., Putnam, R. and McLain Smith, D. 1985 *Action science*, San Francisco: Jossey-Bass

Argyris, C. and Schon, D. 1978 *Organisational learning: a theory of action perspective*, Reading, MA: Addison Wesley

Ashkenas, R., Ulrich, D., Jick, T. and Kerr, S. 1995 *The boundaryless organization: breaking the chains of organizational structure*, San Francisco: Jossey-Bass

Bacharach, S. 1989 Organizational theories: some criteria for evaluation, *Academy of Management Review*, 14, 4: 496–515

Bacharach, S., Bamberger, P. and Sonnenstuhl, W. 1996 The organizational transformation process: the micro politics of dissonance reduction and the alignment of logics of action, *Administrative Science Quarterly*, 41: 477–506

Balogun, J., Huff, A. and Johnson, P. 2003 Three responses to the methodological challenges of studying strategizing, *Journal of Management Studies*, 40, 1: 197–224

Balogun, J. and Johnson, G. 2004 Organizational restructuring and middle manager sensemaking, *Academy of Management Journal*, 47: 523–49

2005 From intended strategies to unintended outcomes: the impact of change recipient sensemaking, *Organization Studies*, 26, 11: 1573–601

Barker, R. 1997 How can we train leaders if we don't know what leadership is? *Human Relations*, 50: 343–62

Barley, S. 1986 Technology as an occasion for structuring: evidence from observations of CT scanners and the social order of radiology departments, *Administrative Science Quarterly*, 31, 1: 78–98

1990 Images of imaging: notes on doing longitudinal fieldwork, *Organization Science*, 1, 2: 220–47

Barley, S. and Tolbert, P. 1997 Institutionalisation and structuration: studying the links between action and institution, *Organization Studies*, 18, 1: 93–117

Barnard, C. 1938 *The functions of the executive*, Cambridge, MA: Harvard University Press

Barnard, H. 1990 Bourdieu and ethnography: reflexivity, politics and practice. In R. Harker, C. Mahar and C. Wilkes (eds.), *An introduction to the work of Pierre Bourdieu: the practice of theory*, 58–85, London: Macmillan

Barney, J. 1986 Organizational culture: can it be a source of sustained competitive advantage?, *Academy of Management Review*, 11, 3: 656–65

1991 Firm resources and sustained competitive advantage, *Journal of Management*, 17: 99–120

2002 Strategic management: from informed conversation to academic discipline, *Academy of Management Executive*, 16, 2: 53–7

Baron, J., Dobbin, F. and Jennings, P. 1986 War and peace: the evolution of modern personnel administration in US industry, *American Journal of Sociology*, 92: 350–83

Barry, D. and Elmes, M. 1997 Strategy retold: towards a narrative view of strategic discourse, *Academy of Management Review*, 22, 2: 429–52

Bartlett, C. and Ghoshal, S. 1989 *Managing across borders: the transnational corporation*, Cambridge, MA: Harvard Business School Press

Bartunek, J. 1984 Changing interpretive schemes and organizational restructuring: the example of a religious order, *Administrative Science Quarterly*, 29: 355–72

Bartunek, J., Rynes, S. and Ireland, R. 2006 What makes management research interesting, and why does it matter?, *Academy of Management Journal*, 49, 1: 8–15

Bate, S., Khan, R. and Pye, A. 2000 Towards a culturally sensitive approach to organisation structuring: where organisation design meets organisation development, *Organization Science*, 11, 2: 197–211

Becker, M., Lazaric, N., Nelson, R. and Winter, S. 2005 Applying organizational routines in understanding organizational change, *Industrial and Corporate Change*, 14, 5: 775–91

Berger, P. and Luckmann, T. 1966 *The social construction of reality*, London: Penguin

Bettenhausen, S. and Murnighan, K. 1985 The emergence of norms in competitive decision making groups, *Administrative Science Quarterly*, 30: 350–72

Bittner, E. 1973 The concept of organization. In G. Salaman and K. Thompson (eds.), *People and organizations*, 264–76, Milton Keynes: Open University Press

Blackler, F., Crump, N. and McDonald, S. 2000 Organizing processes in complex activity networks, *Organization*, 7, 2: 277–91

Boden, D. 1994 *The business of talk*, Cambridge: Polity Press

Bourdieu, P. 1977 *Outline of a theory of practice*, trans. Richard Nice, Cambridge: Cambridge University Press

1988 *Homo academicus*, Cambridge, Polity Press

1990 *The logic of practice*, Cambridge, MA: Harvard University Press

1991 *Language and symbolic power*, Cambridge, MA: Harvard University Press

1993 *The field of cultural production*, New York: Columbia University Press

Bourdieu, P. and Wacquant, L. 1992 *An invitation to reflexive sociology*, Oxford: Polity Press

Bourgeois, L. and Eisenhardt, K. 1988 Strategic decision processes in high velocity environments: four cases in the microcomputer industry, *Management Science*, 34: 816–35

Bourgeois, L. 1979 Toward a method of middle-range theorizing, *Academy of Management Review*, 4, 3: 443–7

Bower, J. 1972 *Managing the resource allocation process: a study of corporate planning and investment*, Homewood, IL: Irwin

1982 Business policy in the 1980's, *Academy of Management Review*, 7, 4: 630–8

Bowman, E. and Helfat, C. 2001 Does corporate strategy matter?, *Strategic Management Journal*, 22, 1: 1–24

Bowman, E., Singh, H. and Thomas, H. 2002 The domain of strategic management: history and evolution. In A. Pettigrew, H. Thomas and R. Whittington (eds.), *Handbook of strategy and management*, 31–51, London: Sage

Boydston, J. 1970 *Guide to the works of John Dewey*, Carbondale and Edwardsville: Southern Illinois University Press

Brews, P. and Hunt, M. 1999 Learning to plan and planning to learn: resolving the planning school/learning school debate, *Strategic Management Journal*, 20, 10: 889–913

Bromiley, P. 2004 *Behavioural foundations of strategic management*, Oxford: Blackwell

Brown, J. and Duguid, P. 2000 *The social life of information*, Boston, MA: Harvard Business School Press

Brown, S. and Eisenhardt, K. 1997 The art of continuous change: linking complexity theory and time-paced evolution in relentlessly shifting environments, *Administrative Science Quarterly*, 42: 1–34

1998 *Competing on the edge*, Cambridge, MA: Harvard Business School Press

Brunsson, N. and Jacobsson, B. 2000 *A world of standards*, Oxford: Oxford University Press

Burgelman, R. 2002 *Strategy as destiny: how strategy-making shapes a company's future*, New York: Free Press

Burgess, R. 1984 *In the field: an introduction to field research*, London: Allen and Unwin

Bürgi, P., Jacobs, C. and Roos, J. 2005 From metaphor to practice in the crafting of strategy, *Journal of Management Inquiry*, 14, 1: 78–94

Bürgi, P. and Roos, J. 2003 Images of strategy, *European Management Journal*, 21, 1: 69–78

Burns, J. 1978 *Leadership*, New York: Harper Colophon

Burrell, G. and Morgan, G. 1979 *Sociological paradigms and organizational analysis*, London: Heinemann

Cailluet, L. and Whittington, R. 2007 The crafts of strategy, *Long Range Planning* (forthcoming)

Calhoun, C. 1995 *Critical social theory: culture, history, and the challenge of difference*, Cambridge, MA: Blackwell

Callero, P. 2003 The sociology of the self, *Annual Review of Sociology*, 29, 1: 115–33

Callon, M. and Law, J. 1997 After the individual in society: lessons on collectivity from science, technology and society, *Canadian Journal of Sociology*, 22, 2: 16–82

Carnegie, G. and Wolnizer, P. 1996 Enabling accountability in museums, *Accounting, Auditing and Accountability Journal*, 9: 84–99

Chakravarthy, B. and Doz, Y. 1992 Strategy process research: focusing on corporate self-renewal, *Strategic Management Journal*, 13, Special Issue: 5–14

Chakravarthy, B. and White, R. 2002 Strategy process: changing and implementing strategies. In A. Pettigrew, H. Thomas and R. Whittington (eds.), *Handbook of strategy and management*, 183–206, London: Sage

Clark, A. and Fujimoto, J. 1992 *The right tools for the job: at work in twentieth century life sciences*, Princeton, NJ: Princeton University Press

Clark, T. 2004 Strategy viewed from a management fashion perspective, *European Management Review*, 1, 1: 105–11

Clark, T. and Fincham, R. (eds.) 2002 *Critical consulting*, Oxford: Blackwell

Cohen, M., Burkhart, R., Dosi, G., Egid, M., Mareno, L. and Winter, S. 1996 Routines and other recurring action patterns of organizations: contemporary research issues, *Industrial and Corporate Change*, 5, 3: 653–98

Cohen, M. D. and March, J. G. 1974 *Leadership and ambiguity: the American college president*, New York: McGraw-Hill

Collier, J. and Collier, M. 1986 *Visual anthropology: photography as a research method*, Albuquerque: University of New Mexico Press

Conrad, C. F. 1982 Grounded theory: an alternative approach to research in higher education, *Review of Higher Education*, 5: 259–69

Contu, A. and Willmott, H. 2003 Re-embedding situatedness: the importance of power relations in learning theory, *Organization Science*, 14, 3: 283–96

Cooper, D. and Dean, N. 1996 Accounting interventions. Paper presented at the Critical Perspectives on Accounting Conference, New York, April

Cyert, R. and March, J. 1963 *A behavioural theory of the firm*, Englewood Cliffs, NJ: Prentice-Hall

Daft, R. L. and Weick, K. E. 1984 Towards a model of organizations as interpretation systems, *Academy of Management Review*, 9: 284–95

D'Aveni, R. (with Gunther, R.) 1995 *Hypercompetitive rivalries*, New York: Free Press

Davis, G,. Dieljam, K. and Tinsley, C. 1994 The decline and fall of the conglomerate firm in the 1980s: the deinstitutionalisation of an organizational form, *American Sociological Review*, 59: 547–70

Dawes, P. 1987 Snowball sampling in industrial marketing, *Australian Marketing Researcher*, 11: 26–35

de Certeau, M. 1998 *The practice of everyday life*, Berkeley: University of California Press

de Certeau, M., Giard, L. and Mayol, L. 1998 *The practice of everyday life*, vol. 2, *Living and cooking*, trans. T. Tomasik, Minneapolis: University of Minnesota Press

Deephouse, D. 1999 To be different or to be the same? it's a question (and theory) of strategic balance, *Strategic Management Journal*, 20: 147–66

Denis, J., Langley, A. and Pineault, M. 2000 Becoming a leader in a complex organization, *Journal of Management Studies*, 37, 8: 1063–99

Denis, J., Langley, A. and Rouleau, L. 2007 Strategizing in pluralistic contexts: rethinking theoretical frames, *Human Relations*, 60, 1: 179–215

Denzin, N. 1989 *The research act: a theoretical introduction to sociological methods*, Englewood Cliffs, NJ: Prentice-Hall

Dewey, J. 1938 *Experience and education*, New York: Touchstone

Dillon, J. 1990 *The practice of questioning*, London: Routledge

DiMaggio, P. 1991 Constructing an organizational field as a professional project: U.S. art museums, 1920–1940. In W. Powell and P. DiMaggio (eds.), *The new institutionalism in organizational analysis*, 267–92, Chicago: University of Chicago Press

DiMaggio, P. and Powell, W. 1983 The iron cage revisited: institutional isomorphism and collective rationality in organizational fields, *American Sociological Review*, 48: 147–60

 1991. Introduction. In W. Powell and P. DiMaggio (eds.), *New institutionalism in organizational analysis*, Chicago: University of Chicago Press

Dinning, J. 1993 *A financial plan for Alberta: Budget '93*, Edmonton: Alberta Treasury, May 6

Djelic, M. 1998 *The export of the American model*, Oxford: Oxford University Press

Donnellon, A., Gray, B. and Bougon, M. 1986 Communication, meaning, and organizational action, *Administrative Science Quarterly*, 31: 43–55

Dougherty, D. 1992 A practice-centred model of organizational renewal through product innovation, *Strategic Management Journal*, 13, Summer Special Issue: 77–96

Dougherty, D., Barnard, H. and Dunne, D. 2004 Exploring the everyday dynamics of dynamic capabilities. Paper presented at the 3rd Annual MIT/UCI Knowledge and Organizations Conference, Laguna Beach, CA, March

Drew, P. and Sorjonen, M. 1997 Institutional dialogue. In T. van Dijk (ed.), *Discourse as social interaction*, 92–118, London: Sage

Dugdale, A. 1999 Materiality: juggling sameness and difference. In J. Law and J. Hassard (eds.), *ANT and after*, 113–35, Oxford: Blackwell

Dutton, J. and Dukerich, J. 1991 Keeping an eye on the mirror: image and identity in organizational adaptation, *Academy of Management Journal*, 24, 3: 517–54

 2006 The relational foundation of research: an underappreciated dimension of interesting research, *Academy of Management Journal*, 49, 1: 21–6

Dutton, J. E. and Duncan, R. B. 1987 The creation of momentum for change through the process of strategic issue diagnosis, *Strategic Management Journal*, 8: 279–95

Dyer, W. and Wilkins, A. 1991 Better stories, not better constructs, to generate better theory: a rejoinder to Eisenhardt, *Academy of Management Review*, 16, 3: 613–19

Edelman, M. 1964 *The symbolic uses of politics*, Urbana: University of Illinois Press

Egginton, W. and Sandbothe, M. 2004 *The pragmatic turn in philosophy*, Albany, NY: SUNY Press

Eisenhardt, K. 1989a Making fast strategic decisions in high-velocity environments, *Academy of Management Journal*, 32, 3: 543–76

 1989b Building theories from case study research, *Academy of Management Review*, 14, 4: 532–50

 1991 Better stories and better constructs: the case for rigor and comparative logic, *Academy of Management Review*, 16, 3: 620–7

Eisenhardt, K. and Bourgeois, L. 1988 Politics of strategic decision making in high velocity environments: toward a midrange theory, *Academy of Management Journal*, 31, 4: 737–70
    1989 Charting strategic decisions: profile of an industry star. In M. Van Glinow and S. Mohrmann (eds.), *Managing complexity in high technology organizations, systems, and people*, 74–89, New York: Oxford University Press
Eisenhardt, K. and Brown, S. 1999 Patching: restitching business portfolios in dynamic markets, *Harvard Business Review*, 77, 3: 72–83
Eisenhardt, K. and Martin, J. 2000 Dynamic capabilities; what are they?, *Strategic Management Journal*, 21: 1105–21
Elsbach, K., Barr, P. and Hargadon, A. 2005 Identifying situated cognition in organizations, *Organization Science*, 16, 4: 422–33
Engeström, Y. 2001 Expansive learning at work: toward an activity theoretical reconceptualisation, *Journal of Education and Work*, 14, 1: 133–56
Fairclough, N. 1995 *Critical discourse analysis*, Harlow: Longman
    2005 Discourse analysis in organization studies: the case for critical realism, *Organization Studies*, 26, 6: 915–39
Feldman, M. 2003 A performative perspective on stability and change in organizational routines, *Industrial and Corporate Change*, 13, 4: 727–52
    2004 Resources in emerging structures and processes of change, *Organization Science*, 15, 3: 295–309
Feldman, M. and Pentland, B. 2003 Reconceptualising organizational routines as a source of flexibility and change, *Administrative Science Quarterly*, 48: 94–118
Feldman, M. and Rafaeli, A. 2002 Organizational routines as sources of connections and understandings, *Journal of Management Studies*, 39, 3: 309–31
Fiol, M. 2002 Capitalizing on paradox: the role of language in transforming organizational identities, *Organization Science*, 13: 653–66
Fiol, M. and Huff, A. 1992 Maps for managers: Where are we? Where do we go from here?, *Journal of Management Studies*, 29: 267–85
Fligstein, N. 1990 *The transformation of corporate control*, Cambridge, MA: Harvard University Press
    1997 Social skill in institutional theory, *American Behavioural Scientist*, 40, 4: 397–405
Foucault, M. 1977 *Discipline and punish: the birth of the prison*, London: Penguin
    1978 *The history of sexuality*, vol. 1, *An introduction*, London: Penguin
Fredrickson, J. and Iaquinto, A. 1987 Incremental change, its correlates, and the comprehensiveness of strategic decision processes, *Academy of Management Proceedings*, 12: 26–30
Fredrickson, J. and Mitchell, T. 1984 Strategic decision processes: comprehensiveness and performance in an industry with an unstable environment, *Academy of Management Journal*, 27: 399–423
Fry, L. 1982 Technology-structure research: three critical issues, *Academy of Management Journal*, 25: 532–52
Gal, R. and Lazarus, R. 1975 The role of activity in anticipating and confronting stressful situations, *Journal of Human Stress*, 2: 4–20
Galunic, C. and Eisenhardt, K. 1994 Renewing the strategy–structure–performance paradigm, *Research in Organizational Behavior*, 16: 215–55

Garfinkel, H. 1967 *Studies in ethnomethodology*, Englewood Cliffs, NJ: Prentice-Hall (1984 edition, Cambridge: Polity Press)

Gavetti, G. 2005 Cognition and hierarchy: rethinking the microfoundations of capabilities' development, *Organization Science*, 16, 6: 599–617

George, A. 1980 *Presidential decision making in foreign policy*, Boulder, CO: Westview Press

Gephart, R. 1993 The textual approach: risk and blame in disaster sensemaking. *Academy of Management Journal*, 36: 1465–514

    1997 Hazardous measures: an interpretive textual analysis of quantitative sensemaking during crises, *Journal of Organizational Behaviour*, 18: 583–622

Giddens, A. 1976 *New rules of sociological method*, London: Hutchinson

    1979 *Central problems in social theory*, Berkeley: University of California Press

    1984 *The constitution of society*, Oxford: Polity Press

    1987 *Social theory and modern sociology*, Oxford: Polity Press

Gioia, D. and Chittipeddi, K. 1991 Sensemaking and sensegiving in strategic change initiation, *Strategic Management Journal*, 12: 433–48

Gioia, D. and Poole, P. 1984 Scripts in organisational behaviour, *Academy of Management Review*, 9, 3: 449–59

Gioia, D. A. and Thomas, J. B. 1996 Identity, image, and issue interpretation: sensemaking during strategic change in academia, *Administrative Science Quarterly*, 41, 3: 370–403

Gioia, D., Thomas, J., Clark, S. and Chittipeddi, K. 1994 Symbolism and strategic change in academia: the dynamics of sensemaking and influence, *Organization Science*, 5: 363–83

Glaser, B. and Strauss, A. 1967 *The discovery of grounded theory: strategies for qualitative research*, London: Weidenfeld and Nicolson

Goffman, E. 1983 The interaction order, *American Sociological Review*, 48: 1–17

Goodman, L. 1961 Snowball sampling, *Annals of Mathematical Statistics*, 32: 148–70

Grant, R. 1995 *Contemporary strategy analysis: concepts, techniques, applications*, 2nd edition, Oxford: Blackwell

    2002 Corporate strategy: managing scope and strategy content. In A. Pettigrew, H. Thomas and R. Whittington (eds.), *Handbook of strategy and management*, 297–321, London: Sage

    2003 Strategic planning in a turbulent environment: evidence from the oil majors, *Strategic Management Journal*, 24: 491–517

Grant, R., Jammine, A. and Thomas, H. 1988 Diversity, diversification and profitability among British manufacturing companies, 1972–84, *Academy of Management Journal*, 31, 4: 771–801

Greenwood, R. and Suddaby, R. 2006 Institutional entrepreneurship in mature fields: the big five accounting firms, *Academy of Management Journal*, 49, 1: 27–48

Greiner, L. and Bhambri, A. 1989 New CEO intervention and dynamics of deliberate strategic change, *Strategic Management Journal*, 10, Special Issue: 67–86.

Greiner, L., Bhambri, A. and Cummings, T. 2003 Searching for a strategy to teach strategy, *Academy of Management Learning and Education*, 2, 4: 402–19

Guba, E. and Lincoln, Y. 1994 Competing paradigms in qualitative research. In N. Denzin (ed.), *Handbook of qualitative research*, 105–17, Thousand Oaks, CA: Sage

Guillory, J. 1993 *Cultural capital: the problem of literary canon formulation*, Chicago: University of Chicago Press

Hafsi, T. and Demers, C. 1989, *Le changement radical dans les organisations complexes: le cas d'Hydro-Québec*, Montréal: Gaétan Morin Éditeur

Hambrick, D. and Chen, M. 2005 New academic fields as social movements: the case of strategic management, *Academy of Management Proceedings*, E1–E6

Hambrick, D. and Mason, P. 1984 Upper echelons: the organization as a reflection of its top managers, *Academy of Management Review*, 9: 195–206

Hamel, G. and Prahalad, C. 1990 The core competence of the corporation, *Harvard Business Review*, 68, 3: 79–88

Hardy, C., Langley, A., Mintzberg, H. and Rose, J. 1984 Strategy formation in the university setting. In J. Bess (ed.), *College and university organization: insights from the behavioural sciences*, 169–210, New York: New York University Press

Harris, L. and Ogbonna, E. 2002 The unintended consequences of culture interventions: a study of unexpected outcomes, *British Journal of Management*, 13, 1: 31–49

Harris, S. 1995 Pragmatics and power, *Journal of Pragmatics*, 23: 117–35

Hart, S. and Banbury, C. 1994 How strategy-making processes can make a difference, *Strategic Management Journal*, 15: 251–69

Hayes, J. 1981 *The complete problem solvers*, Philadelphia: Franklin Institute Press

Hellgren, B. and Melin, L. 1991 Business systems, industrial wisdom and corporate strategies – the case of the pulp-and-paper industry. In R. Whitley (ed.), *The social foundations of enterprise: European comparing perspective*, 47–68, London: Sage

Hendry, J. and Seidl, D. 2003 The structure and significance of strategic episodes: social systems theory and the routine practices of strategic change, *Journal of Management Studies*, 40, 1: 175–96

Hickson, D., Butler, R., Cray, D., Mallory, G. and Wilson, D. 1986 *Top decisions: strategic decision making in organizations*, San Francisco: Jossey-Bass

Hodgkinson, G. and Sparrow, P. 2002 *The competent organization*, Buckingham: Open University Press

Hodgkinson, G., Whittington, R., Johnson, G. and Schwartz, M. 2006 The role of strategy workshops in strategy development processes: formality, communication, coordination and inclusion, *Long Range Planning*, 39, 5: 479–96

Hodgkinson, G. and Wright, G. 2002 Confronting strategic inertia in a top management team: learning from failure, *Organization Studies*, 23, 6: 949–78

Holm, P. 1995 The dynamics of institutionalisation: transformation processes in Norwegian fisheries, *Administrative Science Quarterly*, 40: 398–422

Howard-Grenville, J. 2005 The persistence of flexible organizational routines: the role of agency and organizational context, *Organization Science*, 16, 6: 618–36

Huber, G. 1985 Temporal stability and response-order biases in participant descriptions of organizational decisions, *Academy of Management Journal*, 28: 943–50

Huff, A. 1999 *Writing for scholarly publication*, Thousand Oaks, CA: Sage

Hutchins, E. 1996 Learning to navigate. In J. Lave and S. Chaiklin (eds.), *Understanding practice: perspective on activity and context*, 35–63, New York: Cambridge University Press

Huxham, C. and Vangen, S. 2005 *Managing to collaborate: the theory and practice of collaborative advantage*, London: Routledge

Isabella, L. 1990 Evolving interpretations as change unfolds: how managers construe key organizational events, *Academy of Management Journal*, 33: 7–41

James, W. 1975–88 *The works of William James*, ed. Frederick H. Burkhardt, Cambridge, MA: Harvard University Press

Janis, I. 1982 *Victims of groupthink*, revised edition, Boston: Houghton-Mifflin

Jarzabkowski. P. 2003 Strategic practices: an activity theory perspective on continuity and change, *Journal of Management Studies*, 40, 1: 23–56

2004 Strategy as practice: recursiveness, adaptation and practices-in-use, *Organization Studies*, 24, 3: 489–520

2005 *Strategy as practice: an activity-based view*, London: Sage

Jarzabkowski, P., Balogun, J. and Seidl, D. 2007 Strategizing: the challenges of a practice perspective, *Human Relations*, 60, 1: 5–27

Jermier, J. and Berkes, L. 1979 Leader behavior in a police command bureaucracy: a closer look at the quasi-military model, *Academy of Management Journal*, 37: 350–82

Johnson, G. 1987 *Strategic change and the management process*, Oxford: Basil Blackwell

Johnson, G. and Huff, A. 1997 Everyday innovation/everyday strategy. In G. Hamel, C. Prahalad, H. Thomas and D. O'Neill (eds.), *Strategic flexibility*, 13–27, Chichester: Wiley

Johnson, G., Melin, L. and Whittington, R. 2003 Micro strategy and strategizing: towards an activity-based view, *Journal of Management Studies*, 40, 1: 3–22

Johnson, G., Smith, S. and Codling, B. 2000 Micro processes of institutional change in the context of privatisation, *Academy of Management Review*, Special Topic Forum, 25, 3: 572–80

Jones, R., Jimmieson, N. and Griffiths, A. 2005 The impact of organizational culture and reshaping capabilities on change implementation success: the mediating role of readiness for change, *Journal of Management Studies*, 42, 2: 362–86

Judge, W. and Miller, A. 1991 Antecedents and outcomes of decision speed in different environmental contexts, *Academy of Management Journal*, 34: 449–63

Khandwalla, P. 1974 Mass output orientation of operations technology and organizational structure, *Administrative Science Quarterly*, 19: 74–97

Kuhn, T. S. 1970 *The structure of scientific revolutions*, Chicago: University of Chicago Press

Kincheloe, J. and McLaren, P. 1994 Rethinking critical theory and qualitative research. In N. Denzin and Y. Lincoln (eds.), *Handbook of qualitative research*, 138–57, Thousand Oaks, CA: Sage

Kinsey, A., Pomeroy, W. and Clyde, M. 1948 *Sexual behavior in the human male*, Philadelphia: Saunders

Knight, F. 1941 Anthropology and economics, *Journal of Political Economy*, 49, 2: 247–68

Knights, D. and Morgan, G. 1991 Corporate strategy, organizations and subjectivity: a critique, *Organization Studies*, 12, 2: 251–73

Knorr-Cetina, K. 1995 Laboratory studies: the cultural approach. In S. Jasanoff, G. Markle, J. Petersen and T. Pinch (eds.), *Handbook of science and technology studies*, 140–66, London: Sage

Kostova, T. and Roth, K. 2002 Adoption of an organizational practice by subsidiaries of multinational corporations: institutional relational effects, *Academy of Management Journal*, 45: 215–33

Labianca, G., Gray, B. and Brass, D. 2000 A grounded model of organizational schema change during empowerment, *Organization Science*, 11: 235–57

Langer, E. 1975 The illusion of control, *Journal of Personality and Social Psychology*, 32: 311–28

Langley, A. 1986 The role of formal analysis in organizations. Unpublished PhD thesis, HEC Montréal.

1989 In search of rationality: the purposes behind the use of formal analysis in organizations, *Administrative Science Quarterly*, 34, 4: 598–631

1999 Strategies for theorizing from process data, *Academy of Management Review*, 24, 4: 691–710

Langley, A., Mintzberg, H., Pitcher, P., Posada, E. and Saint-Macary, J. 1995 Opening up decision making: the view from the black stool, *Organization Science* 6, 3: 260–79

Latour, B. 1987 *Science in action: how to follow scientists and engineers through society*, Cambridge, MA: Harvard University Press

1992 Where are the missing masses? The sociology of a few mundane artefacts. In W. Bijker and J. Law (eds.), *Shaping technology/building society*, Boston, MA: MIT Press

1999 *Pandora's hope: essays on the reality of science*, Cambridge, MA: Harvard University Press

2005 *Reassembling the social: an introduction to actor-network-theory*, Oxford: Oxford University Press

Latour, B. and Woolgar, S. 1979 *Laboratory life: the social construction of scientific facts*, Sage: London

Lave, J. and Wenger, E. 1991 *Situated learning: legitimate peripheral participation*, Cambridge: Cambridge University Press

Law, J. and Callon, M. 1988 Engineering and sociology in a military aircraft project: a network analysis of technological change, *Social Problems*, 35, 3: 284–97

Lawrence, P. and Lorsch, J. 1967 *Organization and environment*, Boston, MA: Harvard Business School Press

Lincoln, Y. and Guba, E. 1985 *Naturalistic enquiry*, Beverly Hills, CA: Sage

Lisac, M. 1995 *The Klein revolution*, Edmonton, Alberta: NeWest

Lorenzoni, G. and Lipparini, A. 1999 The leveraging of interfirm relationships as a distinctive organizational capability, *Strategic Management Journal*, 20, 4: 317–39

Luhmann, N. 1995 *Social systems*, Stanford, CA: Stanford University Press

Lynch, M. and Peyrot, M. 1991 Introduction: a reader's guide to ethnomethodology, *Qualitative Sociology*, 15, 2: 113–22

Maguire, S., Hardy, C. and Lawrence, T. 2004 Institutional entrepreneurship in emerging fields: HIV/AIDS treatment advocacy in Canada, *Academy of Management Journal*, 47, 5: 657–81

McAdam, D., McCarthy, J. and Zald, M. 1996 *Comparative perspectives on social movements: political opportunities, mobilizing structures, and cultural framings*, Cambridge: Cambridge University Press

McKinley, W. and Scherer, A. 2000 Some unanticipated consequences of organizational restructuring, *Academy of Management Review*, 25: 735–52

MacLean, C. and Hassard, J. 2004 Symmetrical absence/symmetrical absurdity: critical notes on the production of actor-network accounts, *Journal of Management Studies*, 41, 3: 493–519

Maitlis, S. 2005 The social process of organizational sensemaking, *Academy of Management Journal*, 48, 1: 21–49

Maitlis, S. and Lawrence, T. 2003 Orchestral manoeuvres in the dark: understanding failure in organizational strategizing, *Journal of Management Studies*, 40, 1: 109–40

Mangham, I. 2005 The drama of organizational life, *Organization Studies*, 26, 6: 941–58

Mangham, I. and Pye, A. 1991 *The doing of managing*, Oxford: Basil Blackwell

Mann, W. and Thompson, S. (eds.) 1992 *Diverse analyses of a fund-raising text*, Amsterdam: John Benjamin

Manning, P. 1977 *Police work*, Cambridge, MA: MIT Press

Mantere, S. 2005 Strategic practices as enablers and disablers of championing activity, *Strategic Organization*, 3, 2: 157–84

March, J. and Simon, H. 1958 *Organizations*, New York: Wiley

March, J. and Sutton, R. 1997 Organizational performance as a dependent variable, *Organization Science*, 8, 6: 698–706

Markides, C. and Williamson, P. 1996 Corporate diversification and organizational structure: a resource-based view, *Academy of Management Journal*, 39: 340–67

Mead, G. 1934 *Mind, self and society*, ed. Charles W. Morris, Chicago: University of Chicago Press

Meyer, J. and Rowan, B. 1977 Institutionalized organizations: formal structure as myth and ceremony, *American Journal of Sociology*, 83, 2: 340–63

  1991 Institutionalized organizations: formal structures as myth and ceremony. In W. Powell and P. DiMaggio (eds.), *The new institutionalism in organizational analysis*, 41–62. Chicago: University of Chicago Press

Mezias, S. 1990 An institutional model of organizational practice: financial reporting at the Fortune 200, *Administrative Science Quarterly*, 5: 431–57

Michael, M. 1996 *Constructing identities*, London: Sage

Miles, M. and Huberman, A. 1994 *Qualitative data analysis*, Newbury Park, CA: Sage

Miles, R. and Snow, C. 1978 *Organizational strategy, structure, and process*, New York: McGraw-Hill

Miller, C. and Cardinal, L. 1994 Strategic planning and firm performance: a synthesis of more than two decades of research, *Academy of Management Journal*, 37, 6: 1649–65

Miller, V., Johnson, J. and Grau, J. 1994 Antecedents to willingness to participate in a planned organizational change, *Journal of Applied Communication Research*, 22: 59–80

Mintzberg, H. 1973 *The nature of managerial work*, New York: Harper and Row

  1979 An emerging strategy of 'direct' research, *Administrative Science Quarterly*, 24, 4: 580–9

  1987 Crafting strategy, *Harvard Business Review*, 65, 4: 66–75

  1994 *The rise and fall of strategic planning*, New York: Free Press

Mintzberg, H., Ahlstrand, B. and Lampel, J. 1998 *Strategy safari: a guided tour through the wilds of strategic management*, New York: Prentice Hall

Mintzberg, H. and McHugh, A. 1985 Strategy formulation in an adhocracy, *Administrative Science Quarterly*, 30, 2: 160–97

Mintzberg, H., Raisinghani, D. and Theoret, A. 1976 The structure of 'unstructured' decision processes, *Administrative Science Quarterly*, 21: 246–75

Mintzberg, H. and Rose, J. 2003 Strategic management upside down: tracking strategies at McGill University from 1829 to 1980, *Canadian Journal of the Administrative Sciences*, 20, 4: 270–90

Mintzberg, H. and Waters, J. 1982 Tracking strategy in an entrepreneurial firm, *Academy of Management Journal*, 25: 465–99

  1985 Of strategies deliberate and emergent, *Strategic Management Journal*, 6, 3: 257–72

Moch, M. and Fields, W. 1985 Developing a content analysis for interpreting language use in organizations, In S. Bacharach and S. Mitchell (eds.), *Research in the sociology of organizations*, vol. 4, 81–126. Greenwich, CT: JAI Press

Mohr, L. 1982 *Explaining organizational behavior*, San Francisco: Jossey-Bass

Molloy, E. and Whittington, R. 2005 Organising organising: the practice inside the process, *Advances in Strategic Management: Strategy Process*, 22: 491–515

Molotch, H. and Boden, D. 1985 Talking social structure: discourse, domination and the Watergate hearings, *American Sociological Review*, 50: 273–88

Morgan, D. 1997 *Focus groups as qualitative research*, London: Sage

Morgan, G., Frost, P. and Pondy, L. 1983 Organizational symbolism. In L. Pondy, P. Frost, G. Morgan and T. Dandridge (eds.), *Organizational symbolism*, 3–35, Greenwich, CT: JAI Press

Nelson, R. and Winter, S. 1982 *An evolutionary theory of economic change*, Cambridge, MA: Harvard University Press

Noda, T. and Bower, J. 1996 Strategy making as iterated processes of resource allocation, *Strategic Management Journal*, 17: 159–92

Nonaka, I. and Takeuchi, H. 1995 *The knowledge creating company*, Oxford: Oxford University Press

Nordqvist, M. 2005 *Understanding the role of ownership in strategizing*, JIBS Dissertation Series, 29, Jönköping University

Normann, R. 1977 *Management for growth*, New York: Wiley

Nutt, P. 1976 Models for decision-making in organizations and some contextual variables which stipulate optimal use, *Academy of Management Review*, 1: 147–58

Nystrom, P. and Starbuck, W. 1984 To avoid organizational crises, unlearn, *Organizational Dynamics*, 12, Spring: 53–65

Oakes, L., Townley, B. and Cooper, D. 1998 Business planning as pedagogy: language and control in a changing institutional field, *Administrative Science Quarterly*, 43, 2: 257–92

Orlikowski, W. 2002 Knowing in practice: enacting a collective capability in distributed organizing, *Organization Science*, 13, 3: 249–73

Orr, J. 1996 *Talking about machines: an ethnography of a modern job*, Ithaca, NY: Cornell University Press

Palmer, D., Jennings, P. and Zhou X. 1993 Late adoptions of the multidivisional form by large US corporations: institutional, political and economic accounts, *Administrative Science Quarterly*, 46, 1: 100–31

Papadakis, V., Lioukas, S. and Chambers, D. 1998 Strategic decision making processes: the role of management and context, *Strategic Management Journal*, 19: 115–47

Patton, M. 2002 *Qualitative research and evaluation methods*, 3rd edition, Thousand Oaks, CA: Sage

Payne, J., Bettman, J. and Johnson, E. 1988 Adaptive strategy selection in decision making, *Journal of Experimental Psychology*, 14: 534–52

Pels, D. 1995 Knowledge politics and antipolitics: towards a critical appraisal of Bourdieu's concept of intellectual autonomy, *Theory and Society*, 24: 79–104

Perlow, L. 1997 *Finding time: how corporations, individuals and families can benefit from new work practices*, Ithaca, NY: ILR Press

1999 The time famine: toward a sociology of work time, *Administrative Science Quarterly*, 44: 57–81

Perlow, L., Okhuysen, G. and Repenning, N. 2002 The speed trap: exploring the relationship between decision making and temporal context, *Academy of Management Journal*, 45, 5: 931–55

Peteraf, M. 1993 The cornerstones of competitive advantage: a resource based view, *Strategic Management Journal*, 14: 179–90

Pettigrew, A. 1973 *The politics of organizational decision making*, London: Tavistock.

1977 Strategy formulation as a political process, *International Studies of Management and Organisation*, 7, 2: 78–87

1985 *The awakening giant: continuity and change in ICI*, Oxford: Blackwell

1990 Longitudinal field research on change: theory and practice, *Organization Science*, 1, 3: 267–92

1992a On studying managerial elites, *Strategic Management Journal*, 13, Special Issue: 163–82

1992b The character and significance of strategy process research, *Strategic Management Journal*, 13: 5–16

Pfeffer, J. 1981 Management as symbolic action: the creation and maintenance of organizational paradigms, *Research in Organizational Behavior*, 3: 1–52

1993 Barriers to the advance of organizational science: paradigm development as a dependent variable, *Academy of Management Journal*, 18, 4: 599–620

Phillips, N. 2003 Discourse or institution? Institutional theory and the challenge of critical discourse analysis. In S. Clegg and R. Westwood (eds.), *Debating organization: point-counterpoint in organization studies*, 220–31, Malden, MA: Blackwell

Phillips, N. and Hardy, C. 2002 *Discourse analysis: investigating processes of social construction*, London: Sage

Phillips N., Lawrence, T. and Hardy, C. 2004 Discourse and institutions, *Academy of Management Review*, 29, 4: 635–52

Polanyi, M. 1966 *The tacit dimension*, Garden City, NY: Doubleday

Pondy, L. 1978 Leadership as a language game. In M. McCall Jr. and M. Lombardo (eds.), *Leadership: where else can we go?*, 87–101, Durham, NC: Duke University Press

1983 The role of metaphors and myths in organization and in the facilitation of change. In L. Pondy, P. Frost, G. Morgan and T. Dandridge (eds.), *Organizational symbolism*, 157–66, Greenwich, CT: JAI Press

Poole, P., Gioia, D. and Gray, B. 1989 Influence modes, schema change, and organizational transformation, *Journal of Applied Behavioural Science*, 25: 271–89

Porac, J., Thomas, H., and Baden-Fuller, C. 1989 Competitive groups as cognitive communities: the case of Scottish knitwear manufacturers, *Journal of Management Studies*, 26: 397–416

Porras, J. and Robertson, P. 1992 Organizational development: theory, practice and research. In M. Dunnette and L. Hough (eds.), *Handbook of industrial and organizational psychology*, 2nd edition, vol. 3, 719–822, Palo Alto, CA: Consulting Psychologists Press

Porter, M. 1980 *Competitive strategy: techniques for analysing industries and competitors*, New York: Free Press

1985 *Competitive advantage*, New York: Free Press/Collier Macmillan

Powell, T. 2002 The philosophy of strategy, *Strategic Management Journal*, 23, 9: 873–90

2003 Strategy without ontology, *Strategic Management Journal*, 24, 3: 285–92

Pozzebon, M. 2004 The influence of a structurationist view on strategic management research, *Journal of Management Studies*, 41, 2: 247–72

Priem, R. and Butler, J. 2001 Is the resource based view a useful perspective for strategic management research?, *Academy of Management Review*, 26, 1: 22–40

Putnam, H. 1995 *Pragmatism: an open question*, Oxford: Blackwell
    2004 *Ethics without ontology*, Cambridge, MA: Harvard University Press
Rabinow, P. and Sullivan, W. M. (eds.) 1979 *Interpretive social science*, Berkeley: University of California Press
Ranson, S., Hinings, C. R. and Greenwood, R. 1980 The structuring of organizational structures, *Administrative Science Quarterly*, 25: 1–17
Reason, P. (eds.) 1994 *Participation in human inquiry*, London: Sage
Reckwitz, A. 2002 Toward a theory of social practices: a development in cultural theorizing, *European Journal of Social Theory*, 5, 2: 243–63
Regnér, P. 2003 Strategy creation in the periphery: inductive versus deductive strategy making, *Journal of Management Studies*, 40, 1: 57–82
Ridgway, V. 1956 Dysfunctional consequences of performance measurements, *Administrative Science Quarterly*, 1, 2: 240–7
Rigby, D. 2005 *Management tools 2005: an executive guide*, http://www.bain.com/management_tools/home.asp
Roos, J., Victor, B. and Statler, M. 2004 Playing seriously with strategy, *Long Range Planning*, 37, 6: 549–68
Rorty, R. 1980 *Philosophy and the mirror of nature*, Oxford: Blackwell
    1998 *Truth and progress: philosophical papers*, Cambridge: Cambridge University Press
    1999 *Philosophy and social hope*, London: Penguin
Rouleau, L. 2005 Micro-practices of strategic sensemaking and sensemaking: how middle managers interpret and sell change every day, *Journal of Management Studies*, 42, 7: 1143–441
Rumelt, R. 1974 *Strategy, structure and economic performance*, Cambridge, MA: Harvard University Press
Rumelt, R., Schendel, D. and Teece D. 1994 Fundamental issues in strategy. In R. Rumelt, D. Schendel and D. Teece (eds.), *Fundamental Issues in Strategy*, 9–47, Boston, MA: Harvard Business School Press
Sacks, H. 1992 *Lectures on conversation*, vols. 1 and 2, ed. G. Jefferson, Oxford: Basil Blackwell
Sacks, H., Scheloff, E. and Jefferson, G. 1974 A simplest systematics for the organization of turn-taking for conversation, *Language*, 50, 4: 696–735
Salaman, G. and Thompson, K. 1980 *Control and ideology in organizations*, Cambridge, MA: MIT Press
Salvato, C. 2003 The role of micro-strategies in the engineering of firm evolution, *Journal of Management Studies*, 40, 1: 83–108
Samra-Fredericks, D. 1996 The interpersonal management of competing rationalities: a critical ethnography of board-level competence for 'doing' strategy as spoken in the 'face' of change. Unpublished PhD thesis, Brunel University/Henley Management College
    1998 Conversation analysis. In G. Symon and C. Cassell (eds.), *Qualitative methods and analysis in organizational research: a practical guide*, 161–89, London: Sage
    2000 An analysis of the behavioural dynamics of corporate governance – a talk-based ethnography of a UK manufacturing board-in-action, *Corporate Governance, an International Review*, 8, 4: 311–25
    2003 Strategizing as lived experience and strategists: everyday efforts to shape strategic direction, *Journal of Management Studies*, 40, 1: 141–74

Schank, R. and Abelson, R. 1977 *Scripts, plans, goals and understanding*, Hillsdale, NJ: Erlbaum

Schatzki, T. 2001 'Introduction: practice theory'. In Schatzki et al. 2001

2005 The sites of the social, *Organization Studies*, 26, 3: 465–84

Schatzki, T., Knorr-Cetina, K. and Von Savigny, E. (eds.) 2001 *The practice turn in contemporary theory*, London: Routledge

Schendel, D. and Hofer, C. 1979 *Strategic management: a new view of business policy and planning*, Boston: Little Brown

Schiffrin, D. 1987 *Discourse markers*, Cambridge: Cambridge University Press

Schutz, A. 1932 (1972) *The phenomenology of the social world*, London: Heinemann

Schwarz, M. 2004 Knowing in practice: how consultants work with clients to create, share and apply knowledge, *Academy of Management Proceedings*, D1–D6

Schwenk, C. 1985 The use of participant recollection in the modelling of organizational decision processes, *Academy of Management Review*, 10: 496–503

Scott, W. 2000 *Institutions and organizations*, London: Sage

Seidl, D. 2007 General strategy concepts and the ecology of strategy discourses: a systemic-discursive perspective, *Organization Studies*, 28: 197–218

Seo, M. and Creed, W. 2002 Institutional contradictions, praxis and institutional change: a dialectical perspective, *Academy of Management Review*, 27: 222–47

Silverman, D. 1971 *The theory of organizations*, New York: Basic Books

1985 *Qualitative methodology and sociology*, Aldershot: Gower

Simon, H. 1987 Making management decisions: the role of intuition and emotion, *Academy of Management Executive*, 1: 57–64

Smircich, L. 1983 Implications for management theory. In L. Putnam and M. Pacanowsky (eds.), *Communication and organization: an interpretive approach*, 221–41, Thousand Oaks, CA: Sage

Smith, D. 1965 Front-line organization of a state mental hospital, *Administrative Science Quarterly*, 10: 381–99

Spender, J. 1989 *Industry recipes: the nature and sources of managerial judgement*, Oxford: Basil Blackwell

Spradley, J. P. 1980 *Participant observation*, New York: Holt, Rinehart and Winston

Stearns, L. and Allen, K. 1996 Economic behavior in institutional environments: the corporate merger wave of the 1980s, *American Sociological Review*, 61: 699–718

Stolte J., Fine, G. and Cook, K. 2001 Sociological miniaturism: seeing the big through the small in social psychology, *Annual Review of Sociology*, 27, 1: 387–413

Strauss, A. 1978 *Negotiations: varieties, contexts, processes and social order*, Washington, DC: Jossey-Bass

1982 Inter-organizational negotiations, *Urban Life*, 11, 3: 350–67

Strauss, A. and Corbin, J. 1990 *Basics of qualitative research: grounded theory and techniques*, London: Sage

Stronz, M. 2005 Strategic learning in the context of strategy implementation: a case study of implementers in action. Unpublished PhD thesis, Columbia University

Suddaby, R. and Greenwood, R. 2005 Rhetorical strategies of legitimacy, *Administrative Science Quarterly*, 50: 35–67

Sutton, R. and Callahan, A. 1987 The stigma of bankruptcy: spoiled organizational image and its management, *Academy of Management Journal*, 30: 405–36

Taylor, C. 1993 To follow a rule. In C. Calhoun, E. LiPuma and M. Postone (eds.), *Bourdieu: critical perspectives*, 45–60, Chicago: University of Chicago Press

Taylor, S. and Bogdan, R. 1984 *Introduction to qualitative research methods: the search for meaning*, 2nd edition, New York: Wiley

Teece, D., Pisano, G. and Shuen, A. 1997 Dynamic capabilities and strategic management, *Strategic Management Journal*, 18, 7: 509–33

Terkel, S. 1972 *Working: people talk about what they do all day and how they feel about what they do*, New York: New Press

Tolbert, P. and Zucker, L. 1996 The institionalisation of institutional theory. In R. Clegg, C. Hardy and W. Nord (eds.), *A handbook of organization studies*, London: Sage

Toulmin, S. 1991 *Cosmopolis: the hidden agenda of modernity*, Chicago: University of Chicago Press
2001 *Return to reason*, Cambridge, MA: Harvard University Press

Townley, B. 1995 Know thyself: self-awareness, self-formation and managing, *Organization*, 2: 271–89

1996 Accounting in detail: accounting for individual performance, *Critical Perspectives on Accounting*, 7: 565–84

Tsoukas, H. and Chia, R. 2002 On organizational becoming: rethinking organizational change, *Organization Science*, 13, 5: 567–82

Tsoukas, H. and Cummings, S. 1997 Marginalisation and recovery: the emergence of Aristotelian themes in organization studies, *Organization Studies*, 18, 4: 655–84

Turner, J. 1988 *A theory of social interaction*, Chichester: John Wiley and Sons

Vaara, E., Kleyman, B. and Seristö, H. 2004 Strategies as discursive constructions: the case of airline alliances, *Journal of Management Studies*, 41, 1: 1–35

Vaara, E., Tienari, J., Piekkari, R. and Santti, R. 2005 Language and the circuits of power in a merging multinational corporation, *Journal of Management Studies*, 42, 3: 596–624

van de Ven, A. 1992 Suggestions for studying strategy process: a research note, *Strategic Management Journal*, 13, Special Issue: 169–88

van de Ven, A. and Scott, P. 2005 Alternative approaches to studying organizational change, *Organization Studies*, 26, 9: 1377–404

Van Maanen, J. 1977 Experiencing organization: notes on the meaning of careers and socialisation. In J. Van Maanen (ed.), *Organizational careers: some new perspectives*, 15–45. New York: Wiley

1979 The fact of fiction in organizational ethnography, *Administrative Science Quarterly*, 24: 539–50

1995 Style as theory, *Organization Science*, 6, 1: 133–43

(ed.), 1998 *Qualitative studies of organizations*, Thousand Oaks, CA: Sage

Wally, S. and Baum, J. 1994 Personal and structural determinants of the pace of strategic decision making, *Academy of Management Journal*, 37, 4: 932–56

Walsh, J. 1995 Managerial and organizational cognition: notes from a trip down memory lane, *Organization Science*, 6, 3: 280–321

Walsh, J. P. and Fahey, L. 1986 The role of negotiated belief structures in strategy making, *Journal of Management*, 12: 325–38

Weber, R. and Crocker, J. 1983 Cognitive processes in the revision of stereotypic beliefs, *Journal of Personality and Social Psychology*, 4: 961–77

Weick, K. 1979 *The social psychology of organizing*, 2nd edition, Reading, MA: Addison-Wesley

Weick, K. 1993 The collapse of sensemaking in organizations: the Mann Gulch disaster, *Administrative Science Quarterly*, 36: 628–52

1995 *Sensemaking in organizations*, Thousand Oaks, CA: Sage

Weick, K. and Roberts, K. 1993 Collective mind in organizations: heedful interrelating on flight decks, *Administrative Science Quarterly*, 38: 357–81

Wenger, E. 1998 *Communities of practice: learning, meaning and identity*, Cambridge: Cambridge University Press

Westley, F. 1990 Middle managers and strategy: micro dynamics of inclusion, *Strategic Management Journal*, 11: 337–51

Whitley, R. 1999 *Divergent capitalisms: the social structuring and change of business systems*, Oxford: Oxford University Press

Whittington, R. 1992 Putting Giddens into action: social systems and managerial agency, *Journal of Management Studies*, 29, 6: 693–712

2002 Corporate structure: from policy to practice. In A. Pettigrew, H. Thomas and R. Whittington (eds.), *Handbook of strategy and management*, 113–38, London: Sage

2003 The work of strategizing and organizing: for a practice perspective, *Strategic Organization*, 1, 1: 117–26

2004 Strategy after modernism: recovering practice, *European Management Review*, 1, 1: 62–8

2006 Completing the practice turn in strategy, *Organization Studies*, 27, 5: 613–34

Whittington, R., Jarzabkowski, P., Mayer, M., Mounoud, E., Nahapiet, J. and Rouleau, L. 2003 Taking strategy seriously: responsibility and reform for an important social practice, *Journal of Management Inquiry*, 12, 4: 396–409

Whittington, R. and Mayer, M. 2000 *The European corporation: strategy, structure and social science*, Oxford: Oxford University Press

Whittington, R. and Melin, L. 2003 The challenge of organizing/strategizing. In A. Pettigrew, R. Whittington, L. Melin, C. Sanchéz-Runde, F. van den Bosch, W. Ruigrok and T. Numagami (eds.), *Innovative forms of organizing: international perspectives*, 35–48, London: Sage

Whittington, R., Pettigrew, A., Peck, S., Fenton, E. and Conyon, M. 1999 Change and complementarities in the new competitive landscape, *Organization Science*, 10: 583–600

Wicks, A. and Freeman, R. 1998 Organization studies and the new pragmatism: positivism, anti-positivism and the search for ethics, *Organization Science*, 9, 2: 123–41

Wildavsky, A. 1973 If planning is everything, maybe it's nothing, *Policy Sciences*, 4, 2: 127–53

Wolfe, R., Gephart, R. and Johnson, T. 1993 Computer-facilitated qualitative data analysis: potential contributions to management research, *Journal of Management*, 19: 637–61

Yin, R. 1984 *Case study research: design and methods*, Beverly Hills, CA: Sage

2003 *Case study research*, Newbury Park, CA: Sage

Young, G., Charns, M. and Shortell, S. 2001 Top manager and network effects on the adoption of innovative management practices: a study of TQM in a public hospital system, *Strategic Management Journal*, 21, 10: 935–52

Yukl, G. 1999 An evaluation of conceptual weaknesses in transformational and charismatic leadership theories, *Leadership Quarterly*, 10, 2: 285–305

Zenger, T. and Hesterly, W. 1997 The disaggregation of corporations: selective intervention, high-powered incentives and molecular units, *Organization Science*, 8, 3: 209–25

Zollo, M., Reuer, J. and Singh, H. 2002 Interorganizational routines and performance in strategic alliances, *Organization Science*, 13, 6: 701–14

Zollo, M. and Singh, H. 2004 Deliberate learning in corporate acquisitions: post-acquisition strategies and integration capability in US bank mergers, *Strategic Management Journal*, 25: 1233–56

Zollo, M. and Winter, S. 2002 Deliberate learning and the evolution of dynamic capabilities, *Organization Science*, 13, 3: 339–51

Zorn, D. 2004 Here a chief, there a chief: the rise of the CFO in the American firm, *American Sociological Review*, 69, 3: 345–64

Index

Academy of Management 209
action research 55
    study example 197–203
activities
    and institutional forces 83–100
    hands-on strategizing 197–203
    influence on organization 83–100
activity focus
    practice in social theory 35–6
    pragmatism 32–5
actor-network theory (ANT) 37–8, 45–7
    approach to strategic planning research 49
actors
    agency attributable 33, 35–6
    non-human 46–7
agency attributable to actors 33, 35–6

Balogun and Johnson (2004), research illustrative
        paper 179–96
Barley (1986)
    research illustrative paper 83–100
    study design 63–5
bounded rationality 40
Bourdieu, Pierre, social theory 152–64
Burgelman, Robert 205
Bürgi, Jacobs and Roos (2005), research
        illustrative paper 197–203
business planning
    as pedagogy in action 152–64
    changing the capital of a field 152–64
    cultural and economic capital 152–64
    language and control 152–64
    shifts in values of a field 152–64
Business Policy approach 4–5, 6

Carnegie School 37–8, 40–2
case comparison study (example) 101–20
CEO
    role in change initiation 137–51
    role in strategizing 137–51
    sensegiving in organizational change
        137–51

change
    and speed of strategic decision-making 101–20
    sensegiving by CEO 137–51
    sensemaking by middle managers 179–96
comparison
    case comparison study (example) 101–20
    study design for 62
competences 39, 42
content and process, emphasis in theoretical
        traditions 37–8
content and process divide, actor-network theory
        45–6
conversation analysis 44, 50, 55
    ethnomethodology/conversation analysis
        165–78
core competences 39
corporate diversification research 9–10
corporate structures research 10

data collection 68–70
    through diaries (example) 179–96
decision making
    and organizational structure 121–36
    uses and purposes of formal analysis 121–36
descriptive contributions to research 72–3
Dewey, John 32, 33
dialectics 44
discourse analysis 44, 50, 55
    ethnomethodology/conversation analysis
        165–78
documentation, as research data 69–70
dramaturgy 50
dynamic capabilities 9, 18, 42

Eisenhardt (1989), research illustrative paper
        101–20
empirical research, themes from theoretical
        resources
        47
ethical issues in research 70–1
ethnographic field work (example) 137–51
ethnographic studies of strategy practice 42, 43–4

240